INSIDE THE CULT OF KIBU

ALSO BY LORI GOTTLIEB

Stick Figure: A Diary of My Former Self

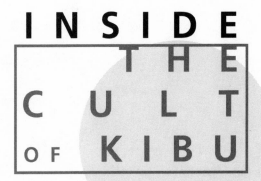

INSIDE THE CULT OF KIBU

AND OTHER TALES OF THE MILLENNIAL GOLD RUSH

LORI GOTTLIEB & JESSE JACOBS

PERSEUS
PUBLISHING

A Member of the Perseus Books Group

Library of Congress Control Number: 2002105969
ISBN 0–7382–0691–1

Perseus Publishing is a member of the Perseus Books Group.
Find us on the World Wide Web at http://www.perseuspublishing.com
Perseus Publishing books are available at special discounts for bulk purchases in the U.S. by corporations, institutions, and other organizations. For more information, please contact the Special Markets Department at the Perseus Books Group, 11 Cambridge Center, Cambridge, MA 02142, or call (800) 255–1514 or (617) 252–5298, or e-mail j.mccrary@perseusbooks.com.

Text design by Jeffrey P. Williams
Set in 10.5-point Weiss by the Perseus Books Group

First printing, August 2002

1 2 3 4 5 6 7 8 9 10—04 03 02

For my 16-year-old cousin Shira Berenson,
who, when I asked what she thought of Kibu
two weeks after I joined the teen startup,
candidly replied via email: "It sucks."

LORI GOTTLIEB

For My Mother

JESSE JACOBS

CONTENTS

INTRODUCTION

"Madness is a rare thing in individuals—but in groups,
parties, peoples, and ages it is the rule."
—Friedrich Nietzsche, *Beyond Good and Evil,* 1886

The question I'm asked most often these days, after "Are you ever going back to Hollywood?"; "Are you ever going back to medical school?"; and my mother's perennial "Are you ever getting married?" is "Are you ever joining another startup?" Despite the dot-bomb headlines, the startup question seems reasonable.

For three ludicrous but lucrative months in the spring of 2000, I was lured away from Stanford Medical School to become vice president and editor-in-chief of an Internet startup for teen girls. Never mind that I had no Web experience and could barely figure out how to use my garden-variety word-processing program. Armed with seventy thousand stock options and a staff of eager twenty-somethings, I was given the opportunity to "influence an entire generation," "shape a revolutionary global frontier," and make a large fortune in the process. This was no pipe dream: I'd seen several friends leave stable jobs with benefit packages, move out west or up north from L.A., toil in the endlessly exciting Internet trenches until their startup's flashy IPO made national headlines a year later, and become instant millionaires.

Who wouldn't chuck everything for that?

The startup I joined—dubbed at various points in the make-it-up-as-you-go-along Internet Zeitgeist as "a community," "a destination," "a portal," "a multimedia enterprise," "a digital lifestyle brand," "a digital hangout," and "Yahoo! for Gen-Y, with an estrogen slant"— was officially called Kibu, the Japanese word for "foundation." Ironically, Kibu itself had no foundation. Sure, the company was financed to the tune of a $22 million first-round investment by the likes of the colorful billionaire Jim Clark (of Silicon Graphics and Netscape fame and the subject of Michael Lewis's best-seller *The New New Thing*) and Kleiner, Perkins, Caulfield & Byers, Silicon Valley's "It" venture-capital firm (the backers behind successful startups such as Handspring and Travelocity). But mere months after a shaky launch, Kibu's hollow structure—lacking, among other things, a viable business plan—came crumbling down.

Before you could say "dot-gone," Kibu's demise was posted on FuckedCompany.com, the irreverent death-watch site gawked at weekly by over a million rubberneckers at a superhighway crash site. Many were Schadenfreude-filled risk-averse types who'd stayed put in their button-down law firms, Old Media jobs, medical practices, and tenure-track teaching gigs while we millennial cowboys and cowgirls set out to strike gold in the Web's Wild West. Yet another high-profile startup, the site gleefully announced, had bitten the bytes.

What to do?

Within days of the FuckedCompany.com obit posting, job offers from other startups came pouring in. This may seem counterintuitive, but having just worked at a failed dot-com actually *increased* my marketability (much like the convoluted argument that if you're still single after age 40, having been divorced makes you seem *more* qualified to be in a relationship than never having tied the knot at all). According to the digerati conventional wisdom, at least I'd had some experience. So what if my "experience" consisted of a few months in a company even more dysfunctional than the Burnham family in *American Beauty*? Courted by the hottest startups in cyberspace, I was treated to lavish lunches and promised perks like an onsite masseuse, lunchtime yoga and Tae Bo sessions (this *was* Northern California), plus even more zeroes added to the figure in my would-be stock-option package.

But each time I said no.

You see, I had a bad case of PTSD (post-traumatic startup disorder). So while others gamely jumped from startup to startup, leveraging each so-called experience for both a more inflated title and financial offer, I needed time to regroup my senses and regain my sanity. Instead of hopping on the next dot-com bus—hoping for early retirement but willing to play musical URLs if need be—I decided to write about the wreckage instead. I turned off my phone, cranked out an article, jumped into bed, and crashed.

And so did my AOL.

Hours after my essay, "Inside the Cult of Kibu," hit newsstands in *The Industry Standard's* "Year-in-Review 2000" issue, my e-mail box overflowed with hundreds of messages, temporarily knocking out my system. These electronic missives came from fellow startup refugees, CEOs, investment bankers, venture capitalists, sociologists studying "mass delusion," social workers interested in workplace dynamics, business school professors, doctors, lawyers, novelists, journalists, even Hollywood film and TV agents. They originated from laptops in the Midwest and the South, from keyboards as far east as Boston and as far west as Hawaii.

Hmm.

In writing the Kibu piece, I thought I was recounting a very specific, very surreal story about how a startup whose goal of "empowering" teen girls devolved into the behind-the-scenes equivalent of *Heathers* meets *Lord of the Flies*. But after receiving these e-mails, I realized the extent to which widespread knowledge of—and fascination with—this online universe had become.

No wonder *New York* magazine dubbed the 1990s the "e-Decade": Ordinary folks followed the Net the way they followed Hollywood in the tabloids. Wildly commercial magazines like *People* and *Entertainment Weekly* had "Internet Manners" and "Cyber Digest" columns. Publications ranging from *USA Today* to *The Hollywood Reporter* featured gossip about the Web's young, hip, high-profile players (and many became household names as familiar as Brad Pitt and Jennifer Aniston, who, incidentally, attached herself to the teen-girl Web venture Voxxy.com). Thousands of Americans bought stocks for the first time, gambling their entire nest eggs in the high-technology sector. At cocktail parties, buzzwords like "vested," "cliffs," "IPO," "backer," "scalable," "eyeballs," "hits," "first round," "angel investors" and the dreaded "burn rate" were bandied about near the brie.

"Geeks" were no longer, well, "geeky." Nerd stars were airbrushed to grace *In Style* photo spreads and courted by Hollywood moguls and Fortune 500 CEO's. Sitcoms that traditionally played to Middle America made dot-com gags a new staple. Cartoons in the *New York Times*, the *Washington Post*, the *Boston Globe*, and *The New Yorker* weekly satirized "Silly Valley." Advertising agencies began specializing in creating TV commercials and billboards for companies in the "digital space."

Meantime, the nation's top banking, law, and consulting firms, concerned about losing their most talented recruits to startups, routinely offered stock-option pools and higher salaries as incentives. Other conventional work-places, eager to capture the high-flying success of these startups, attempted to mimic the free-spirited culture of open spaces instead of closed-door offices, T-shirts instead of ties. It was official: The Web had gone mainstream.

In our new, youth-obsessed "I-nation," the Internet stood for I-dealism. No longer a depressed "Prozac nation" autopathographized in the early nineties, the Internet culture of the late nineties had galvanized us into an almost manic euphoria. Suddenly we had purpose, passion, hope for the future, and unprecedented wealth in one digital package. But the mania couldn't last for-ever. As any psychiatrist will tell you, the Lithium eventually wears off, right?

Sort of.

Although the Internet bubble seemed to have burst by the end of 2000, our national fascination didn't deflate along with it. Thousands of young but more grounded hopefuls still flock to L.A.'s HollyWired, the Bay Area's Silicon Valley, or Manhattan's Silicon Alley to get in on the action, while the more prudent who have crawled back to their stable jobs ("I told you so," their colleagues inevitably gloat) talk endlessly about their friends who "can't get out." Even those who haven't joined a startup themselves always seem to know *someone* who's "been there," like a person afflicted with alcoholism, an eating disorder, or any other common compulsion.

The dot-com drama still makes page one news, the only difference being that now—given our post-9/11 focus on a more pressing "revolution"—it's often under the fold and seen as a frivolous, guilty pleasure, like the latest Madonna album or *Survivor* sequel. We say that the startup saga is *"so over"*— that we've all lost interest—but secretly, we can't get enough.

Which is why I'm still asked that inevitable question: "Are you ever joining another startup?"

Oddly, I can't say that I won't. "Not right now" is my standard reply, letting the unspoken "Maybe, someday" hang in the air. And I'm certainly not alone.

Why not?

"Silicon Valley is not only *not* dead, it's already on the way back," asserted *Newsweek*'s Steven Levy as late as March 25, 2002. "Labeling the current Valley as a bust is almost as wacky as believing all the hype of the boom. While the valuation of high-tech firms went to hallucinatory levels, the benefits people enjoyed from the Internet itself were quite real."

The fact is, the Internet is here to stay, and both it and the innovations associated with it have become inextricable parts of our lives. Despite the scary headlines, there have been some phenomenal successes. And like playing the slot machines in Vegas, hearing about a jackpot winner makes us forget about the losers: one tale of a windfall for a quarter's investment, and there we are, obsessively pulling the lever again.

What's curious about the recent startup phenomenon, though, is that despite the occasional winner, in many cases the people pulling that lever should have known better. Instead of little old ladies with cups of coins, these gamblers were savvy, highly successful entrepreneurs, venture capitalists, and investment bankers with long, enviable track records. How could they make multi-million-dollar commitments to what might have seemed, in the eyes of any rational business person, like idiotic ideas? Or good ideas with idiotic business plans? Or catchy domain names with *no* ideas or business plans, idiotic or otherwise?

These are the questions I asked in my *Industry Standard* exposé, and they're also the questions that Jesse Jacobs, a twenty-six-year-old I hadn't met down in Los Angeles, had been asking. As head of content for the online movie site IFILM (ifilm.com), he too had been thinking about a book that would help make sense of the mysterious allure of the dot-com world.

He too had noticed that at the gym, at work, at parties, and in casual conversations, this seemingly inscrutable realm invariably came up in the form of an opinion, a horror story, a success story, a dropout, someone looking for funding, or a witty one-liner. Even my article about Kibu was mentioned in his office parking lot one day. It being the digital age, Jesse approached me via e-mail.

"Do you want to find answers with me?" he asked.

And with a few quick keystrokes—a Google search (stalker filter), the exchange of JPEG photos (reality check), and several e-mail discussions (Are we on the same page?)—this book was born. It wasn't until after we were committed to write it that Jesse and I finally met face-to-face, in a Hollywood restaurant where the folks on our left were hatching a new online television series while those on the right talked about getting a celebrity-of-the-moment to sponsor a luxury goods consumer Web site.

Idly eavesdropping on these conversations, Jesse and I realized that they mirrored the power, vitality, and madness of the entire Internet saga. Before we even ordered, we'd made a decision: Rather than simply recount our own peculiar experiences, as we'd planned to do—or report on territory thoroughly mined in yesterday's business pages—we wanted to spend the bulk of our book capturing the kinds of voices and stories we couldn't help but listen in on at these surrounding tables.

And so, we went straight to the digital trenches to talk to venture capitalists; entrepreneurs green and seasoned; investment bankers; Old Media types who jumped on the New Media bandwagon; journalists who covered the scene for national newspapers and magazines; Hollywood moguls who started Web ventures; New Economy advertising executives, consultants, attorneys, and agents; CEOs and founders of both the once- and still-popular sites; and the project managers, programmers, designers, and assistants who've had a front-row seat to it all.

Many important sources, we guessed, wouldn't speak to us at all, or would be reticent about what really happened—and what was still happening—in the New Economy. But surprisingly, we found that virtually everyone we approached was willing not only to talk, but to talk candidly—to give us the alternately compelling and dish-filled accounts we'd overheard from adjacent lunch tables.

We agreed to divvy up the duties. Jesse, based in Los Angeles, would interview everyone from the New Economy's movers to the people who decided where the gilded salt shakers would go at one of the early startups' fabled bacchanals. Meantime, from Silicon Valley I would share my experiences watching and participating in one of the bizarre but all-too-familiar launches and crashes that fill the annals of dot-com history. Then, together, we'd create an oral mosaic of this period by connecting my story with those unearthed in Jesse's archaeological digs.

What you're about to read is a collective memoir of our capitalist culture at its wackiest, a very personal backstage pass to a national rave—the pursuit of the American Dream fueled by somebody else's Ecstasy.

INSIDE THE CULT OF KIBU

CHAPTER ONE THE IDEA

HAPPY: Wait a minute! I got an idea. I got a feasible idea.
Come here, Biff, let's talk this over now, let's talk some sense
here. When I was down in Florida last time, I thought of a
great idea to sell sporting goods. It just came back to me. You
and I, Biff—we have a line, the Loman Line. We train a couple of weeks, and put on a couple of exhibitions, see?

WILLY: That's an idea!

HAPPY: Wait! We form two basketball teams, see? Two
water-polo teams. We play each other. It's a million dollars'
worth of publicity. Two brothers, see? The Loman Brothers.
Displays in the Royal Palms—all the hotels. And banners
over the ring and the basketball court: "Loman Brothers."
Baby, we could sell sporting goods!

WILLY: That is a one-million-dollar idea!

—Arthur Miller, *Death of a Salesman*, 1949

"The shattering effects of Willy [Loman]'s flawed dream
should resonate today, with young dot-commers."

—*The New York Times*, August 5, 2001

There's a reason I'd never heard of the woman who came up with the idea for
Kibu until after I published my piece in *The Industry Standard*. Quite simply, her
story didn't make a good Idea Story.

Idea Stories, of course, aren't unique to New Economy startups: most
American companies boast epic tales of How We Came To Be. From the
1950s, for instance, comes the legend of middle-aged traveling milkshake-

machine salesman Ray Kroc buying out for virtually nothing Mac and Dick McDonald's popular San Bernardino, California, hamburger stand because he fell in love with their French fries. Later came Bill Gates, who alchemized from a Harvard dropout to the grand poohbah of Microsoft, a benign-seeming genius who looked like such a doofus he might have been excluded from the corporate softball game—if he didn't own most of the company.

How We Came To Be legends, naturally, took hold *after* a company's success. But for late-nineties startups, whose nonexistent products and revenue were mere millennial forecasts, Idea Stories came first—because, well, they had to.

If your startup didn't have a catchy Idea Story, it wouldn't register on the media radar. And like the proverbial tree that falls in the forest, if no one heard about you—if your publicity kit wasn't better thought out than your product—you didn't exist.

In short, a startup *was* its Idea Story.

But an Idea Story had to be a certain kind of tale. The most popular, those discussed both over Silicon Valley Foosball tables and in *Wall Street Journal* story conferences, shared certain elements. Usually they involved an eager twenty-something whose "aha moment" was triggered by:

1. Remembering a dream
2. Taking an especially long shower
3. Cruising down the Bay Area's Highway 101 at 90 miles per hour
4. Shooting the shit with a friend at a bar
5. Whining by the water cooler at a boring entry-level corporate job ("Screw this! I'm gonna start my *own* company!")
6. Having a flashback to childhood (which wasn't that long ago)

Suddenly . . . *voila!* Like a genie from a bottle, The Idea—a simple concept that would make other folks slap their foreheads à la those old V–8 Juice commercials and exclaim, "Why didn't *I* think of that?"—popped out. This story then became the tale that captured the public's imagination and created public awareness of (and thus anticipation for) the promised future products and revenue streams.

In the case of Kibu, there was nothing terribly wrong with the actual Idea Story, which was told to me later by the actual Idea Person and confirmed by the company's actual original employees. But the Idea Story needed the right characters. After the publication of my *Industry Standard* article, I learned of several original "first-hireds" who'd been disposed of early on and never mentioned again, only to be replaced by new *official* "first-hireds," who became characters in the new *official* Idea Story. (Oddly, this sounded like a practice straight out of the *old* Old Economy, when Stalin consolidated his power by purging his co-revolutionaries and airbrushing them out of group photographs.)

As it happens, the real Kibu Idea Story went something like this: A smart young woman named Susan Scarpa had been working in the beauty industry in Manhattan, paying her dues at Revlon, L'Oréal, and Redken. She finally broke through to the corporate management level at Chanel, but her position was demanding. By 1999, Scarpa was thinking about having a baby, and she wondered whether there was something beauty industry–related that she could do from home.

Maybe, she thought, she'd start her own business.

Her husband, a young Merrill Lynch investment banker, suspected an answer might lie in the Web. Scarpa wasn't so sure. She knew nothing about the Internet, didn't even have e-mail, and beauty-industry experts she talked to understood the online world no better than she. "Some very intelligent people could not understand what I was about to do. And neither could I," she explained later—in an e-mail.

Then, kismet. Scarpa's husband, Rudy, had been the lead banker for Silver Lake Partners, the Silicon Valley tech fund then in the process of raising their eventual $2.2 billion and co-managed by venture capitalist Dave Roux. Seated together on a plane in 1999, Rudy told Roux that his wife, Susan, worked at Chanel, and was contemplating creating a hair and makeup Internet site for teen girls. According to Scarpa, her husband came up with the idea of a teen site because he guessed that teen girls did a lot of surfing the Net. "And," adds Scarpa, "we both knew they had money to spend."

Well, at least a certain type of teen girl did—like Dave Roux's daughter. Apparently, she and all her Silicon Valley girlfriends logged onto the Net each day, but—*total bummer!*—had nowhere to go. They'd already clicked through all the virtual shopping malls. What was a girl with money to *do*?

Daddy Warbucks to the rescue. Cradling an air phone, Roux dialed his buddies down on the gilded venture capitalist strip known as Sand Hill Road and immediately began asking for startup money. This display, Scarpa mused at the time, could only mean one thing: If not just Roux, but also his equally wealthy and powerful colleagues, got excited by the fledgling concept, then maybe the Internet really *was* the answer. "I thought," says Scarpa, "it was our destiny!"

Within months, Susan and Rudy Scarpa moved west; she would oversee the startup, while he temporarily transferred to Merrill Lynch's San Francisco office. The agreement was that after Kibu took off in Silicon Valley, Scarpa could come back to New York within the year and work from home. Before having her baby, she would first midwife this teen-girl startup.

And so, Kibu's Idea Story.

Almost.

This is the Kibu Story that nobody talks about and few have heard. In truth, it wasn't the classic Idea Story for several reasons. First, Scarpa wasn't a single twenty-something, but in her thirties (gasp!), married (double gasp!), and hoping to have a baby (how Old Economy—to have time for a child!). But the biggest problem was that six months after Kibu had hatched, Scarpa left the company, thanks to Molly Lynch. Molly had been brought in as cofounder by Tom Jermoluk, a Kibu director and the former Excite@Home chairman who later became a general partner at the venture-capital firm Kleiner, Perkins, Caulfield & Byers. At this point, according to several original first-hireds, it was decided that a brand-new Idea Story should be spun— with Molly as the starring character.

(Interestingly, I did once hear the name Susan slip out at a meeting, but when another member of the Kibu management team asked, "Who's Susan?" the room went silent and Looks were exchanged. Like a shameful family secret, Susan was never mentioned again.)

Kibu's new Idea Story, sent out in splashy press releases and told ad nauseam at sales meetings and media junkets, is what I heard the first day I interviewed to be the site's editor-in-chief at the company's Redwood City, California, offices, located on the ground floor of the Excite@Home Building. It was the story that Molly and Judy MacDonald, who had been brought in as CEO by Kleiner, Perkins, shared with all potential Kibu employees, as if to say, "Hop aboard! We're the stuff legends are made of!"

Molly's version, told between teensy-weensy bites of sushi washed down with copious quantities of Evian, went something like this: So, I was working with Tom Jermoluk at Excite@Home (she was his secretary, but who has time for details). I mentioned that jillions of teen girls had nowhere to go on the Net, that there was no site that was, like, *theirs*. So I thought, why hasn't anyone done this? Tom and I talked about the idea, and he loved it. But because I didn't have any business experience, we brought on Judy as our CEO. (In every iteration of this fable, Judy's full name seemed to be Judy-who-sold-her-Portland-based-company-PrintPaks-to-Mattel-for-$26-million.)

As Idea Stories go, Kibu's fictional version trumped reality, particularly since Molly, who resembled a popular teenage girl, and Judy, a thirty-something trying to resemble a popular teenage girl (think Britney Spears with crow's feet) made for good press. The dynamic duo rewrote Kibu's history, regaling the media with buzzwords like "empowerment" and waxing poetic about the online personalities, or "Faces," who would mentor teen girls in areas ranging from friendship to fashion. The Idea, they said, was to attract "Girls Who Get It."

It sounded good in theory, but something didn't seem quite right. I wasn't sure that these women, well, "got it." Molly and Judy certainly could swing their pom-poms and cheerlead, but could they run a company, create a product, and produce revenue? I wasn't so sure.

One Sunday, while taking a walk on the beach in Sausalito, I mentioned these concerns to my then boyfriend. At thirty, he had just resigned as the lead banker on communications services at Goldman Sachs, the prominent New York investment banking firm, to become one of the first-hireds at a San Francisco startup—leaving behind, the hot industry magazine *Red Herring* reported, "a few million dollars in unvested equity."

"Only sign on if you truly believe in the idea," he told me as we strolled along the sand. In taking his own several-million-dollar gamble, he certainly believed in his startup's idea. The company, named Epoch (by me, and for which I was to be compensated with 10,000 shares that I never received), had a sexy idea: make IPOs—those daily instant-millionaire-producing phenomena—available to regular Joe's and Jane's clamoring to get in on the action. With partners like T. D. Waterhouse and Charles Schwab, it seemed like a solid premise. And in theory, so did a unique Web community for teen girls. *If done well*, I thought, it had potential.

The only problem was the gaping hole in Kibu's Idea. Beyond the "teen girl Web site" part, not much had been worked out. Would it target younger teens or older teens? How would the interactivity work? How would it make money? What would prevent a competitor from registering a URL and inviting fickle "girls who get it" to its online slumber party as well?

Basically, there was a great Story, but no real Idea. When I brought this up to Judy and Molly during the interview process, they explained enthusiastically that that was why they needed people like me: I could be instrumental in building the company. This is the Internet! There are no boundaries! We concocted the Idea, now you bring us your ideas!

Okay, I thought, this might be an exciting challenge.

Around the same time, though, I was also offered an editor position at a startup called UBUBU. UBUBU had a promising Idea Story, too, having been cofounded by photogenic, fresh-faced, Harvard Business School graduates who'd been dorm buddies. Josh Keller, one of these cofounders, explained the concept: "We wanted to turn your flat, boring, Microsoft-issued desktop into this colorful 3-D environment. We used a planetary metaphor. The way we made money was to go to companies and say that you could own the desktop and theme it entirely in your brand." With *Star Trek* celebrity Patrick Stewart as their spokesperson and several solid partnership deals signed, they seemed legitimate.

But while I felt that these UBUBU people could manage, their Idea didn't trip my trigger. Planets and interfaces just weren't my thing. The teen-girl Idea, on the other hand, seemed like a perfect fit—I'd just published my teen diaries, and I wrote regularly for magazines and newspapers about teen issues. And Kibu was saying that their site wouldn't be about barrettes and boys, but about self-confidence and community.

"We're going to change girls' lives," Judy told me as I tried to decide between the two gigs. "It's a chance to make a difference."

And with that one phrase, *"chance to make a difference,"* I took my first toe dip into the cult. Like every other newbie dot-commer, I was hooked by the notion that, on some level, I could make a difference. That difference might be "empowering" teen girls, creating a "revolutionary" new platform, or breaking down "brick-and-mortar barriers." It might even be making a six- or seven-figure difference on my bank statement.

Whatever that difference we'd all supposedly make was, the Idea would take us there. In its name we recruits accepted stock options that would soon turn as worthless as Confederate money, worked inhumane hours, and spouted ridiculous catchphrases in public with a straight face. The Idea wasn't just a cool company concept—it was a ticket to something Bigger Than Us.

Which is why so many people tried to come up with one.

There were so many Ideas floating around, in fact, that to break through the clutter, each had to be shortened into a recognizable phrase, often cannibalizing other successful brand-name startups. The telephone service auction site called Keen.com, for instance, was billed as the "eBay of 900-number calls." A startup that sold only balls, called JustBalls.com, was dubbed the "Amazon.com of Balls." A funeral planning site, HeavenlyDoor.com, became known as the "Geocities of Funerals."

Before attending medical school I had worked briefly in the film business, so I was used to this practice of describing, say, slam-dunk ideas for the next wildly commercial screenplay: "It's *Die Hard* on a bus!" "It's *Titanic* on Mars!" It all sounded eerily familiar. But what resonated most was the concept used in Hollywood called "suspension of disbelief"—roughly translated to mean "dismissing initial skepticism."

In the startup world, "suspension of disbelief" allowed hundreds of would-be Thomas Edisons to put their ideas down on cocktail-party napkins, punch in 1-800-Dial-A-VC, and head straight for a Nasdaq IPO. Instead of being called crazy, these purveyors of pie-in-the-sky ideas were now considered "visionary."

And for one simple reason: With technology creating entirely new money-making possibilities seemingly every second, "pie-in-the-sky" became relative. After all, had *Death of a Salesman's* Willy Loman suggested auctioning off tchotchkes that were cluttering up people's basements as being a "million-dollar idea," attention would not have been paid. Yet eBay wasn't just a million-dollar idea—it was a *billion*-dollar idea.

Nor was eBay a lone luck-of-the-draw lottery winner. Remember the far-fetched "million-dollar idea" to sell sporting goods, the so-called "Loman Line"? In 1995, Jim Medalia, a New Jersey entrepreneur, had a similar notion. At the time, Medalia and his wife were running a successful computer graphics company in New York, but, he says, building Web sites for large corporations had become "insane."

"One of my best examples," Medalia recalls, "is that we were invited to talk to one of the largest insurance companies in the U.S. In the meeting room, there were fifty people, including my wife and one of our designers. We didn't get to say *one word* in over two hours! They just sat there arguing with each other: Who was going to control the Web site? What was it going to *do*? We never even got to make our presentation!"

So Medalia and his wife decided to build their own site—with one slight problem. Like many budding Internet entrepreneurs, they hadn't actually decided what kind. E-commerce came to mind, but what the heck to sell? "We thought it was important to develop a new niche," explains Medalia, "so we looked at books and CDs and wrote down what they had in common." Medalia's list went like this:

- They're affordable.
- They're easy to ship.
- They have a long shelf life.
- There are more book and CD titles than what could reasonably fit into a store.
- There's little after-market support.

Evaluating their scribbles, Medalia and his wife then asked themselves, "What's a really big industry that meets all of these criteria?" They settled on sporting goods. Yet even that seemed too general. "What is there more of than any other item in the sporting goods business?" Medalia wondered. His answer: balls. "Actually," he concedes, "the real answer was athletic shoes, but somebody was already doing that. So, we said—*balls*. Just balls!"

JustBalls.com has since raised $17 million from investors including David Wetherell of CMGI, Blue Rock Capital, Zesiger Capital Group, and Japan's JAFCO American Ventures. Even Medalia seems surprised by the company's success. "We found that people usually buy *multiple* balls, not just one," he says. "It turns out that the ball business is about a five-billion-dollar business worldwide! Who knew?"

That's the thing about these Ideas: You just never knew.

Auren Hoffman, now the CEO of BridgePath.com, a staffing exchange site, discovered firsthand how difficult it became to distinguish between the diamonds and the cubic zirconium. When Hoffman was an undergraduate at Berkeley in 1996, he was part of a small group of students who used to meet every few weeks to bounce business ideas off each other. One day, his buddy Kevin Brown said that he was thinking of joining a company called Inktomi.

"I said, 'Inktomi—you mean that search engine company?' I told him, 'Don't do it. This is stupid.' "

Brown ignored Hoffman's advice and became employee number five, Inktomi's first nonengineer. He helped to write their business plan and ended up getting a sizable interest in the company, whose market cap, even as late as Spring 2002, still exceeded $500 million. "Every time I see him," Hoffman admits sheepishly, "I remind him that he's very lucky not to have listened to me."

David Neuman, the former head of Disney Television who later became president of the now-defunct online entertainment site Digital Entertainment Network (DEN), recalls that even the most well-respected business people misjudged dot-com ideas in the early days. Neuman cites the trouble that DEN's cofounder Marc Collins-Rector experienced when seeking support for what turned out to be the Web's first—and very successful—Internet service provider (ISP), Concentric Networks.

"Marc claimed that when he went to former Secretary of the Treasury Robert Rubin, who was at the time the head of one of the largest investment banks on Wall Street [Goldman Sachs], Robert sort of patted him on the head and said, 'You seem like a smart young man, but nobody is going to want to type to each other on the Internet.' "

Some ideas, however, sounded impractical even to the idealistic. Take Sang Lee, an early Net enthusiast who back in 1992 was building Web pages and "playing with HTML" as an undergraduate at the University of Pennsylvania. Dabbling in online poker chat rooms, Lee excitedly watched the evolution from dial-up bulletin boards to Web sites and later "put off an MBA to pursue the dot-com craze."

As a lead project manager in the New York office of Rare Medium, an Internet consultancy, Lee remembers his Web shop colleagues standing near the bar at late-nineties launch parties saying, "Yeah, I might leave Rare, because I have the next great idea."

One such harebrained idea, Lee says, involved connecting all the city's Asian grocers and deli owners via the Web by handing out wireless Palm Pilots so they could trade goods. "Conceptually," Lee says, "it sounded like it might work, but these grocers can barely speak English. These people at Rare Medium didn't even understand that there was a whole market of Korean grocer suppliers out there who'd never *heard* of the Web."

New York grocers aside, by the time Lee's coworkers began dreaming about the next big Idea, many people had, in fact, heard of the Web, and new business plans were being bandied about by the cappuccino machine along with the latest stock quotes. But just a few years earlier, Web-heads were mostly to be found in academia. From Hoffman's group of Berkeley friends, for instance, everyone went on to found a company—some, three or four.

Like Hoffman's pal Noah Doyle, who in 1996 cofounded an online direct marketing company called IntelliPost (later renamed MyPoints.com) that was sold to United NewVentures for over $100 million in the summer of 2001. "It was pretty exciting stuff," says Hoffman. "There weren't that many people who were into it back then."

Alex Cohen, a professor at Berkeley in 1993, was one of the few. Cohen's résumé reads like a timeline of the most successful (and *un*-successful) Internet companies: The McKinley Group, Excite, Netscape, CNET, and Pop.com. Still, when he came to Berkeley armed with a comparative litera-ture doctorate from SUNY Buffalo, he thought he'd be teaching film and rhetoric—not hopping aboard the Internet roller coaster.

ALEX COHEN

I started teaching a course called "Cinema and Beyond" at UC Berkeley in 1993 that talked about the transformation of society in the digital era. The course was a runaway hit—600 students tried to take it! A lot of my students ending up working in the Net, the most well-known being Janelle Brown at *Salon* magazine. Others went on to work at ILM, Pixar, and CNET. Christine Maxwell of the Maxwell publishing family heard about my course and want-ed me to help her with an Internet project called The McKinley Group. I avoided her at first because I didn't want to consult.

But then I ran into her husband at a party—he was a scientist at Berkeley doing satellite research. He said, "Have you met my wife?" I said I hadn't. It turned out to be Christine Maxwell. Oops! I felt bad about dissing her, so I visited her at work and met her whole crew. And then I thought, "Oh my God, you have so much stuff to do!"

She actually owned a Yellow Pages directory, and they were trying to build a directory of the Net. I started getting involved with some very interesting peo-ple there. David Hayden was our CEO, and he, of course, went on to become the CEO of Critical Path [the once high-flying San Francisco–based provider of e-mail and messaging services that later came under attack from investors claim-ing that the company had artificially inflated its stock price].

Meantime, I set up a Web server called Cinema Space. It was designed to be the first online magazine for film and technology, but I could get nobody to write for it because everyone was afraid that if they did, they couldn't get tenure. They were all, "What does it mean to have your text everywhere? What is the Web? What are you *talking* about?"

But I knew that the Web was going to be *huge!* Because if you indexed all these texts, you could run a Spider. Someone was already doing it, this guy called WebCrawler up in Washington, and then Lycos suddenly came out, and I started playing with the software, but they didn't quite have it right yet. So, when Christine Maxwell said "Internet directory" to me, I said, "Got it—that's what we have to do! A site where you could get to everything on the Web!"

I wasn't a businessman. I didn't care about money. For me, it was the idea of all the databases in the universe known to man, available for indexing! But David Hayden said, "Alex, I gotta find a business here." We were getting a cup of coffee in that weird area of Berkeley near Fourth Street that David Lynch used to have coffee in. Finally he goes, "Aha! We'll pay for traffic." I said, "What are you talking about? That's insane, because that's like negative." He said, "No, you don't understand. You'll get it." And actually, that became the model for the IPO market: negative revenue.

So we started building up the company—which we eventually sold to Excite on September 3, 1996, for something like $10 million in stock.

Cohen wasn't alone in venturing online in a seemingly Stone Age time before Web sites became as integral to our daily lives as Chinese takeout: "Meet me there at eight—get the directions on Mapquest"; "The new Stephen King book is out—I just saw it on Amazon"; "You've got to hear this Moby tune I downloaded from Morpheus."

In fact, there are so many active Web sites today that keeping track of where you've been can cause a bad case of what Cohen later called "Internet amnesia." But back in 1994, when there were virtually no sites, a twenty-two-year-old University of Pennsylvania graduate, Adeo Ressi, and his college cohorts Ted Werth, Andrew Wanliss-Orlebar, and Paul Glanzrock decided to create their own: They named it Total New York (totalny.com).

Little did Ressi know that Total New York would soon grow into AOL Digital Cities, after its sale to America Online and Tribune, and that the twenty-something postgrad would go on to become an Internet millionaire.

ADEO RESSI

We literally started one of the first Web companies that I know of. There were ISPs that were selling access, and there were magazines such as *Wired* that had launched sites, but we were Web-only.

At the time, all that was on the Net was stuff like someone's research paper linked to someone's bio. There were no such things as tables or graphics. We thought there was an opportunity to produce better content.

Our idea was to create a really good city guide that would also cover culture. It worked pretty well because by 1994 and 1995, we were definitely the most high-profile site out there. We had major publications like *Time*, the *New York Times*, and *Business Week* writing full-page articles on us. But it was ironic, because you had major media outlets reporting on the Net, and no one knew what it was! No one even knew how to get *access*.

A lot of people think it was such a big deal, but when we had the idea, it was the furthest thing from a big deal imaginable. I mean, our first investor was a brain surgeon and avid art collector who put $50,000 into the idea, and looked at this as a philanthropic venture.

———————

Auren Hoffman was also one of the early "kids" experimenting online.

AUREN HOFFMAN

I founded Kyber Systems in May of my junior year at Berkeley to help pay my tuition. It was 1995, and I thought that we would first build Web sites for politicians. Which was a really stupid idea because I didn't realize that politicians have no money! There was a mayor's race in San Francisco, and I called a candidate, Frank Jordan, trying to get him as a client, thinking that would be a big name and we'd be able to get bigger clients.

I told them, "Listen, you guys should really get a Web site. Even if the site isn't great, you'll get so much press for it, it'll be worth the money that you pay me to build it." Every single day, like clockwork, I called and left that message. Nothing, nothing, nothing, nothing, nothing. For months!

Then one day, the third candidate in the campaign, Roberta Achtenberg, put up a Web site. That day she was on two TV stations, she was on the radio, she was in all the dailies and weeklies. The next night, I got a call from the Jordan campaign saying the other candidate, Willie Brown, is going to have a Web site done in eleven days, so we need ours in ten. We got it done in nine. Willie Brown got it done in twelve. There was an article in the *San Francisco Chronicle* comparing all three, which said that Frank Jordan's was by far the best. That was the first and last political client for KS. We sold the company to Human Ingenuity in 1997 for lots of stock but not much cash, and I left to start BridgePath.

It wasn't just professors and postgrads pursuing new ideas on the Web. Also typing in "www" were traditional boardroom executives like Andrew Anker, the former CS First Boston and PaineWebber investment banker who cofounded *Wired* Digital, Inc.; successful Hollywood executives like Kevin Wendle, cofounder of the Fox Broadcasting Network, CNET, E! Online, and IFILM, who back in 1993 became the first senior entertainment executive to make the move to the Web; and music club owners like Andrew Rasiej (pronounced Ra-shay), who started the live music site Digital Club Network.

Not that offline talent necessarily translated into online brilliance. Dan Adler, head of New Media at Hollywood's Creative Artists Agency (CAA), notes that many of the early pioneers came up with "thought-piece demo tapes that took this view that you'd be cooking in your kitchen with a touch-screen refrigerator while your friend, who was rock-climbing, would call you on the screen and you would communicate via video."

But folks like Anker were shaping what would become hallmarks of the digital revolution.

ANDREW ANKER

I was in a banking stage in my career and Jane Metcalfe and Louis Rossetto came to my door around early August 1992 with the idea of building a magazine to capture this thing they called the "digital revolution" that was about to happen. I had spent my career as a banker in media—advertising, cable—and I had been a computer guy since I was a teen. So I was like, "Cool—I want this magazine."

We raised six or seven hundred thousand dollars to help them launch *Wired*. We didn't make any money on it, but it was really fun. By mid-'93, the magazine had a very successful launch. Clinton and Gore were starting out with their information superhighway idea, so taking the magazine and brand online was the obvious next step.

Wired had been the first to dip their toes into a lot of waters. They were the first magazine to have content on AOL. If you go back to AOL's annual report in '94, we were higher up on their partner list than *Time!* I began attending these weekly meetings called Online Brain Trusts to figure out what *Wired* should do, and the idea was to spend half our money on the magazine, and half online.

Kevin Wendle remembers "completing a whirlwind of excitement and success at Fox"—where he had programed hit series like 21 *Jump Street, The Simpsons, Married with Children,* and *Beverly Hills 90210*—and wondering what to do next. "I was thinking—what a shame, never again will I have the same rush as starting the Fox Network."

A phone call from startup entrepreneur Halsey Minor would change all that. When Wendle left Los Angeles to join Minor in founding CNET, he recalls that his Hollywood friends "thought I was nuts." In fact, one Hollywood mogul said to a friend of Wendle's, "Kevin Wendle is out of his mind. He's out of the business."

Not exactly. Wendle had no idea what CNET was when Minor approached him, but it would soon make him far wealthier than the Hollywood naysayers who stayed behind.

KEVIN WENDLE

I was producing some television stuff, and I got a phone call from Halsey Minor. He said, "I'm the CEO of a company called CNET and I want to talk to you about possibly being a consultant to my company."

I said, "CNET? Is that in the *marine* business?"

He said, "No, no, it's CNET as in the Computer Network, and I'm starting a cable network about technology." He said that I was highly recommended as a TV exec by a number of people, so he was hoping that I would read his business plan and give him some advice.

I really liked the notion of a TV network that was able to capitalize on the high CPMs that computer magazines were getting. And the notion that computer products for the first time needed more than magazines to be exposed to the world. One idea was to have an online component to the network, though we didn't know how that was going to work at the time. Being somewhat of a Luddite, I wanted to immerse myself. I remember saying to Halsey on the phone, "How many people are in your company?", and he said, "It's just really me right now."

So I spent a lot of time with Halsey, and he introduced me to something called "the WELL," one of the first ever online communities for people who were passionate about technology, but who were also intellectual and interesting. And I also found out about MUDs and MOOs and all these other connected communities online. So when Halsey said, "Why don't you come and do this with me full-time?", I was intrigued.

All these sites were launching that would focus on wine or flowers or whatever, but our view was that we had the best category—technology—because if you're online in the first place, we know that you have a browser, we know that you have e-mail. Our audience was the largest possible audience. We knew about Jeff Bezos who was pursuing something with books. We knew about Jerry Yang and David Filo with Yahoo!, who were pursuing this Internet directory. But we were just focused on our category.

Andrew Rasiej, whom *New York* magazine described as looking "a little like George Clooney," had a successful career in real estate development (South Street Seaport, World Financial Center) and live music (former owner of Irving Plaza) before he got hooked on the Web in the days when things didn't quite yet *work*.

ANDREW RASIEJ

This idea to do concerts on the Web started in 1994, when Michael Dorf [founder and CEO of the popular club The Knitting Factory] and I did the Mac Festival, which was a multiclub New York music festival that was broadcast online. Students at NYU would file reports online every fifteen minutes. There was a Web site, but it was very rudimentary—I think Mosaic was the browser.

Streaming didn't exist, but we thought it was really cool that you could do a linked event. We got an e-mail from some kid in Singapore saying, "Hey, I feel like I'm club-hopping in NYC!" The following year, we did the festival again and used a technology called Xing, the predecessor to Real Networks. And we installed all these ISDN lines into the clubs, with the effect of streaming these live concerts online.

But, a week before the event, we found that Apple machines don't support ISDN modems! We went ahead and did it anyway—half the shows crashed and half the shows went up. We were criticized by some for presenting a lot of hype and of not being able to deliver, but we were saying that this was an *experiment*. I'm sure that the first time Edison tried to do a recording, it didn't work, but do we crucify him now?

Well, no. Nor did you have to be Edison to hop on the Web. According to Courtney Pulitzer, founder of Cocktails with Courtney, a networking event for Silicon Alley dot-commers, "Everyone had this ability to show the world who they were with their homepage." Having a background in theater, Pulitzer says, "I thought of changing Shakespeare's 'All the world's a stage' to 'Everyone has their homepage.' "

Homepage schmomepage. Soon, everyone had an idea for a full-fledged business. And in keeping with the biblical passage that "there is no new thing under the sun," many came up with almost identical ideas. Not only was there fierce competition across categories to gain market share, but companies also had to overcome the multitude of players on their own turf.

In true Darwinian fashion, casualties abounded. Within the online sports category, ESPN.com and CBSSportsline.com had to battle the heavily funded upstart Quokka Sports, which fizzled out after a nearly $200 million fight and a last-ditch effort to save itself through a 1-for-50 reverse stock split. Amazon.com went head-to-head with BarnesandNoble.com and Borders.com. DrKoop.com, represented by CAA's Dan Adler, vied for elbow room with WebMD and CBSHealthWatch in the health and wellness space. But less than two years after a surging IPO in June 1999—

almost doubling its price by the end of the day—DrKoop was delisted from the Nasdaq, and announced in December of 2001 that it would cease operations.

Ideas, it seemed, many of which were conceived in the local bar, were like darts thrown at a board—some hit the bull's-eye, while others followed a trajectory straight to the sawdust floor. Yet no one could predict where any one dart would land.

The author and journalist Po Bronson, who writes about Silicon Valley, believes that his "head was screwed on okay" during the Internet boom. But analogous to the rule that you should start selling your stocks when your cab driver starts giving *you* tips, Bronson "knew that things were going wrong when other writers started coming up with ideas" for companies. Still, it wasn't just writers who, perhaps too eagerly, blindly bought into the boom.

PO BRONSON

I met two guys at a cocktail party who worked for an Israeli high-tech company. One was the local biz-dev guy and the other guy was the COO. It was a solid technology play—they were making switches or routers or something.

On a plane, one of them met the wife of Dr. Spock. He sort of sidled up to her and got her talking. Just recently, DrKoop.com had gone public and was worth an enormous amount of money. She was like, "Dr. Koop, come on, what's the one name that people know more than Dr. Koop? It's *Dr. Spock.*"

So this guy comes back from this cross-country flight with the rights to Dr. Spock! I had just seen these guys two weeks before and they were telling me about their company, and I thought it was pretty cool, that what these guys were doing was solid. Now, two weeks later, they're about to quit their jobs and are saying, "If DrKoop.com is worth this amount of money, then DrSpock.com is a six-hundred-million-dollar idea."

They didn't have anything except for sitting next to Mrs. Spock on a plane! But they were like, "The name brand, the name brand. . . "

Unlike Bronson, Dan Roach doesn't make his living as a writer, but the former managing director at Garage Technology Ventures does tell stories—Idea Stories. After hearing too many cockamamie idea pitches as a venture capitalist, Roach came up with a spoof of his own.

DAN ROACH

There were plenty of ideas that looked ludicrous but got funding, so I conceived of my own company called BaloneyNet.com. I actually bought the Web site name. The company was focused on the high-end gift market for sending baloney. In essence, we had, in layman's terms, a baloney scanner and a baloney printer.

When I'm giving the pitch, I hold up whatever I have in my hand—it could be a pen or a glass of water—and I say, "What is this? This is energy! There's nothing here but quarks, charms, photons, you name it. This can be packetized. And there's no reason that we can't do the same thing with baloney: break it down, packetize it, and send it. Then it can be reassembled after it's been sent through the wire on a rapid prototyping machine called a baloney printer. You put in a printer cartridge and reassemble the baloney." It was an extremely silly goof.

Anyone who had anything to do with the Net thought it was really funny. But once I was having dinner with a friend of mine, and I'm giving the BaloneyNet.com pitch. I'm going through the private label strategy because we don't want to alienate Oscar Meyer or any of the big names. You know, the whole thing with blades and razors—you give away the baloney printer and make money on the baloney cartridges. There was going to be a BaloneyNet.com printer in every office building so you could send a personalized corporate gift of baloney. But the key was that you had to buy the cartridges and keep them *refrigerated*.

So my friend's wife, who knew nothing about the Internet, goes, "Why do you need to spend the money to develop the scanner, printer and all the infrastructure to deliver baloney to someone's office if the poor SOB has to go to the grocery store to buy the refrigerated cartridges in the first place?"

It was this just classic moment where the whole table goes silent and everyone says to her, "You just don't get it, do you?"

But in fact, she hit the nail on the head: The economics of so many ideas didn't make any sense.

Other ideas might as well have been lampoons. Lew Harris, who came to the Web with over twenty years of media experience, including stints as editor-in-chief at *Los Angeles* magazine and entertainment editor for *People* magazine in New York, remembers the supposedly "big, bold plans" he heard while serving as founding editor of E! Online.

"Audio chat was the most ludicrous idea I'd ever heard," says Harris. "They were calling it 'audio instant messaging.' I was like, that's why we have the *phone!*"

Although *The Internet for Dummies* handbook lacked an "Ideas" chapter to guide aspiring CEOs away from dopey ideas, many hopefuls turned to the online Goliath Amazon.com to look to for the secret of startup success. The independent bookseller became the industry paragon, conceived and grown in garage-band style by Jeff Bezos, a young entrepreneur who later experienced the American capitalist orgasm when he appeared on *Time* magazine's cover as their Man of the Year.

Those attempting to imitate the niche-player-gone-big—and even those who simply observed—spent endless hours trying to figure out what had gone right with Amazon. One journalist, Rebecca Eisenberg, who began covering the industry in 1995, couldn't resist comparing her Stanford buddy's idea to Amazon's.

REBECCA EISENBERG

Amazon made sense, but people were raising tons and tons of money for niche players that I never understood. Someone I knew from Stanford started a site that was dedicated just to hosiery. He managed to raise some money, but I truly wondered how it would be able to stand on its own. I mean, maybe a site that sells a lot of things to women. But a one-niche small-market product didn't strike me as something that could get that big.

Amazon got big because the book market is big. But the hosiery market is tiny! Maybe I'm biased in saying this, because I hate wearing hosiery, and have gone great lengths to avoid it. Still, I just didn't see the site becoming the Amazon of hosiery.

Steven Overman, who moved from New York to San Francisco in 1994 to work as the executive assistant to *Wired* magazine cofounders Louis Rossetto and Jane Metcalfe, also recalls Amazon's influence.

STEVEN OVERMAN

I remember hearing, "Amazon, Amazon. . . "—all the editors at *Wired* were talking about Amazon. I asked, "What is this Amazon thing?" and Louis said, "Well, they sell books," and I remember thinking that sounded like a really terrific idea and wondering if we should write about them. My first impression was an image of a dusty little hippie bookstore in Portland.

We heard new ideas all the time at the magazine, and Amazon sounded like a good one. It fit in with what Louis deeply believed in: When you create a truly networked society, the way goods and services are exchanged will change, and so will the whole economy.

DAN ADLER

During the boom, everyone had an idea. Ultimately, because many of the ideas that had succeeded had been back-of-the-envelope crazy ideas that no one thought would work—often by people who had not a lot of experience in doing them—when you looked at pitches, you had to say, "Okay, I can't turn down this idea that may not make a lot of sense, from someone who may not have the credentials, because maybe it's the next Amazon or Yahoo! or eBay." That made it all the more chaotic.

It wasn't just Amazon or Yahoo! or eBay: any even seemingly successful startup became an instant target for copycats, resulting in a comical herd mentality. Suddenly the Internet became less a place for brilliant innovators and more a mecca for me-toos, also-rans, and never-weres who emerged on the scene.

"One idea would come up and then you would see thirty proposals for the same thing," remembers Peter Seidler, former chief creative officer of the once powerful Web shop Razorfish.

Doug Levin, a former Microsoft executive, had also been around technology and the Internet long enough to have seen his fair share of imitators.

DOUG LEVIN

There was a whole series of pet-related types of investments. Pets.com, Petstore.com, PetStation.com, In-Memory-Of-Pets.com, PETsMART.com, PetVacations.com, and Petagonia.com—it eventually reached *twelve* types of Pet startups. In fact, there was a business plan being passed around, now I don't know if it was specious or not, but it was called Cement.com. The thinking was, if you could believe in a 50-pound bag of dog food being shipped, you could also deliver a 50-pound bag of cement.

The most successful ideas, it seems, were born not of a what's-hot-this-second mindset but of that good old-fashioned entrepreneurial stalwart—passion. Lack of passion, in fact, could often kill a company faster than a bad Idea Story. The Ziff-Davis ad executive Jennifer Musillo remembers when her family came up with an idea for a service called Secretary.com, "where all kinds of resources for secretaries, including restaurant listings, dictionaries, and travel booking services, could be filtered through one site." But when it was discovered that the URL was taken, "that was the end of it," Musillo says regretfully. "No one cared enough to pursue it."

That can't be said of Lynn Harris, a 1990 Yale grad who launched BreakupGirl.com as a "labor of love."

LYNN HARRIS

I co-created the BreakupGirl character and Web site with my college buddy, Chris Kalb. I was words, Chris was pictures and concept. We invented this animated, irreverent, advice-spewing character as part of a book that I was writing. Because, you know, we need a superhero for relationships, don't we?

We had a great property in two dimensions, a character that people really liked, so we thought, "Wouldn't it be great if she could give relationship advice in an ongoing interactive format, and maybe even one day have an animated cartoon adventure? And wouldn't it be cool if there was some kind of medium where we could do that by ourselves right now?" Then a second later, it was like, "OH, WAIT!"

We launched the site in 1997 when the Internet was a quaint community, seemingly held together with duct tape and run by a steam engine. But because of the grassroots spirit of the Web, we deliberately didn't mention the book for six months, so that we could develop street credibility on our own.

Shortly after we launched, we were approached by ChickClick and that's how we started making money. We joined their consortium of sites that shared their ad revenue. We didn't make salaries that way, but we made operating costs and when we revamped, we doubled our revenue and were able to hire an assistant. Then, in 1999, Oxygen asked us to become its relationship brand.

We accepted, but it was only after three months of agonizing and negotiating. After all, this was our *baby!* We weren't willing to sell the BreakupGirl character outright, because, really, the only people who could do her was us. She was our vision.

Auren Hoffman also worked from the passion platform when he started a new industry institution.

AUREN HOFFMAN

In 1998, I started this thing called Silicon Forum for people passionate about the industry. I was sick of going to these events where all they would talk about was Amazon's stock price, or who got what in their Series B financing, or the future of B2B. So we decided to start this organization because there wasn't anything like it.

I cold-called Tim Draper, the famous VC in the Valley. A common tactic of mine is to call five hundred times until I'm so annoying that they finally take my call. I basically told his assistant that she'd keep hearing from me for the next thirty years unless I got to talk to him, so finally, he calls me one day and I convince him to be our first speaker at the Silicon Forum.

We limited it to forty people, and it's now an institution. We generally hold them in a back room in a Chinese restaurant in Palo Alto. The criteria for coming to the Forum are that the person is passionate, and has an opinion. The lucky thing is that the first one we had was supersuccessful. Guy Kawasaki, one of the people responsible for the success of the Macintosh, came, and so did Chris Alden, the editor of *Red Herring*.

Craig Johnson, probably the most famous lawyer in Silicon Valley—he runs Venture Law Group [which helped to start Yahoo!, WebTV, and Hotmail, among others]—comes to quite a few, and he actually started a company called GrassRoots.com at a Silicon Forum. He was sitting next to another guy, they decided to start it, and two months later, they had raised $30 million for it! He says the reason he likes Silicon Forum is that it's his break away from "work."

LEW HARRIS

What I remember as sparking my interest in the potential of the Web was the Oklahoma City bombing. I got to the office and at ten-thirty, I went to AOL to see if there was any news on it. Already there were twenty chat rooms, twenty bulletin boards asking, "Have you seen so-and-so?" People were talking about who they thought had done it.

Keep in mind, at this point, there was not a newspaper published on this. But when I went back at three or four in the afternoon, AOL had the latest news, and now there were many more chat rooms, bulletin boards, lots of photos. An entire community had been built, and it wasn't just a newscaster blabbing at you. People were giving their opinions, posting things. It was the most fascinating thing I had ever seen! I was mesmerized.

I thought, wouldn't it be amazing if you could have a writer post a story, then get immediate feedback from the readers, and have the writer actually join in on the dialogue? It was something I put into practice years later at E! Online.

It was also something that a Los Angeles teenager, Ashley Power, put into practice in the late nineties. Growing up surrounded by both T–1 lines and teen magazines, Power started posting snippets of her adolescent angst online. Her ramblings resulted in a deluge of posts from fellow digital diarists and gave her the idea for the teen entertainment site Goosehead.com.

ASHLEY POWER

The idea for Goosehead came about three years ago, when I was in eighth grade. I got my first computer when I was eight years old, and I took a Photoshop class when I was in fifth grade, because both my parents were really into graphic art. So I was on the Internet a lot just for school stuff and chatting, and I came across a lot of different Web sites that I could tell were done by young people. I thought if *they* could do it, *I* could do it, too!

So I bought *HTML for Dummies,* taught myself how to program, and e-mailed a lot of Webmasters. I had a lot of people helping me, and I put together this little site. Pretty soon I was getting 40,000 hits a day!

At first, I just started writing what I thought about everything. I put up a chat room, and got some message boards, but then I heard about broadband, which got me interested in doing my own shows online. At that point, I went to my parents and said, "This is my idea, and can you help me?"

As soon as I told my stepdad, he called all these Webmasters I'd been e-mailing and asked them, "How old are you?" "Do you go to church?" "Are you married?" "Do you have kids?" We talked to all of them and then we got together in Vegas.

Finally my stepdad said, "All right, if you really want to do this, we need to all get together and put in a little bit of money." I had to pitch my idea to everyone, and they liked it and agreed to support me in creating a teen entertainment network.

We do the shows I've created, but it's also become a real teen community online. When I have a chemistry test or break up with my boyfriend, everyone knows. It's very cool to be able to talk to people in Australia, New Zealand, Canada, and Japan. Sometimes I get e-mails in different languages, so I go to a translator site to figure out what they're saying.

If teenagers could create their own thriving online entertainment companies, why shouldn't major media get in on the action? It wasn't long before conglomerates and individual film, music, and publishing moguls alike queued up at what they believed might be the next big premiere.

"The cliché is that everyone in L.A. has a screenplay," says the L.A.-based screenwriter and former DEN producer Bob Makela, "but back then, it was, 'Everyone in L.A. has a business plan'" for an online entertainment site. Sadly, the content turned out to be not *Citizen Kane* but more like *Police Academy* sequels. Dubbed. In Spanglish.

Time Warner—first with Pathfinder and then with Entertaindom—failed twice in its attempt to create the leading online entertainment destination. NBC's NBCi.com went public only to quickly flame out following a misguided ad campaign that led most to think the site was an informational labyrinth instead of an easy-to-use, functional portal. Disney's Go.com served mostly to provide fodder for pun-hungry headline-writers, who derided it as, among other things, "Go.com's Mickey Mouse Strategy" (*The Industry Standard*) and "GO.com to STOP" (*E-Commerce Times*).

The former Sony Pictures Entertainment chairman Peter Guber, who now runs Mandalay Pictures, decided not to follow his Hollywood coterie along the New Economy red carpet.

PETER GUBER

I was constantly presented with ideas for companies that wanted our financial capital, our intellectual capital, our Rolodex, our content, or wanted me to be on their board.

I saw many thrilling concepts—some for which the technology has not been fully realized; some of which require an intensive amount of capital; some of which need the infrastructure to be built up before all the pieces can work in some sort of symmetry; and some of which had a lamebrained management, even though it was a good idea.

So I didn't bet the farm on trying to find the Holy Grail. I've continued my core business, producing movies. But what the Internet really allows, unlike the other mediums, is for one person to reach an audience of millions.

Exactly. The Internet allowed the then NBC Studios chief Dave Bartis to resurrect an idea that he and Doug Liman, the director of *Swingers* and *Go*, had been tossing around since their days at Brown University in the mid-eighties.

DAVE BARTIS

Doug Liman and I had been talking about doing something together. He had just released the movie *Go*, and I was getting to the end of a TV season. So in March 1999 we went to the Aspen Comedy Festival together and informally started sketching out a company. Literally, sketching it out on paper.

Doug had been talking to his cousin Liz Hamburg, who'd been working a lot in the Internet space, and she began telling us the profile of a successful Internet venture: it would be grassroots and would take advantage of all the aspects of the Net. It was this tool that could give phenomenal access, no matter who you were.

Well, in college, a group of us had done a TV and radio station called UNET. Doug and I stayed on after college to build it into a network of college stations. Our big problem had been that distribution was very difficult. So I realized that the Internet might provide a distribution means for that demo, and we thought about going back to that network, because we liked that audience of new creators. Liz told us that no one had really done this idea of looking for grassroots content creators to put work online. So that became the model for Nibblebox.com.

Bartis wasn't the only successful media figure to partner with a long-time friend in starting an Internet company. Kurt Andersen, the former editor of *New York* magazine and cofounder of *Spy*, watched the Internet explosion from the sidelines as he worked on his novel *Turn of the Century*. But a call from his pal Michael Hirschorn led to the birth of what became the extremely popular media news site, Inside.com.

KURT ANDERSEN

As I was finishing my book, happily locked up in a room for a year, I was also observing this sort of rock-'n'-roll moment. I had a friend, Jim Cramer, who founded TheStreet.com. I thought TheStreet.com was good and interesting, and I thought that he should extend it beyond the world of technology stocks into the worlds that I'm more interested in, of the media and entertainment businesses. I certainly wasn't looking into starting anything on my own.

Then, in early 1999, Michael Hirschorn, my friend and former colleague at *New York* magazine, called and had this idea of an online publication covering the entertainment and media businesses. I said, "Funny you should say that. I had that same idea and talked about it last summer with Cramer and

Flatiron Partners." Everyone got excited about it, and my notion of my involvement was to be a godfather, adviser, helper—not really to be operationally involved. So Michael recruited Deanna Brown, whom he had worked with at *Esquire*. The Flatiron folks really liked her, and in the summer of '99, they declared their willingness to get behind this.

It wasn't like I was sitting around thinking, "God, how can I get into the Internet revolution?" It wasn't like there were twelve ideas that I bandied around and this was the remaining one. This was a thing that I wished existed. I wanted an online service that would cover the things that I cared about with wit and intelligence. I sort of stumbled into this, and I think that we went into it with the requisite combination of confidence and terror.

David Neuman, on the other hand, then a Disney executive in Hollywood, was itching to move online: "I wished that someone would offer me the kind of job that my boss had just interviewed for as CEO of PointCast. The Web seemed so much more exciting than trying to develop another comedy about a single mom."

DAVID NEUMAN

So here I am at Disney with these two competing screens—the Internet with my AOL account and Netscape browser, and a big-screen TV with prime-time programming. It was increasingly apparent to me that my creative soul was drawn to the new medium.

On a panel discussion, I met Marc Collins-Rector, who was just leaving Concentric Networks, where he was the cofounder and CEO, and he was talking about a new company he was starting called Digital Entertainment Network. He identified these subgroups and subcultures that he was going to create original, TV-style, half-hour programming for, and distribute it over the Net: senior citizens, skateboarders, anything smaller than the discrete units currently served by cable TV. What a *radical model!* It made sense because there were cost problems in primetime TV, and he said he would make money if 50,000 people watched his shows.

We ended up having lunch, and he asked me to join this company. He had no experience in TV and I had no experience in the Internet. His idea for

DEN was: there is this new medium, and you no longer have to depend on cable TV to distribute original content. There is now a way to get directly to consumers and to organize communities virtually. That was a very powerful idea, and presented an unexpected opportunity.

———————

For 25-year-old Jeff Malkin, unexpected opportunity knocked when his old high-school buddy, "a financial hedge guy," called him because he had registered the domain name FreeSamples.com but "didn't know what to do with it."

His friend had picked FreeSamples.com because his father was a dermatologist who wanted to distribute samples of a line of skin-care products he'd developed. His son thought the Web might be the solution; Malkin, who'd been helping companies build databases, refined the idea into "a tremendous database by using traditional sampling." The site would later become an online marketing services company.

Like Malkin, many newly minted CEOs stumbled upon startup ideas. Not even thinking that the only sure things in life were death and taxes, Helen Maynard, a new Zealand native, says she "accidentally" founded HeavenlyDoor.com, a funeral services Web site.

HELEN MAYNARD

My father-in-law passed away and my husband and I came to the United States for his funeral. We were met by this family member who said, "I've got this wonderful idea, and if you two move here, you will become dot-com millionaires." He thought that the way to make money was for people to be able to plan a funeral online in the privacy of their own homes.

At the time, everybody was making money on the Internet. So we packed up our life and moved to Florida. I was only here three weeks when I went to my very first funeral industry trade show. That was an experience that you just cannot *imagine*. They have everything from urns to cosmetics to make the bodies look better, to devices used to hoist dead bodies into caskets. It was the most unbelievable thing.

When we went to that first trade show and were trying to sell people memorial Web sites for $1,299 a year, people actually believed that this was feasible. But I had a huge career in New Zealand in the home appliance industry and then a very successful uniform business, and I couldn't for the life of me understand how on earth we could sell this. There was no business plan that made sense, but it was typical of the dot-coms. You sat down and you said, "There are this many people in the country who die every year, and if we tag one percent of that market and sell memorials at this dollar value, this is how many millions we are going to make."

For Chuck D, frontman of the influential rap group Public Enemy and founder of the hip-hop sites Rapstation.com and Slamjamz.com, it wasn't about the millions, but about the digital distribution of music online. Hoping to reach and interact directly with fans, Chuck D has been outspoken in his goal of turning the Internet into what he calls "the radio of the future." But in 1994, the rapper says, he was as clueless about the Net as the rest of us.

CHUCK D

This guy Harry Allen, a hip-hop journalist, gave me a phone call and invited me to the New Music Seminar panel, which also had Adam Curry, the Beasties. A lot of us were sitting on this panel not knowing what the fuck to say, but knowing that this was some kind of door into the future, because it went from the artist directly to the public. And when I was on that panel, the light bulbs started to click on.

A lot of the ideas I had in '94 and '95 were still far-fetched. Can we have a video station on this thing that goes over the phone lines? Can a person press a button and then get their music right away? I didn't know how to go about it.

But at least with the idea, I knew that when it came down to servicing hip-hop from a radio or video standpoint through the MTVs or the BETs—even in print which had its *Source's* and *Rap Sheet's*—we had to borrow some service area to get exposure to the music we were producing. I knew it wouldn't be done through traditional media. So I thought, this is the thing to be involved with because it connects all the dots. That's why I became involved with it, not because it was the trendy thing to do.

Of course, creating a dot-com business lost its trendiness factor right around the time the Y2K craze engendered a collective yawn. With the buzzards of a full-blown recession picking at the bones of so many dead New Economy companies, the idea of attempting another startup might seem to make as much sense as trying to reintroduce the Stutz Bearcat to the auto market-place. Funding is more difficult to secure, and national security has supplanted stock-option packages as the main topic of conversation among Americans, twenty-somethings and older folks alike. But that hasn't damp-ened the power of the Idea that gained so much traction in the minds of entrepreneurial hopefuls.

Matt Welch, an industry journalist and former consultant at DEN, recent-ly realized just how profound an effect the past several years of idea genera-tion have had on the American psyche.

MATT WELCH

Not long ago, we had two friends visiting—they're French and work at *Libération*, which is kind of a left-leaning daily there started by the '68ers. They were sitting around and complaining about the paper, how the old guard never listens to what the young kids have to say, how people get paid and don't do any work, and how there's all this intrigue in the office.

As always, my reaction was, "Well, why don't you start your *own* paper?"

They looked at me as if I'd just landed from the moon. It never occurs to anyone outside the U.S. that "the idea" is a viable option. But I think that any-one who has been touched at all with the craziness that happened here will have that attitude programmed into their DNA from now on: *Anyone can have an idea.* They may not execute it, but it always seems in the realm of real this-could-actually-happen possibility.

I mean, shit, isn't that *terrific?*

CHAPTER TWO THE MONEY

It's not a smart risk to take a URL, an MBA student who has
no operating experience, and a thirty-page business plan that
doesn't have clear value. . . and fund it.
                    —Venture capitalist John Doerr,
                       December 2000, on CNET.com

There's a rule of venture capital that your first deals don't
work out. I think John Doerr said that it's like crashing an F15
fighter plane. Until you've crashed it, you can't be good at
flying it.
              —Andrew Anker, partner at August Capital

After Dave Roux made those 1999 air-phone calls in which he evangelized
the company that would be Kibu, he and Susan Scarpa became lead stock-
holders in a startup that raised $22 million in just four months from superstars
including Netscape's cofounder Jim Clark; former Excite@Home chairman
Tom Jermoluk; and the Silicon Valley venture-capital firm of Kleiner, Perkins,
Caulfield & Byers. Kibu also had a powerhouse board boasting the Hollywood
heavyweight Jeffrey Berg, chairman of International Creative Management
(ICM); and CNET chairman Shelby Bonnie.

What caught people's attention wasn't really the amount of money—after
all, $22 million hardly seemed outrageous at the time—but where it came
from. Kibu's backers were the equivalent of Internet royalty, with Kleiner,
Perkins embodying the deep pockets of the Medicis and the glamour of the
Kennedys in one cyber power package. KP, as the firm was nicknamed, had
put their beknighting sword on the shoulder of entrepreneurs behind many
of the Internet's most successful and name-brand companies, including
Google and Amazon.

CNET.com's Troy Wolverton likened an investment from Kleiner, Perkins to "the Good Housekeeping seal of approval," but in practical terms, it was probably closer to an unknown novel being tapped as an Oprah's Book Club selection. Just as viewers loyally heeded Oprah's choices in the latest weepy-woman's novel, virtually anyone hoping to file an S-1 implicitly trusted KP's mass-market taste in startups.

A KP imprimatur meant prestige, splashy publicity, instant name recognition, and the assumption that *this* business meant serious business. It was permission to speed along to riches on the shoulder of Highway 101, past the dot-com gridlock that had turned the Web autobahn into a veritable parking lot.

"A lot of it was about who's backing you," admits the former *Industry Standard* columnist Laura Rich. "We gave more coverage to a KP-backed company than to a no-name company."

Kibu got coverage, all right, and not just in *The Industry Standard*. From the *Wall Street Journal* to *Fortune*, a flurry of alliterative headlines ("KP-backed Kibu") appeared, followed by column inches that were less stories than glowing benedictions to the union. The $22 million was mentioned in passing, but few, if any, publications reported how the money had been distributed. In fact, according to an insider close to the process, Roux and Scarpa originally took a quarter of the company each; Molly Lynch and Roux's associate at Silver Lake Partners, Egon Durbon, split a quarter; and the remaining quarter was earmarked for to-be-hired employees and future investors.

Once those investors ponied up, however, it was like musical shares in the Kibu boardroom. "Percentages of the company were being redistributed every week," says this source. "They'd take shares away willy-nilly" to accommodate the influx of backers, and soon there weren't many left for the not-yet-materialized Kibu staff.

"This was ridiculous from the start," this insider believes. "It was greedy. How could four people have three fourths of the stock in the company with only one fourth left over for potentially hundreds more?" Those involved didn't question the equation, however, probably because two of them, Molly Lynch and Susan Scarpa, had no experience starting a Web company. (Silver Lake's Durbon even bought Scarpa *The Internet for Dummies* on her first trip to Silicon Valley to help her bone up on the medium she was about to venture into.) Nevertheless, this source insists, the result was "a cap table doomed for infighting."

This kind of quibbling wasn't a New Economy phenomenon, of course. If infighting and money weren't already as inextricably linked in American culture as baseball and hotdogs, there would be fewer divorces in this country, not to mention fewer lawsuits. But both terms took on new meaning in an era when John Doerr, KP's most influential venture capitalist, acquired the habit of proclaiming, "The Internet is the greatest legal creation of wealth in the history of the planet."

So what if, in a later apologia, the charismatic VC added the words "and evaporation" after "creation"? For many, Doerr seemed simply to be announcing the obvious. Elizabeth Collet, a Harvard Business School graduate and one of the first forty employees at Yahoo!, remembers an interoffice bet made when her company's stock was rising faster than the morning mercury in the Mojave.

"A guy named John Briggs made a public statement: 'If Yahoo!'s stock ever hits one hundred, I'll get "Yahoo!" tattooed on my ass,' " she recalls. "So we had a tattooing party when it hit one hundred, but then it became a macho issue of one-upmanship." A couple of months later, Collet says, Briggs's colleague made a similar challenge: If the stock ever hit 200, he'd shave his head. Sure enough, the company gave him a hair-shaving party not long after.

But not all startups performed like Yahoo!, and Peter Heinecke, an attorney at the Silicon Valley law firm Wilson Sonsini Goodrich & Rosati, was one of many who marveled at the money being squandered. "In 1999, five online pet-related companies were funded simultaneously with huge amounts of money," he says with astonishment. "I thought, You've got to be *kidding*." ("The Pet Space was 'in,' so we funded it," one embarrassed VC admits, perhaps explaining how in the world the four largest "pet" players raised anywhere from $50 million to $150 million *each*.)

Of course, that was when VCs felt invincible and, as the former Wall Street strategist Elizabeth Mackay said in a *New York Times Magazine* interview, "Investing became more like entertainment." But by the summer of 2001, *Business Week* reported that venture capitalists had posted negative returns in their portfolios for two consecutive quarters—for the first time in almost thirty years!

What gives? Long before that manic time of free-flowing cash and generous stock-option packages, venture capitalists made profits by carefully doling out their dollars. But in the late 1990s, they acted less like Rockefeller and more like Shel Silverstein's *The Giving Tree*. And as the financial columnist James Surowiecki wrote in *The New Yorker*, "The easier it is for startups to raise. . . money, the harder they find it to manage that money wisely."

Indeed.

Perhaps having learned from the wreckage of the dot-bombs, one young entrepreneur, Surowiecki reported, toyed with the idea of using the infamous Pets.com "sock puppet" as a warning sign to employees—a reminder of the heavily funded startup that went public and bankrupt in the span of a year. Instead of an "employee of the month" plaque, a wasteful employee would receive the shameful mascot.

But former *Wired* executive assistant Steven Overman remembers when money wasn't even the point. "The original angel investor in *Wired* was Charlie Jackson," says Overman. "He made money from inventing SuperPaint and Supercard in the early days of the Mac software business." At the same time, Jackson was "your classic non-VC," the kind of guy who "decided in his fifties that he wanted to be in the Olympics, so he became an expert sharpshooter just so he could participate."

According to Overman, Nicholas Negroponte of MIT's Media Lab also gave money to *Wired*—$10,000 to get it started, about the same amount that Jackson contributed. "Compare that with the scale of investment in startups I worked at later, nine million dollars in their first round," sighs Overman. "It was such a different spirit back then. These guys didn't know if they'd make big money from *Wired*, but just wanted to see it happen. Their attitude was: I want to invest in something because it's a good idea."

That soon changed, as VCs chased after windmills of cash with the fervor of Don Quixote. Still, according to former *Wired* Digital CEO Andrew Anker, now a partner at the venture firm August Capital, it would take some convincing before VCs began begging entrepreneurs for the "privilege" to invest.

ANDREW ANKER

When I raised money for *HotWired* in 1995, the first question I asked investors was, "Do you believe in the Internet?" You either had been on the Net and felt you had to be a player there, or no amount of my time could convince you of that.

I'd call up and say, "Hey, I've got this online product that I want to sell," and people would either go, "What?" or "Yeah, come in." If they'd say,

"What?" we would make no effort to go see them, because there was absolutely no way that you could make a credible case for the Internet.

A philanthropic neurosurgeon may have been one of the few willing to put money into the Internet when Adeo Ressi needed backing for his online cultural guide, Total New York. Five years later, however, while raising money for the Web shop Methodfive, Ressi would have no trouble making a "credible case for the Internet." In fact, in 1999, Methodfive received over $8 million in cash and services from Price Waterhouse Coopers—the first time that a Big Five accounting firm had invested in a Web-development company.

"It was really strange," says Ressi, "because I met nearly the entire senior management team of PWC to approve the deal, and they were trying to get us to allow them to invest more than we were asking for. We were being courted by the biggest investors out there, and they're trying to invest more than we even *want!*"

In a most unusual power shift, the courted became the suitors.

"It was definitely a time when dot-com companies could get really selective about who they got money from," says Gong Szeto, the former chief creative officer at the New York Web shop Rare Medium. "It was a role reversal—we would have to pitch startup companies to be able to invest in their idea." High on the fumes of tomorrow's fortunes today, investors were standing in line to give their money away.

Wilson, Sonsini attorney Peter Heinecke watched as checks were made out to startups who not only no longer needed to grovel, but didn't even have to return VCs' phone calls.

PETER HEINECKE

There was definitely a herd mentality among the VCs, so they'd throw money at the company-of-the-month. You talk about these road shows where the books were forty times oversubscribed? Back in the late eighties, if we could get things *two* times oversubscribed that was a home run. Those were the days that if you got fifteen to twenty percent bump up, you were doing really well, and even then they were saying, "Wow, they're leaving money on the table." But those guys in the eighties, they didn't see returns on investment like with TheGlobe.com [Internet start-up founded by two Cornell students that opened on November 13, 1998, with the then largest IPO in stock history], which was a completely different story.

DAVE BARTIS

In 1999, I signed a two-year deal with 3Arts Entertainment to be President of the TV division, because I figured that it would take at least a year and a half to raise money for Nibblebox.

We kept working on the plan and it got better, so we wanted to show it around for feedback. When Doug Liman and I did UNET at Brown, one of the people who had given us money was Michael Milken. Now, I think Doug's mom suggested that we go back to Milken. So, Doug and his cousin, Liz Hamburg, came out to L.A. to set up a meeting with Mike, who thought it was very interesting. He responded very quickly to Doug and Liz, and told them that he was interested in financing this, and that we shouldn't go anywhere else. By this time, it's only October and I'm going, "Holy shit, this is *weird!*"

We had another meeting with Mike; Terry Semel, the former Warner Bros. chairman who's now the Yahoo! chairman; and Sandy Climan, the managing director of Entertainment Media Ventures. They basically validated the plan, and said that their respective funds would all contribute, following Mike's lead. This was shocking to me, but we're hearing about all these online entertainment companies like Icebox, IFILM, and Atom Films, so it was sort of in the air.

We started these negotiations, and I had to go to 3Arts and tell them that the plan was getting some traction. I knew I had literally just signed a deal with them, but this was my dream project. They were pissed at first, but they came back later and were very cool about it. I agreed to stay until the end of that TV season.

We closed our financing the day after Christmas, and had to fire one set of attorneys who had a problem working through the holidays. I was on the chairlift in Aspen, and I'm calling real estate agents from the lift because I realized we needed an office in two weeks!

Bartis's experience was hardly unusual. "There were more fundraising deals going down than there were people to do them," says Andrew Brenner, who left his Chicago law firm in 1997 to work in Silicon Valley. "If it had an *e* or an *I* at the front of it, it got funded."

ANDREW BRENNER

Things would get funded, but they're not still around. Furniture.com seemed a little far-fetched: Okay, we're going to ship *furniture* to you.

I remember one company founded by five people with pretty decent backgrounds—all had worked at big consultancies. They didn't have a name for the company, and didn't have any idea what they wanted to sell, but they wanted to do some e-commerce type of site. They finally came up with one thing that they wanted to sell—I can't remember now, but it certainly wasn't an original idea. I was thinking, "Yeah right, they'll never get funded." Two weeks later, they had three term sheets on the table.

Even in this giddy environment, not every hopeful with no business plan and an uninspired idea landed term sheets from venture capitalists. Sometimes, says JustBalls.com's founder, Jim Medalia, "you needed a bit of luck."

Enter "angel" investors with shamrocks around their necks and gold coins in their pockets ready to swoop down on some unsuspecting entrepreneur. So what if the term "angel" originally applied to turn-of-the- century wealthy businessmen funding Broadway productions, frequently with the proviso that their girlfriends be given the leading role? These millennial angels were no mistress-appeasers, nor were they the little old ladies swindled by producer-shysters like Leo Bloom and Max Bialystock in Mel Brooks's *The Producers*.

Now, according to the Small Business Administration, there are at least 250,000 angels funding an estimated 30,000 U.S. companies annually. But while this largely behind-the-scenes angel community invests an estimated $20 billion a year in new business startups, the VC community nevertheless steals the media's center stage.

And that's not the only difference: Whereas VCs—sometimes called "vulture capitalists"—prefer that new business plans be pitched to them over their own granite tables in intimidating conference rooms, angels often seem to appear by mere magic.

JIM MEDALIA

Part of our graphics and Web site business was something called the Internet Business Center in New York. We had probably forty computers with twenty-one-inch monitors hooked up to the Net. The place was very, very chic-looking and we rented it out for people to present new products. One day there was an interesting demo going on, so I called up my mentor, John Evans, to tell him to come take a look at this technology.

I'm standing by the front door with John, and all of a sudden this tall guy walks in and John says, "Oh, Dave, how are you?" This tall guy says, "John, good to see ya. How ya doing?" It turned out to be Dave Wetherell, the CEO of an Internet incubator called CMGI. Talk about luck! Dave had been invited to this particular presentation, and, in fact, had an appointment to meet with John later in the day.

So I start to tell Dave about JustBalls.com, and I show him sketches of what the site was going to look like. He immediately got what I was talking about. He said, "Listen, come and see me as soon as you can." I said, "Wait a minute, we don't even have a *business plan*." He said, "Don't wait for a business plan." All we had was the concept and the name JustBalls, and we'd also reserved seventy-five other names: JustBats, JustGloves, JustSticks, you name it.

The second week of January 1998, we go to CMGI in Boston. Dave said that he talked to some of his partners, and they really liked the idea. How quickly could we get him a business plan? At that point he said, "If CMGI doesn't fund this, I'll put a group together myself." By March, we had a business plan. So we met with Dave again, and made a presentation.

On June first, we had a million dollars. CMGI passed, but Dave put together a group of some of his friends—investors and angels—and funded it privately. I was very lucky because the group included people like Bob Davis, [the former president and CEO of Lycos] and Ted Phillips [another former CEO of Lycos].

AUREN HOFFMAN

We tried to raise money for BridgePath, but we didn't know what we were talking about. I didn't know what a cap table was, I didn't know what a P&L was. We ran our business on all cash.

We were basically a little job board—a HotJobs—but we saw this much bigger opportunity to become an exchange for staffing firms. We couldn't do both, so we decided to focus our entire attention on the exchange, but to do that we had to raise money.

We had the classic story—we were oversubscribed, we had no business plan. We actually didn't know what we were doing at the time. We knew we were changing our models, we knew that it had something to do with the recruiting industry, and we knew that we were figuring it out. The VCs wouldn't look at us, so we raised about $850,000 from a bunch of different angels—guys like Alan Silverman [former director of the American Cancer Society and National Association of Theatre Owners], Walter Baumgartner [former partner at Sequoia Capital], and Terry Brookshire [former Vice Chairman of the Pacific Stock Exchange].

JEFF MALKIN

For six months, I was on the road in New York and Connecticut trying to get funding for FreeSamples.com. I had a pretty bad experience with a small firm that verbally committed to funding in the summer of '99, and then over the next eight weeks they went back on everything they promised. In September I got fed up and said we wouldn't be doing business together, and was about to give up entirely. But, serendipitously, I met a guy in New York named Doug Mellinger, a partner at Interactive Capital Partners, and it was sort of love at first sight.

He brought me around to well-known angels. There were three things I was up against: I needed to have clients to get funding; in order to have clients, I needed to have funding and a fulfillment partner; and in order to get a fulfillment partner, I needed to have clients and money. Thank God for these guys! We were finally able to close on a $1.8 million angel round in October.

Once those deals were closed, the wizardry continued in the New Economy's form of fairy dust: stock options and shares. If you had 'em, you undoubtedly played the Math Game over and over in your head: "Let's see. If Ashford.com is valued at one hundred million, and Amazon.com is valued at ten billion, and Pets.com is valued at eighty-five million, then our online store that sells mood rings for cats should be worth *twice* that!"

Delusional? Perhaps. Yet it's easy to see why so much blood, sweat, and bullshit went into the illusion. As Humphrey Bogart explained at the end of *The Maltese Falcon*, when the supposedly priceless statue was discovered to be worthless lead: "It's the stuff dreams are made of."

Alan Citron, a thirteen-year veteran of the *Los Angeles Times* who was lured to the Web after getting a call from Ticketmaster chief Fred Rosen, witnessed the delirium firsthand. He remembers seeing "a lot of blank stares" when he decided to join the ticketing giant to run their online initiatives. "The big question that I got was, 'Why would anyone want to work in the Net?'" Later, however, these same reformed know-it-alls would have gladly exchanged their initial skepticism for some "friends-and-family" shares.

The frenzy only increased. Citron recalls the intoxicating nature of company stock during the funding process.

ALAN CITRON

It wasn't as if you could just go out and say, "I know we're supposed to be pitching you, but let's have a drink and when it's over, you can buy some stock." You had to go through the pitch.

But at the same time, the whole pitching process was a farce, because you could read in people's eyes that they just wanted to get the stock. They wanted to know how much they could have, and wanted to know how quickly they could sell it. I think if we pitched roughly twenty-five companies to fund Ticketmaster on our road show, I'd say two expressed any cynicism at all. The rest were nodding politely and waiting for us to end so they could put in their order. The pitch was a formality, more or less.

———————

Perhaps, but not for Dan Myrick, the director of *The Blair Witch Project*, whose online trailer and Web site for the film became cult sensations. He figured what he didn't know *could* hurt him, ignorance *wasn't* bliss, and if something sounded too good to be true, it probably *was*.

DAN MYRICK

We were going to do a deal with an online entertainment site, but they wanted the rights to all of our ideas. Well, what do we get in return? They said, "Oh, you get shares in the company." Well, if you've ever studied any law, you know that it's a lot harder for us to get our rights wrangled back if they go defunct than it is getting no money for shares. We didn't want to give rights to our ideas for shares in some business plan that hadn't been proven yet.

We almost struck a deal with Shockwave, because we were going to do some online comic mythology for our next film. But at that point, no one was offering us cash, it was always stock options. You have to keep in mind that we're five broke filmmakers, and we're talking about stock options. It was like, "What does that *mean*? Can I buy lunch?"

———————

It depends on where you ate. "Some companies kept their options very close, and others threw them around," says Harold Mann, an Internet consultant in San Francisco. "We typically took cash with a small option part, since we were experienced enough not to drink the Kool-Aid along with everyone else."

Good thing, because someone had to remain straight enough to help companies raise the money in the first place. Through their consultancy, Mann and his younger brother Alex helped prepare funding presentations for startups. "Our niche," he says, "was basically coming up with quick prototypes for companies that didn't have their acts together."

HAROLD MANN

People would have an idea, talk to funders, and the funders wanted to see a bit more of the idea beyond the business plan, so they could take it to the partners.

We were already friends with people who became EIRs—entrepreneurs in residence, like "trainees"—for top-tier venture-capital firms. Companies like Softbank, which had backed Yahoo! and E*Trade, and Kleiner, Perkins. We were brought into their offices, and they told us the idea.

We were amused by some of the ideas. "This is going to revolutionize the way people are going to shop online," or "This is the way people are going to share ideas online." The partners would really force the EIRs to stretch the idea to a massive scale. In order to get funded, ideas couldn't simply make your life a little bit *better*. They had to change your life *entirely*.

Beyond a "change-your-life" idea, did the VCs, lawyers, and agents really know what they were looking for? A solid business plan? Experienced management? An identifiable path-to-profitability? Or were they after "sexy" marketing strategies, youthful MBAs, and growth-in-lieu-of-value?

"The mentality back then was: page views equals better," says August Capital partner Andrew Anker. "People didn't realize that certain page views and certain audiences are worth more than others."

But Anker and his colleagues did realize that experienced management teams trumped pubescent ones. "We did very little of the, 'This is my first job, I'm twenty-five years old, right out of B-School or college. Now give me twenty million to start a company.' "

Even so, concedes Anker's colleague David Hornik, once a lawyer at the top-tier Valley firm Venture Law Group, the decision to dole out dough—or services to companies hoping to get some—often came down to little more than instinct.

DAVID HORNIK

At Venture Law Group, there were about ten companies for every one that we could take on. Even with us recruiting like crazy and trying to build the practice, we didn't have the staff. We had to make these decisions very quickly, and we were completely ill suited to do that. Now that I'm a VC, I see that. The criteria were arbitrary. Everything was working, so it didn't matter. It was what your gut said. They were definitely not deep decisions.

Caveat emptor clearly wasn't the credo of many plunking down millions for a slice of the digital pie. "It was pretty crazy, man," says Dan Myrick about a time when "money was just flying around" and he and his partner, fresh off the *Blair Witch* bonanza, "were like gods for a while. . . doing the victory lap in L.A."

Courted by anyone with a bank account, the "Blair Witch guys," as they were called, didn't quite know what to make of all the wining and dining. "Everyone had a fifty-million-dollar backer, or there was a twenty-four-year-old with fifty million in his pocket, saying 'I'm gonna do an online entertainment this-and-that, and I'll give you guys money to do this,' " says Myrick.

Posturing, perhaps, but even from the other side of the bargaining table, some of what DEN's David Neuman calls "hubris" was strategic. In order to get money from the networks, he and his DEN colleagues presented themselves like a digital mafia offering an opportunity that the TV folks couldn't refuse. "Gen-Y wants to be on the Net and if you want to stick with them, you need to start spending money with us," was the message, Neuman says, recalling DEN's intimidation tactics. "DEN had to be deliberately arrogant and chest-beating because otherwise there'd be no money for us to make the product."

Swagger aside, however, funding wasn't always a fancy dinner, phone call, or e-mail away. "It's a false perception that it was that easy to raise money," asserts Josh Keller, a Harvard MBA, speaking about getting funding for his startup UBUBU. "Obviously, it was easier to raise money than it is now, and it was probably easier than in other periods. But it still wasn't easy."

JOSH KELLER

Media notions of, "You've got a bunch of Harvard MBA's and some pretty cool ideas, so we'll just throw money at you and be done with it," are pretty false. It still took us several months of talking to a variety of firms, not just about the vision of UBUBU and what a cool idea this would be, but about: How are you guys going to make money? Why is your team qualified to deal with this? Who are going to be your customers? How is the business model working? How are you proving your concept?

HAROLD MANN

We tried to get our application service provider business funded for almost a year. Because we had worked with so many companies that got funded with such inane concepts, we had this false sense of how easy it was going to be. But when we met with VCs, they sent us off with homework: Show me that there's this, this, and this, and we'll talk more. While we were frustrated that they didn't just see the light, it was good for us. It forced us to think, and we became a stronger company. We didn't get too big for our britches, and with funding we might have.

CHUCK D

It was never easy for us to get money because we were black. And also what we was bringing to the table—the rap and hip-hop community—was considered not grandiose enough.

They thought rap and hip-hop was a small aspect. We said it's a seed genre that everything sprouts from. It's not like pop music, but this is a genre that needs a service area. But when it came down to, "Hey, I have an idea and this is our little corner of the world and we need to get funded," it became the same old game. I've been able to build and operate my projects from the lint of my pockets. But I'm looking to the left and the right, and seeing people get the money to fund an idea, when we've got a practicality and can't get funded. Discouraging shit happens.

Shit happens, all right. Like, the moment the market whipped out its existential Exacto knife to drive a big puncture into the dot-com bubble. Doug

Scott, a cofounder of the popular industry magazine *Red Herring* back in 1993, four years later joined the Hollywood Stock Exchange (HSX.com), a virtual stock market and box-office prediction device for movie stars and feature films. But like many entrepreneurs, he remembers feeling "left at the altar" when his funding fell through after Black Friday, April 14, 2000.

DOUG SCOTT

Things started to unravel for us pretty much in line with the economy. In late April, Bear Stearns is working on our round, and the banker calls one day and says, "Look, with the economy what it is, and with the market's being tight, blah blah blah blah blah." The next thing we know, we're sitting there with a half-done prospectus on our next round of capital for $20 million, we've burned through a shitload of our cash, and, what we didn't burn, we were already committed to spend.

DAVID HORNIK

We represented a company called MemoryVine. It was couple of women who had a CD-ROM business where you could encapsulate life stories with photos, music, and voice. They were going to recreate it for the Web, so you can do it yourself. It was a great idea. You could add all the media, characterize it ("This is Aunt Sue in 1953 at a family reunion with Jack, Frank, etc."), and correlate it into a timeline that was cross-referenced.

Other people had raised money around related ideas, but these women were at the tail end of the bubble, and people were already becoming skeptical about consumer business models. Earlier sites like BlueMountain had been valued based upon their user acquisition, and not on their business models. But by the time MemoryVine finally got out on the money-raising circuit, companies were no longer being valued merely for user acquisition, and they weren't able to describe a business model in which they'd be paid for the site.

AUREN HOFFMAN

We started raising our venture round for BridgePath in January 2000. By then our idea was fairly well fleshed out, we had a good management team behind it, and we had a history of not spending money. We pitched at least a hundred different VCs on the phone.

In the end, we got our term sheet from Charter Ventures one day before the market crashed. We had two other term sheets guaranteed to come in on Monday because that's when the partners meet. The market crashed on Friday. On Monday, we got a call saying "Auren, we can only do about sixty percent of the valuation that we had originally discussed." If the market hadn't crashed, I was expecting them to actually *up* the valuation considerably by playing these folks against each other.

Charter got a little worried, so they asked us to come in again and pitch to the full partnership. We went in and did a really good job—we actually got a standing ovation at the end. We were able to close it, but not until June 2000.

We were definitely freaked out during the two months from April to June, because there were about a hundred different stories in *The Industry Standard*, *Red Herring*, and the *San Francisco Chronicle* about companies that had gotten term sheets, and then their investors backed out.

But here's where inexperience played in our favor. Charter was going to put in $4 million. The day they signed the term sheet, I asked them to give us a check for 10 percent. So they wrote me a check for $400,000.

My lead investor, Alan Silverman, who was this seasoned guy, freaked out when I told him that, because, he said, you don't do that. There was no precedent. He's like, "What are you *doing?* You can't ask for that!" But when the check came, he called me up and said, "Auren, I just want to tell you how happy I am to be in business with someone as inexperienced as you are."

I was just twenty-five at the time, and I *ran* to the bank with that check.

Other budding entrepreneurs, like DutyFreeGuide.com's founder, Bernardo Joselevich, tripped and fell on the way to make a deposit. Joselevich began working on the Net in 1996 while "traveling the world with a laptop selling online advertising to hotels" for HotelGuide.com.

BERNARDO JOSELEVICH

By 1998, HotelGuide.com was going so well that I thought I should have my own company. Maybe, I thought, people would be willing to make their travel plans online. I paid some executive at a bank a thousand dollars to write me a six-page business plan, then I went around peddling it to see if I could get money for DutyFreeGuide.com.

On my first meeting, I still didn't know the paradox of venture capital, which is that if you ask for *less* money, you're *less* likely to get it. They'd rather have five investments of $3 million than thirty investments of $500,000. I was asking for one million. After I made my presentation, I was under the impression that they were very interested. But then they told me that they only invested in companies for a minimum of $5 million because they don't have the attention span for anything less.

So I spoke to someone else who was kind of interested. He said, "What's the minimum that I could give you to get started." I told him it was $300,000 just to get it off the ground, not including any marketing or anything. He said, "Well, if I give you three hundred thousand, will you give me forty percent of your company?"

"Your company" was such an overstatement to me because I only had that flimsy executive summary. So I thought it was a great deal! Later on, everyone thought I'd been idiotic to give away 40 percent of my company for only $300,000.

I moved to New York and started DutyFreeGuide. In March 2000, I had an offer to sell the site for $3 million. We had finalized the contract and it was ready for signing, but then the Nasdaq collapsed and the deal collapsed along with it.

Desperate for funding, some companies, according to the New York attorney Steven Masur, resorted to flat-out lying (or "massaging the numbers," as one entrepreneur corrected us).

STEVEN MASUR

In order to raise money, this one company had to claim a much greater return than they could actually get. It was an online music licensing business, and they could make good money, but it's not one of these businesses that you invest twenty-five cents in and get back a million. The guy insisted that he had to show revenue of $10 million in the next few years, and we kept fighting with him that it would never happen, but he said to just make the case.

Finally, we sat this guy down and said, "Look. In order to make this money you have to sell $30,000 worth of licenses 365 days of this year. And you only have five people working for you." But he said, "It doesn't matter. We need to show these projections to get the investment." He was really forced into this position because the VCs just wouldn't listen to him otherwise.

———————

Fortunately, not everyone in the dot-com world was born yesterday, even if many looked like they'd just stepped off the set of the teen drama *Roswell*. Sure, some devised—and even fell for—the kinds of tricks Masur refers to. But though the word "sensible" may not have rung cool, even at the height of Web mania, several entrepreneurs and VCs shunned imprudent spending and questionable investments.

ANDREW RASIEJ

I was definitely from the old school. I used to run music clubs. I was not someone who knew all these financiers. I sold Bud out of garbage cans for five dollars a pop, so I was always terrified of raising money because, unlike a lot of other people, I looked at it as a loan—like, I actually had to pay this *back*.

AUREN HOFFMAN

When we raised our angel round for BridgePath, a friend of mine was bragging to an investor in his company that he had a friend—me—who was really frugal. So the investor, Alan Silverman, cold-called me. He calls me at like eight P.M. at the office—it was sort of a test to see if I worked long hours—and says, "Auren, tell me a little bit about your business." He was living in Palm Springs at the time, and he says, "Why don't you come down to Palm Springs sometime in the next couple of weeks and give me a bit more information." I did some background on this guy and found out that he was well known in the Valley, so I figured it was worth the risk.

I flew to San Diego on the cheapest flight because the parents of a BridgePath employee lived there. I stayed with her parents and was able to borrow the parents' car, drive up to Palm Springs, pitch Silverman, and get a commitment from him on the spot for $200,000. That's what we used to do, even during the boom. We were very sensible.

ANDREW ANKER

I only did one deal in my entire first year at August Capital. I'd have loved to have done two or three more, but my partners were very much of the idea that I should slow down. Let's stick to our guns and focus on the important things.

More than anything else, startups are about time. The more time you have, the more time you have to succeed. But when you're spending your money as quickly as everyone was on Herman Miller chairs and everything else, those were dollars that your customers would never see on your Web site.

Fortune did an article on us as the "Cool VC of 2001." We funded eight companies in the B2C space, the ad-supported business-to-consumer space that everyone hates. Seven are still around. The only one that isn't around is Evite, which we sold to Ticketmaster. I don't know if they'll all be winners, but I think they were worth funding: Topica, Guru, ImproveNet, Emode, Listen.com, CameraWorld, and Ebates.

With journalism's cardinal five *W*'s and one *H*, the digital funding tale can, in its broadest terms, be summed up as six questions:

1. *Who's* going to fund us?
2. *What* valuation should we ask for?
3. *Where's* Paul Allen when you need him?
4. *When* will this round run out?
5. *Why* isn't anyone returning our calls?
6. *How* the fuck did we think that?

But in talking to Inside.com cofounder and *Turn of the Century* author Kurt Andersen, we posed a different "when" question:

Q: When you're looking back thirty years from now, what is the single story or moment that will epitomize the New Media funding environment at the turn of the century?

A: It was the early winter of 2000, and we had just moved into our raw space on West Twenty-sixth Street in New York. There were lots of technology and Internet companies suddenly crowded into this wonderfully exciting, multicultural building filled with all kinds of people—little old bookbinders and new dot-coms. But one day there was a banker from one of the big Wall Street firms literally *walking the hallway*, cold-calling, knocking on doors and, basically, offering funding.

I said to myself, "Okay, this is some high watermark of gold-rush madness."

CHAPTER THREE

THE CULTURE

I think that the Valley was a big Rorschach test. You could
see whatever you wanted to see, and act out whatever you
wanted to act out.
—Journalist and author Po Bronson

"It's high school with money," a producer told me when I worked in
Hollywood as a film and TV executive and complained about the industry's
peculiar culture.

Exactly, I thought. And so I left.

I'd had enough of "doing" lunches, egos that grew like metastatic tumors,
tasteless displays of wealth, and working on fart-joke films. I wanted to do
something more challenging and meaningful. At twenty-eight, I was ready to
make my mark on the world.

Cut, as they say, to 1999. I moved up north to attend Stanford Medical
School, but from the second I arrived in Palo Alto, I was surrounded by
more dot-com folks than doctors. Which felt a lot like living in Los Angeles
and not being in "the biz," except up here "the biz" revolved around a much
smaller screen. If you weren't affiliated with something ending in ".com,"
you were deemed as irrelevant as a 28.8Kbps modem, or in show business
terms, anyone who'd ever appeared on *The Hollywood Squares*.

"What do you do?" people would ask me at parties. "I'm a medical student," I'd reply, and occasionally the person would probe for tips on the
hottest biotech stocks or health-care services that might be made available
on the Web. (In the Hollywood version, you'd be offered a consulting gig
on *ER*.) Most of the time, though, my interlocutor simply looked over my
shoulder for someone more worthwhile to schmooze with. Networking

was, to use the native tongue, "24/7." In NoCal, as in SoCal, there seemed to be no such thing as a purely social gathering.

Which is why, from Whole Foods to Café Barrone to the dog park, I learned a lot about the local culture by osmosis. And the digerati looked remarkably like the glitterati: twenty-somethings cruising in Beemers and walking around with headsets that made them look like well-dressed schizophrenics mumbling to Pluto. ("Is that guy talking to himself?" a friend visiting from the Midwest asked.)

Everywhere, there was the unique sound of wireless devices going off. ("Yours?". . . "No, must be yours". . . "Oh, sorry, mine.") Everywhere, there seemed to be kids with fortunes growing at almost the same exponential rate as their sense of entitlement.

In Hollywood, conventional wisdom has it that you're washed up if you haven't directed your first film by age thirty. In the Valley, you were considered a loser if you didn't go public with your first venture by the big three–oh. In both places, youth predominated because there were no "barriers to entry." College degree? Work experience? Old enough to have a driver's license or grow a beard? *Not necessary*. Welcome to our pubescent country.

Learning the lingo came easily, because I just translated everything into Hollywood-ese. I started a dictionary of analogous phrases, like when I went to Italy after taking French.

"Is it scalable?" = "Does the film have legs?"

"Let's discuss it offline." = "Let's discuss it off-set."

"Eyeballs" = "Box Office"

"KP" = "CAA"

"Dog and pony show" (Remember to say "big," "revolutionary" and make a comparison like "It's eBay meets Evite, but with streaming video. Plus Bill's interested.") = "Pitch meeting" (Remember to say "big," "revolutionary" and make a comparison like "It's *Mission Impossible* meets *Boys Don't Cry*, but with animation. Plus Julia's interested.")

"So, I did Netscape, then went on to do eToys for a while, and I just finished a gig with Jim Clark's new venture." = "So, I was a production assistant on *When Harry Met Sally*, then went on to assistant-direct *Eyes Wide Shut*, and I just wrapped on the new Spielberg vehicle."

Usage note: While some direct translations do exist—such as "ka-ching!" = "ka-ching!"—"the Valley" up north is not synonymous with "the Valley" down south. In Hollywood, avoid "the Valley" at all costs. If you absolutely *must* refer to it, use "Burbank."

Looking through my dictionary, I had to accept reality: I'd left Hollywood for Hollywood With Computers. Still, I hoped it was different somehow. Sure, people flocked to startups for the dough, but didn't I detect an undercurrent of idealism?

"This isn't Hollywood," I'd hear repeatedly (always followed immediately by the phrase "higher purpose"). Everyone I met seemed to care about what they called the Big Picture—and they didn't mean a Zen perspective on life, or even the next *Stars Wars* installment. Rather, they talked about "revolutionizing the way people live," "being on the cutting edge," and "changing the New World Order." When they described their "visionary" new businesses, they gesticulated wildly (one guy accidentally bashed me in the face), and their cheeks flushed with excitement. Their gauche displays of passion seemed refreshing, disarmingly genuine.

So I found myself intrigued when kids in khakis, packing tiny metallic devices, began offering me jobs willy-nilly ("A doctor?" they asked, incredulously, "Why would you want to do *that*?"). A few months later, telling friends back in Hollywood about my new gig at a startup, I heard myself saying, "I'm on the cutting edge! I'm gonna influence an entire generation!" Part of me even believed this.

Then came the headline in *Daily Variety* where it was announced that I had joined Kibu.com as editor-in-chief. I'd been in *Variety* a few times before—for job promotions or selling a screenplay. But for joining a dot-com? What was *that* doing in the Hollywood trades? Like a 911 display on my network-issued pager, the message was loud, clear, and insistent. It was no mere coincidence that a VC friend chose to explain how Silicon Valley operates using—what else?—Hollywood as a model. His version of Valley 101 went something like this:

A VC, he said, is like a "producer," the money guy who brings in the CEO, who in turn is like the "director" for the "project." (Overheard at power breakfasts north and south: "So, yeah, things are crazy busy. I just started working on a new project.") Some directors (CEOs) have their favorite "actors" (CFOs) and bring them along from "project" to "project." (Think Woody Allen and Mia Farrow, pre–Soon Yi.) And, of course, there are the high-profile "players"—targets of reverence, envy, and sightings—all linked to a list of smash startups the way their Hollywood counterparts are to Academy Award–winning movie credits.

If that didn't convince me I was just hopscotching ponds, it was also around this time that I told another VC friend that I was looking to hire a senior editor. His suggestion: Steal "talent" from your competitors, and use your VC firm to help coax them over. "But that sounds so slimy," I said. "And besides, what about loyalty?"

He tried to suppress a smile. "Where did you get your talent when you worked in Hollywood?" he replied rhetorically. He had a point.

Taking his advice, I interviewed a woman who worked at another teen-girl Web site. A sleek, manicured, Kate Spade-toting recent Princeton grad who compulsively name-dropped the CEO with whom she shared a personal trainer, she peppered the conversation with buzzwords and phrases like "convergence," "destination," "new paradigm," "monetizing," "tearing up the old rules," and "leveraging a $60 billion market opportunity." She also said something about "Yahoo! for Gen-Y, with an estrogen slant." (Apparently, she'd spoken with our publicist in the parking lot.)

In any case, she had her pick of hot startups—she'd met a lot of "I-people," she told me, at her trendy day spa in San Francisco—so I asked why she wanted to work at Kibu. Without missing a beat, she replied enthusiastically, "For its monumental impact on the world!" (I had a flashback to Jim Cameron at the 1998 Academy Award ceremony proclaiming, "I'm king of the world!")

I had to admit it: I *was* back in Hollywood, the New Economy version. But this time, I couldn't just pick up and leave. Like every other disillusioned dot-commer, I was waiting for my stock options to vest.

Perhaps, as the business adviser Marc Joseph remarked, the new New Things were actually the oldest of Old Things like fear, greed, hubris, and insecurity dressed up in the latest flat-front chinos. In truth, though, the

Internet culture wasn't merely Hollywood's clone, but a misguided younger sibling searching for a unique identity that became instantly familiar.

Familiar even to Jesse's investment-banker friend in Manhattan, who called after Jesse's first day at IFILM and asked, "So, what's it like?"

"Well," Jesse paused. "It's very dot-commish."

His button-down banker friend immediately knew what Jesse was talking about. This was a business world where their phone call might be interrupted by people playing Ping-Pong in the background. Where CEOs were called "Chief Yahoos" or "Chief Evangelists." Where philosophy geniuses-turned-XML-programmers sped around the office on the scooter-du-jour, and massage times were posted in on the office's online bulletin board.

These New Economy accoutrements had become as standard as the Old Economy's key to the executive washroom: Foosball tables. Red Bull energy drinks. Split screens with personal stock portfolios flashing 24/7. Dirt-encrusted barefeet. Drooling dogs atop sleeping bags under desks. Tae Bo for the wired. Nap rooms for the fried. Polygon-shaped business cards. Free Frappucinos. Skateboard ramps. Weekly companywide All Hands meetings—mandatory pep rallies in which you'd yell "Go team!" and cheer wildly after every announcement.

And noise, always. Random gismos beeping and burping and vibrating. Video games. Mega-earphones on every head. Yelling from work space to work space when Instant Messenger overloads your screen.

But the startup culture was about more than summer camp–like offices. It was an *attitude*. It started with a "we-can-change-the-world" idealism that morphed into a brazen cockiness never before seen in fresh-faced entry-level college grads. This ethos was immortalized by the industry's frantic pace, outlandish offices, and casual clothing, but underneath lay something more substantial and transformative: a spirit of optimism, freedom, and unprecedented openness to new ideas.

For many twenty-somethings jumping on the startup bandwagon, their companies became surrogate families. To outsiders, the digerati seemed like Moonies. It was an upside-down universe in which venture capitalists with premature receding hairlines became rock stars, and a million bucks didn't seem like a lot of money. Some have likened the culture not only to Hollywood, but to Wall Street or Vegas. Yet instead of would-be billionaires pining to become the next Steve Wynn, it was a group of kids on the brink of adulthood, trying to carve out their niche in a manic, surreal world that makes *Alice's Adventure in Wonderland* seem like the simple story of a young girl's day at a local amusement park.

In some respects, going "dot-com" wasn't just about inventing a revolutionary new platform. It was also about the turbulent process of inventing oneself—even if it looked like not much more than a good excuse for protracting adolescence while perhaps socking away a few hundred thousand.

But many who were introduced to the Web early on didn't realize they were on the cusp of a cultural revolution that would soon attract hipsters, celebrities, and soccer moms alike. They thought they were just, well, hanging out with a bunch of tech nerds.

Take Jeff Goodell—a Silicon Valley native who would later write for *Rolling Stone* and pen the best-selling memoir *Sunnyvale: The Rise and Fall of a Silicon Valley Family.* Then a teenager working as a technical writer for Apple, a tiny computer company located in two buildings in the northern California bedroom community of Cupertino, Goodell recalls the days when the neonatal New Economy crawled out of its crib.

"The Apple II had just come out," Goodell says, "and no one had any fucking idea what these things would be used for. The engineers would talk about people using these machines to put kitchen recipes on."

Despite Apple founder Steve Jobs's reputation as a New Age Nostradamus, even he was unable to see into the future. "It's easy to say Steve Jobs had this grand vision," Goodell, who personally admires Jobs, continues. "But it was all just cool toys—these guys loved building stuff and playing with it."

Looking back, Goodell believes that "the cool thing then was this sense of mystery of what this thing could possibly do. Everyone had their own wild ideas, and most of them were totally wrong. The great thing was this conviction that people held on to—even if they had no idea what it would lead to."

Nevertheless, Goodell didn't share his colleagues' boyish enthusiasm. "I didn't get the romance of the culture at all. It was ironic, because here I was at the center of the universe technology-wise, and I was just sitting there looking out the window thinking, 'I gotta get outta here and go where something's *happening.*' "

But the power of this new medium and the tight-knit community that fueled it did hook Lisa Hendricks. Originally a music manager, in 1994 she started BoxTop, an L.A.-based interactive consultancy that helped bring musicians online.

LISA HENDRICKS

In the early days, it was a very dynamic and very, very small community, and there probably were less than 300 sites. Sky Dayton [founder of ISP giant EarthLink at age twenty-three] and those guys from EarthLink were nearby on Melrose. My e-mail address was like number 130 at EarthLink. You could get Sky on the phone no matter what. You could even get *Jerry Yang* on the phone and say, "Hey, I've got a site that I want you to list."

Not anymore. We tried getting Yahoo! cofounder Jerry Yang on the phone to ask for his participation in this book, but a PR person returned our call via brush-off e-mail.

When did the culture change? Michael Krantz, a former *Time* staffer turned Keen.com editor, points to an exact moment; whereas Cathy Brooks, a veteran PR executive, believes that the basement-to-boardroom transformation occurred over time.

MICHAEL KRANTZ

One thing that I never forgot was August 9, 1995. I was working on a piece for *The New Yorker*, a "Talk Of The Town" on Microsoft's CEO, Steve Ballmer. On that day, two things happened and it still astounds me that no one has ever captured this and written about it. That was the day Netscape went public, which to me is as good a marking place as any for the dawn of the dot-com era. And the same day, Jerry Garcia died! It was as though one era of Bay Area culture ended and the next began.

CATHY BROOKS

The culture changed over the years. I was doing PR for a software company on the Sun campus in Mountain View, and they used to do a beer and pretzel mixer every Friday. They had pinball and video-game machines rigged for free play.

They had company gatherings all the time. They had dunk tanks with the CEO and founder in them. The company T-shirt was tie-dye, and the theme was "Stairway to Heaven." It was like a kibbutz with less Jews and more junk food!

Bruce Francis at CNBC came and shot a story on corporate culture. There were Nerf gun fights in the hallways, people shooting Super Soakers outside, people going jogging at lunch and coming right back to work—without showering. It was a very fun environment. That was the culture and what I thought of as Silicon Valley, because to the true geeks, programming is play. It was a vocation and an avocation.

Then later, it became like, "Oh God, we *have* to have a 'culture.' We *have* to be wacky. We *have* to offer food and trips and scooters." But you can't force culture. The way to maintain culture is to let it change as it needs to change, and not to force old culture on new organizations. But eventually the culture became a "thing."

Funky office spaces made culture a "thing" for many New Economy companies. What better way to spit in the face of brick-and-mortar middle managers than to turn their step-and-repeat, office-cubicle-office-cubicle design on its balding head. And while they were at it, why not rip off Dilbert's tie, tear down his partitions, and pour some Jolt down his throat? The challenge was creating an environment that, as Lisa Hendricks says, the "skateboarders, pierced, tattooed, right-out-of-college generation" could feel comfortable in.

That didn't mean facsimiles of the parental workplaces most dot-commers had seen on take-your-child-to-work day. As a twenty-five-year-old former producer at Disney's Go.com noted when she walked into her company's obstacle course of dogs, pool tables, air hockey games, free-play arcades and "aloha Fridays": "Obviously, it wasn't my dad's office."

Not only aesthetics changed; so did a sense of privacy. "The space was so open that you were always looking at other people," says Nicholas Goldsmith, who designed the New York offices of Boo.com, a once highly touted but now defunct fashion startup promising a "gateway to a world of cool." "Nothing was above a forty-two-inch height. With everything at this lower level, sound is traveling back and forth. Everybody is hearing everything."

"We had two attorneys, two paralegals, and a secretary in a space that was probably twenty by thirty," says David Hornik of the offices Perkins Coie created next to those of their client AdAuction.com. "I was spending hours a day recruiting, and these poor people would have to listen to me. Sometimes they'd say, 'That was a great pitch, David,' or more embarrassing, 'You know, man, that wasn't your best pitch.'"

ANDREW ANKER

I don't know if we helped start this open-space concept, but we were one of the first. For the kind of job that *Wired* was doing, it was very easy to get really focused on your computer and eight-by-eight space and lose sight of the fact that we were trying to build community. So very early on, I decreed no offices, no cubicles, no walls, no nothing. And that included me as the CEO. We were clearly overcrowded, and there were times when if OSHA [the Occupational Safety and Health Administration] had come in, we would have been gone.

My lawyer complained more than anyone else. She had certain issues, so eventually we got her a conference room that she could go to for private phone calls. The Human Resources people had some issues, too. I've seen it work well, but the times that I haven't were when the CEO said, "You guys don't get offices, but I do." I made it very clear that I was out in the same bullpen as everyone else.

STEVEN OVERMAN

When I first came to *Wired* we were at a space in San Francisco now called 2 South Park, but then it was 433 Second Street, a beat-up old building. Dave Eggers was running *Might* magazine on the ground floor and we were on floor two. It had crappy wall-to-wall carpet peeling up and *HotWired* was three desks shoved in the back of the office. Everybody called it The Swamp.

When we moved to a bigger space, Bill Gates came to see our office and Japanese guys in suits would come, and I would bring these guys on tours. I'd point to one bank of computers and say, "That's the design department," and point to another bank and say, "That's editorial," and they were scribbling notes like they had never seen an open office before.

JOSH KELLER

Business Week did a feature on UBUBU, and they talked about our bathroom. We had a unisex bathroom where we put in a disco ball and had music going twenty-four hours a day. We took those postcards that are very popular marketing vehicles—we must have had a couple thousand of them—and used them as wallpaper. There were three stalls, but the main door didn't close. So we also had another bathroom which, because it had a door on it and it closed, we actually used also as a private conference room/telephone room. We didn't have any other doors in the office. Our desks were in a big, open room with no walls—not even cubicle walls!

LYNN HARRIS

The offices at Oxygen had lots of open spaces. It's in an old cookie factory, the Nabisco factory, and the renovation was true to the factory. There was this funky pipey look to everything with the girder pipes painted different colors. The top floor was three stories high.

One day there was a blimp in the office—it was a promotional stunt some company sent—but it had plenty of room to fly. We had a DJ because we had live TV going twenty-four hours a day. She spun from the mezzanine during the bumpers, but this got annoying after a while because you couldn't make phone calls. The Bacon Brothers or the Indigo Girls or Marc Anthony would be playing, and I would say, above the din, "Hey, *guess* where I'm calling from?" At first it was totally amusing, but then you realized it was hard to do business.

———————

The open offices—many furnished with rows of "cube farms"—may have compromised both productivity and privacy, but they also made work seem less like a four-letter word, and more like f-u-n. Business development executive Elizabeth Collet remembers that because her office at Yahoo! had no conference room, "a lot of times, you would bring visitors to the lawn because it was the only place that you could be out of your cubicle. Most of the meetings happened in the hallway. There was a deck and barbecue out back and that was where people were having most of their meals. We were working 24/7 at the time, so there was a lot of camaraderie."

Josh Keller believes that the offices mirrored the culture, which seemed more college dorm than corporate command center: loud, informal, and young. "There's something about the spirit of what was going on at that time," says Keller. "You could walk into companies and feel an energy level, and a free-spiritedness. You even heard it in the noise level."

"It was playtime," says Shuli Hallack, a former Rare Medium executive assistant. "I mean, our company meetings always had an open bar. Sure, I'd learn something, but I was going there to drink Heineken."

Hallack's Rare Medium colleague Sang Lee also witnessed life at the New Economy carnival.

SANG LEE

This guy—I didn't even know what he did. He never worked on any projects. But one thing he never forgot was to walk around the office at five P.M. on Fridays with an IOMEGA Zip-drive box with a hole cut out of the picture of the IOMEGA drive where the disk goes in. He would collect money from all the employees to buy beer and wine. The management didn't care. People would just sit there and play hackeysack and Unreal Tournament until eight or nine at night. That was the real time that people got to know each other.

Subj: Only in Silicon Valley
Date: 8/31/00

In a message dated 8/31/00 3:16:43 PM Pacific Daylight Time, Melissa@Epylon.Com writes:

We have a Football team and a Softball team, a game room filled with all sorts of work-distracting toys such as a pool table, foos ball, basketball hoop and video games!! I have a ton of positions open but this email is focused mainly towards finding a dependable receptionist. (We like to refer to him/her as a Manager of First Impressions.) This position includes stock options and full benefits from day one. If you know of anyone who might be interested in this position, please reply.

Job notice for "Manager of First Impressions" (receptionist) sent by Melissa Daimler, former "Director of People" at Epylon.com, touting such cultural perks as "work-distracting toys."

"We wanted a fun workspace to keep good creative people around," says David Epstein, founder of the Kansas City Web shop BlairLake, which Compuware acquired for more than $18 million in February 2000.

DAVID EPSTEIN

We ended up buying a strange 1920s mortuary in Kansas City. We chopped the mortuary up into different offices, and everyone was allowed to paint their own. We actually had an embalming room, and rather than ignore it, we totally took advantage of it. You know, "Todd, you have a call in the embalming room."

Clients first thought it was creepy, and then they kind of got it. The elevators had been designed for coffins, and they were very long and had these railings to hold on to. Our average age was twenty-four, so anyone who walked in was probably not going to be depressed, but we still worked really hard to put up cartoons and funny drawings and paintings. It was kind of like the HBO series *Six Feet Under*, without the dead people.

The dead people, it seems, were those who couldn't find offices in the first place. Because startups were racing to build their "space" so quickly, there was a serious supply-and-demand problem. Who benefited? Designers like Nicholas Goldsmith, real estate agents like Chris Dallas, and property owners. San Francisco rents skyrocketed, while dot-commers asked designers to forget about what Goldsmith calls "function over form" and instead to craft spaces that read like trashy novels. It wasn't uncommon for tyro CEOs to request "a space that's subtly sexy, curved at the edges. Equally penetrable and penetrating. A fine balance between seductive and dismissive."

Um, okay . . . but that'll cost you.

NICHOLAS GOLDSMITH

In designing these firms, the sky was the limit. Investors were willing to jump in and just start spending the money. Initially, it's a lot more than your overhead, but you think you need a space to show that you are really at that level. If they started in a funky place, they felt they would attract talent. And you had to be competitive.

Boo.com wanted to do the whole office with these Swedish birch tables. They were very elegant looking, but they were basically individual desks. I said, "Wait a second, there is no wire management, no way to move these around, there is no *flexibility*, there is no *modularity*. You would have to build all these walls around them and it's kind of a ridiculous idea." But they still wanted the tables.

CHRIS DALLAS

Prospective tenants didn't have a choice. It was, "Do you like it? Because if you don't, it will be leased out to one of the next three people who want it." We had a zero vacancy rate in San Francisco and such a shortage of office space that a lot of startups were also buying up these residential loft buildings and moving their businesses in there. It was a pretty arrogant market. We had a lot of artists or art galleries who had five- or six-year leases and they were coming to term. They were used to paying ten, twelve, twenty dollars a square foot. Now it went up to eighty dollars.

DAVID NEUMAN

We were racing to get more space to expand production capability at DEN, and one of my lieutenants came to me and said, "I found some cheap space, it's in Marina del Rey, we can convert it in a second." I said, "Fine, let's get our real estate agent involved," and he said, "No, no, no—we have no time to do that." This is someone I had worked with in a previous company relationship, so I trusted him, and we ended up getting the new space lickety-split.

A few months passed, and an employee came into my office and said, "Uh, I've become aware of something, and I'm terrified to tell you this, but I feel it's my obligation." He said he had reason to believe that his supervisor had a financial interest in the lease that DEN signed. Basically, this person had gone out and leased a property, then flipped it to DEN.

I was astonished. It was a moment of *et tu, Brute?* I remember confronting this employee and him finally coming clean after denying it for the first couple of meetings. I was like, "How could you do something like this?" and his attitude was, "Well, it just seemed like everyone else was getting rich, so I should too."

Of course, he was prosecuted, but I thought, there's something *very* dangerous about these times.

———————

Dangerous indeed: What to do with the millions left over after the real estate agents and designers got paid? Sharper Image shopping sprees, of course. Think Julia Roberts in the scene in *Pretty Woman* when she goes wild on Richard Gere's credit card. Now multiply that by ten. Got that? Okay, multiply by ten again.

"Aeron chairs were the highlight of the Internet revolution," jokes Shuli Hallack, whose company, Rare Medium, "shepherded in so many" that "people were rolling around the floor in them. It was awesome!"

Or excessive.

"I would love to see someone take Aeron chairs, put them out in concrete and distribute them around Manhattan, like the cows. Have artists spray-paint them," says Jerry Blanton, a former branding specialist at the defunct Web shop March First.

Others who witnessed the green bills flipping by as quickly as calendar pages marking the passage of time in classic movies include Lev Chapelsky, the former marketing director at CarsDirect.com.

LEV CHAPELSKY

My first day at CarsDirect, they took me around and introduced me to "the guy with indiscriminate spending power." They said, "Here's the guy in charge of IT, tell him what you want, Lev." So I went through a wish list: Give me a cell phone, Palm Pilot, a laptop, wireless Internet access. And he said, "Okay, sure." You asked and you got it.

DAN MYRICK

When we took tours of these new startups, our jaws dropped. We went to one place in the Valley, and, man, you're talking Aeron chairs, Herman Miller furniture, top-of-the-line computers. I'm like, "What are you guys doing?" And they go, "We're doing QuickTime movies." So we sit down in this fancy, brand-new, paint-still-wet conference room. They're throwing out all the catchphrases of the day: We're going to do this, we're going to do that.

We're like, "Okay, that's all great, that's excellent, but how do you guys see making money?" They say, "Oh, we're going to put up all this great content, we're going to sell banner space." I said, "Well, you'll have to sell a lot, because you've got half a million bucks in gear here."

DAVID NEUMAN

Marc Collins-Rector flew chartered jets so much that at some point they would throw him freebies. He was launching DEN music in New York and for some reason they had a 737 that they were giving him for the normal price that his six-passenger Lear plane would have been. There are thirty or forty people flying out on a 737 and I remember thinking, "There is something not right about this. This is a <u>737</u>. It just doesn't feel appropriate."

DOUG SCOTT

We do this big, expensive deal to hire a new CEO at Hollywood Stock Exchange, and at the same time, we move into the hot Ritts Furniture building on Santa Monica Boulevard. I had initiated a project to get one of those old Wall Street stock tickers, like you'd find at Merrill Lynch. We'd wire it into one of our computers and feed our celebrity stock prices into it. That became the entryway to our office.

People were in love with it! People would wait in our office for meetings and they'd just stare at the ticker machine watching Tom Cruise's name scroll down a half. That was like, the *ultimate in vanity*. You know, I'm affecting the value of the man! What, he's on the rocks with Nicole Kidman? Drop him, sell him! What, he's *not* a Scientologist? Buy him!

Michael Burns, our cofounder and biggest stockholder, fell in love with the ticker and wanted a 150-foot long and 5-foot-high stock ticker on top of the new building. We spent $500,000 on that stock ticker! We're going out for another round of capital, and next thing we know, $4 million gets plopped into a new office and a big stock ticker on a building that we don't even own.

JEFF GOODELL

The cafeteria at Excite@Home was unbelievably outlandish. They had five different regional cuisines and chefs to cook these regional cuisines to your order. It was great to see janitors go up to chefs—who were undoubtedly making $75,000 a year—and asking them to cook some exotic filet for lunch. Given what happened to Excite@Home, that's quite hilarious. [@Home, a broadband provider, bought Excite, a portal, for $6.7 billion in January 1999 and went bankrupt in October 2001, a month before selling Excite to Infospace and iWon for a comparatively paltry $10 million.]

STEVEN OVERMAN

Wired was one of the first companies to have a chef. His name was Chuck, and he was also on the masthead. We were in this crappy clubhouse, but there was a guy who came in and cooked couscous. It was a beautiful thing.

But something happened right before my first all-company lunch. It was eleven-thirty A.M. and I was really hungry, so I poked into the kitchen and saw a plate of brownies. I grabbed a couple and ate them, and Chuck said, "You didn't just eat those brownies, did you?" I asked why, and Chuck yells out, "Steven ate the brownies!" and everyone said, "Oh my God!" Then he pulls out a sign that said: POT BROWNIES.

I was pissed. I remember thinking, "This is an *office?*" I still had the New York mentality. Louis Rossetto, the cofounder, cracked up. He said, "You're not going to make it through the day." I was catatonic and couldn't do anything. It was my first all-company food gathering, and I was drugged.

Fortunately, not everyone was drugged—or acted as if they were. Some startups chanted the creed of economical prudence in a culture that prided itself on reckless spending.

Alan Citron recalls his days at Real Networks, where "the environment was a bit more subdued and less lavish." Yes, "When you peered under the surface, people had very large bank accounts and tended to live very, very well." And, yes, "Once you got to know people, they started to talk about their wine cellars and boats." But when it came to running the business, he insists, the motto was: frugality.

"We always benefited from being conservative," says Nibblebox.com's Dave Bartis, who paid "only forty-five hundred per month on rent" for his office space. Sure, he admits, his back is "fucked up" from the bargain-basement chairs and no one had company credit cards, but his skinflint strategy made sense. "I was at NBC when we had to cut jobs, and I was at HBO when we had to deal with cable budgets," the veteran television executive explains. "I've always used my own business background in making spending decisions."

JEFF GOODELL

I remember talking to [Netscape cofounder] Marc Andreessen in 1997, and he said to me, "Any company that has a private jet is, by definition, doomed to fail." Because that meant they had all their money in the wrong things. Of course, that's changed, especially post-WTC. All the companies now are scrambling for jets.

JIM MEDALIA

When the VCs came to look at us at JustBalls, the minute they walked in the door they would smile. We literally had twenty people in four eight-by-ten-foot offices. We bought our desks at Sam's Club and each person had to build their own. It was a rite of passage. But the good thing was, it was very convenient and it did have a shower. We hired a couple of guys from the Olympic Rowing Team who worked out early in the morning and in the evening, so the shower was very good for them.

The showers, close quarters, late nights, and group meals created an environment similar to that of a family. In fact, the demographics of the start-up culture—dominated by the young and single who'd ditched their hometowns to conquer the millennial frontier—may have contributed to a longing for familial connection. After all, most had recently left their parents but hadn't yet become parents themselves.

Andrew Anker remembers attending an information presentation about medical benefits at *Wired*, where the representative leading the session announced, "We have family benefits, too." Anker says she asked, "Who here has a family?" but "Kevin Kelly, who was the executive editor at the time, and I were the only two people to raise our hands."

Fittingly, Chris Dallas, the San Francisco real estate broker, noticed that many of his young clients chose to live with roommates—not because they couldn't afford their own places, but because there was a feeling, he recalls, of responsibility for one's friends as if they were family: "Look, okay, I'm worth a million or ten million, but my friend isn't, and I have to take care of him."

It makes sense, then, that home and office became virtually indistinguishable. Nicholas Goldsmith, the designer of the Boo.com offices in New York, believes that the notion of "bringing your residential lifestyle to the office" was a good thing. "The informality actually creates a very healthy environment," he says. Yet while some—like the former Scient receptionist Joanne

Weaver and Live365.com's senior editor J. Betty Ray—liked the collegiality, journalist Jeff Goodell felt that the line between "family" and "cult" could be as thin as a microchip.

"You got the sense that it was a Moonie operation," Goodell says of new recruits he observed at an Austin software company, Trilogy, while reporting an article for *Rolling Stone*. "They really wanted you to drink the Kool-Aid because they really wanted your life and your soul."

JOANNE WEAVER

A lot of the press said, "This is very culty," because you'd go through something called Spark, which is your first week of orientation. They'd give you all the catchphrases for the office, and really instill you with the culture. But people felt as if you'd joined a family, not a cult.

I got promoted into Human Resources, and I started a little thing where after each person got Sparked, I'd introduce them by sending an e-mail. I'd hyperlink their name to their Zone page on our Intranet. It had each person's picture, where they sat in the office, a list of their favorite foods, quotes, what their past jobs had been. I'd put a little creative story at the beginning of it. Anyone could send something out to All Scient Global. A lot of us were young and single and away from our real families, so this was like a halfway house out of the nest.

J. BETTY RAY

When I worked at a small South of Market Web development shop, we had this big, old Victorian house. Everybody who lived there worked together. The boundaries of one's existence were just gone. We'd go to Burning Man together, come home, go to work together, work together at home, go dancing, deals would be cut at parties. You'd be at these pool parties and you'd see the CEO of one company and the CEO of another company talking and they'd both be blitzed. It was so fantastic.

But according to Larry Glenn, the former chief technology officer of Liquid Digital, a Web production company in New York, his work-family more closely resembled the Mansons than the Waltons.

LARRY GLENN

I sat next to a guy, a programmer, who would just randomly scream out the word "crack" during the day. Everyone heard, because we had these open offices. So three times a day he would scream the word "crack," and nobody blinked an eye. It was like, "Oh, he's a programmer, it's some genius thing." There was a little bit of that freaky mystique going on— like the brilliant, eccentric relative you see at family occasions. But I think it was just a regular reference to cocaine. The guy seemed constantly wired.

———

Many dot-commers seemed constantly "wired" as well, which wasn't surprising, given the long hours arising from intense competition to be "first to market." Interestingly, this "24/7" mentality wasn't a dot-com cultural invention so much as a mimicking of earlier roots in the software business.

"If you go back to any of the Microsoft books," notes CNET cofounder Kevin Wendle, "you read stories about the wives and children coming into the commissary to have dinner and then going home so their husbands could get back to work."

But that doesn't mean the digerati appreciated this legacy.

"I did not admire these people's lifestyles at all," says Ted Kruckel, the president of a boutique public relations and marketing firm in New York that began taking on New Economy clients in 1999. "All of these people were getting all glamorous all of a sudden and yeah, *Vanity Fair* was inviting them to the Hollywood Oscar parties, but at what price? These people went from zero to sixty. They were working like dogs."

Cameron Hickey, then a twenty-year-old "Web innovator" at Boo.com, was one of the unfortunate scions.

CAMERON HICKEY

I spent ten weeks in London working 24/7 to get the Boo site up. A lot of it was meetings and then it was straight coding with short breaks to roll joints. We were working until four A.M. I had a girlfriend, and the time that I spent working there was the closest that we came to breaking up.

JOANNE WEAVER

It was a work-hard, play-hard environment. This one guy, Brandon Eiseman, was presented with a pillow for always spending the night at the company. It was considered an honor at Scient.

When I was the receptionist, we had ten people squeezed into this tiny little greeting area. I'm sitting on this little desk 24/7, lines are ringing, and people are filtering in so I had to cater to them first. Faxes are coming in. Things are bleeping. People are shoving things in my face. It's an absolute madhouse. Put you through to Marketing? Put you through to Sales? Can I help you? Finally I put the phone on the cradle, took a deep breath, and sat there. And everyone in the room busts up and starts applauding me! It was my heroic dot-com moment.

As with the frenetic pace, dress code—or lack thereof—was another hand-me-down from the early days. When Greg Deocampo, a young technologist, met with Apple CEO and Chairman John Scully to show him some software he'd developed in college, "It didn't even occur to me to put on a suit." In fact, the programmer's idea of dressing up was putting on his "finest T-shirt." In Deocampo's world, "Does your code work?" beat "dress code."

AUREN HOFFMAN

Back in 1995 and 1996, I used to go to these Internet user group meetings—this was like pocket-protector city! "People who did not tuck in their shirts," would be the polite way to say it. A lot of plaid. A lot of T-shirts that had either obscenities on them or those really long equations that at the bottom said, "Let there be light."

Years later, however, Hoffman says that the group "responsible for the innovations got co-opted by the MBAs," which led to a shift from sartorial cluelessness to stylish self-consciousness.

CATHY BROOKS

It's a better-looking industry now. I'm not saying that people were ugly before, but you can see the yuppification. The people who follow from hip industry to hip industry—all of a sudden they were here. You used to be able to look around at a party and say, "Okay, those are the people who program the stuff, those are the people who sell the stuff, and those are the people who do marketing and PR for the stuff." And they were in three separate little groups.

I first noticed the change in New York, when the whole Silicon Alley industry started to happen. And, let's face it, they dress all in black, they're tragically hip, they go to all the best clubs. You could still go to a tech industry party and tell the people apart today, but the lines are more blurred now.

SANG LEE

You could break people into four groups at Rare Medium:

One, corporate thwarters. The artsy-fartsy guys. You'd see them at Village bars wearing camouflage with spiked, colored hair.

Two, the old people. It was funny to see them show up the first day of work with Dockers slacks and white button-down shirts that they had been wearing their whole lives. Two months later, they'd be wearing TeVa sandals and Camel Light T-shirts.

Three, normal programmers. There were a lot of Middle Eastern and Russian people who just sat there and cranked out code in flannel shirts, jeans, and sneakers.

Four, young, gun 'em and get 'em folks. They shopped at Banana Republic and Barney's. Everyone was wearing the same fly-away collar in some funky color. NetSetGoods.com catered to these people making one hundred K who sold things that they didn't know a lot about, like ten-dollar pens that lit up when your cell phone rang.

––––––––––

While the suit-and-tie culture gave way to corporate casual in many industries besides the Internet, some startup companies took the word "casual" to mean "borderline ratty."

"Being forty and a CEO," says Elizabeth Kalodner of her gig running SocialNet.com, "I didn't really feel too old, but I did feel better dressed than a lot of other people."

"People knew how to buy casual wear or office wear," agrees Amanda Sherman, a Barney's New York buyer, "but didn't understand that there was an in-between."

ANDREW ANKER

There was no dress code at *Wired*. At one point we were talking to the Viacom guys about investing, and Viacom owns MTV. One of the guys came in and said, "Pretty impressive, but I think that MTV has you beat on the piercing per employee." There was definitely the rave culture going on, and definitely too many piercings and tattoos for my taste.

STEVEN OVERMAN

You know how everybody else had casual Fridays? *Wired* had "formal Fridays." It was started by the accounting department. They would wear evening gowns and tuxedos, and soon it took off and the whole company did it.

JOANNE WEAVER

They sold the job to me on the culture. Adam Cunha was the guy doing phones before me. He was this apathetic looking punk-rocker wearing these cute little Adidas, very casually dressed with his hair hanging in his face. I was like, "Cool, I might like it here." The first words I uttered at Scient were, "Nice Adidas."

DAVID HORNIK

At Perkins Coie, I showed up the first day in khakis and what I viewed as a perfectly reasonable collared shirt. And everyone was wearing suits. I looked around, like, this is ridiculous! I'm setting up my office, and someone made a comment: "Hey David, don't ya have any suits?" And I said, "None that I intend to wear." They sort of laughed, thinking I'm full of it, but the next day, I wore the same thing. And they all kind of looked at me again.

The next day, another associate came in khakis. And then, on Thursday, so did another. Friday was casual Fridays and the next Monday, no one wore suits. And that was the end of suits. It was a simple revolution.

But ultimately, I pushed the envelope a bit. We made these black T-shirts for Perkins Coie that said "www.PerkinsCoie.com" on the front and "Legal Minds @ Internet Speed" on the back. This was my idea of marketing for a law firm. Any given day, I was wearing that T-shirt with a black short-sleeve shirt over it and sneakers. Clients liked it because they were our age, mostly kids. So they felt more comfortable that this was someone who was about getting stuff done, not about formalities like suits.

That was the message of the time: If you could get stuff done, you could wear a *tutu*.

It wasn't just grunge versus Gucci that created a rift between Old and New Economy types. Many from publishing, film, and TV flocked to the Internet when the medium began to expand. Some were truly fascinated by the Net's power and opportunity for creative freedom; others were just after a quick buck. But there were also those driven by the Old-Media-is-toast notion, now that kids could click on hyperlinked text on cool color screens.

ANDREW ANKER

Wired was well-known for bashing Old Media. Michael Crichton wrote an article in the first year or two of *Wired* in which he called the *New York Times* a "Mediasaurus" and said that they'd be dead in ten years. There was definitely that "we know, you don't know, how dare you think you know" mentality. It was a great rallying cry. We used to say—it was part of our sales pitch—"Buy one less page in *Time* magazine this year. Buy *HotWired*—*Wired*'s online property—for a year."

KURT ANDERSEN

There was a sense of resentment toward the New Media people on the part of some Old Media people still working in print who felt that the train had left the station—even more than the resentment of first-generation Internet technologists toward Johnny-come-lately media people like me.

There was a combination of bafflement, this sense of "Why are all these people getting all this attention?" and at some point there was also the fear that, "Uh-oh, my world is being rocked and I'm not with the new program." There was some anxiety about, "Oh my God, print is dead. I better get on this train as it's leaving."

"Young people sold fear," says Richard Titus, a former vice president of Razorfish. "It was almost like being in the extortion business in 1990."

Because it was the young people who by and large understood technology, he continues, there was an attitude of, "You old fogies don't have a clue, but it's about to change your business." The twenty-somethings "would point to eToys and how they were gonna crush Toys-'R'-Us—that would generate major fear in brick-and-mortar businesses. Which is ironic, now that eToys has crashed and burned."

CAMERON HICKEY

I was managing at least twenty-five people, so I didn't tell everyone how young I was. But every so often I would have reason to tell my age. I was only twenty, so I wasn't legal to drink or participate in the 401K plan. And there was definitely resentment when people found out how much I was making.

But it went beyond that. The fear we instilled in older people was driven by this exclusive understanding and control over this new technology. We made it seem like magic to them, when all it was, really, was HTML.

ASHLEY POWER

When people come in to Goosehead, they'll talk to my stepfather, who's also the cochair. They'll say, "Who runs the company?" and he'll say, "Ashley—she's the president." And they'll say, "Yeah, but who *really* runs the company." My stepfather says, "Ashley does. She's the president." Then they go, "Well, who makes the decisions? She's only *sixteen!*" And he'll say again, "Ashley does."

I love when they come in the office and don't even talk to me, or don't even look at me when they're talking. They look at my parents because they're the older authority figures in the room. It's *over* then. I don't even *care* what you're saying.

It's about respect, not age. There are thirteen-year-olds who are the most amazing programmers I've ever seen in my entire life. My brother is three and a half and has an iMac and knows how to download MP3s. Our generation, we've just grown up with this.

It's not surprising that one of the "fuck-yous" to the geezers came from Philip "Pud" Kaplan, a programmer and former product manager at the New York Web design firm Think New Ideas who later founded FuckedCompany.com, an online water cooler community where employees ruthlessly ridicule the cyber-challenged fuddy duddies "ruining" their companies.

PHILIP "PUD" KAPLAN

I was on this panel at Internet World, and another guy on the panel was one of the top execs at Time Warner. He was so proud of himself because he started Pathfinder, Time Warner's first online venture. Obviously, it went out of business. I was like, "Dude, what the fuck! I was doing that in *high school!* There were like ten thousand other fifteen-year-old kids fucking making a site like Pathfinder every day. All you need is like Geocities and a freaking copy of FrontPage! There's nothing to be proud of."

The fact that he was some old CEO guy, he was like, "Well, I'm doing a Web site, and people are gonna come." I was, like, "*Of course* you'll get eyeballs, you're fucking *Warner Brothers!*"

If youth operated on "Internet time"—the oft-used phrase to describe the warp speed at which things move in the New Economy—the idea that one could plant a seed and not see its growth for decades seemed unfathomable to Marc Andreessen, the wunderkind Netscape cofounder who grew to power overnight.

JEFF GOODELL

When I was doing a *Rolling Stone* article about Marc Andreessen—this was at the height of the boom—we were driving down El Camino in Palo Alto. We passed this very old hotel in his fancy-ass white Mercedes, the $150,000 one, and he was talking to me about how he took it up to 140 miles per hour on the Bayshore Expressway at two in the morning, and how cool it felt.

But I looked at this hotel and I had a flashback to when I was a kid. I realized that my grandfather, who had been a landscape contractor, had landscaped this hotel. As a four- or five-year-old kid, I had planted some of these trees when I was helping him on the job. So I said, "Marc, look at those trees in front of the hotel." They were giant now. I said, "I planted those when I was a kid." And he looked at me with this expression like I was on fucking *Mars*. Like, "So fucking what? So you planted those trees."

It was this huge disconnect of Marc—who was in his mid-20s—not having any connection with the world around him. He couldn't wrap his head around the idea that there were trees there *at all* and that I had *planted* them and that this had any personal *meaning* to me.

———

"People just starting out in professional life don't really know what life is all about," notes DutyFreeGuide.com's Bernardo Joselevich, who is thirty-nine. "Their attitudes are unmoderated by the hits of life."

"Of course," he concedes, "a lot of them are just assholes."

"Everybody at Rare Medium was twenty-five and people were snotty, immature, and cliquey," says Shuli Hallack. "Everybody knew everybody else's business. There was an 'in crowd' and Nerf footballs would hit me in the head and someone would come to retrieve it without saying a word. It was just like high school."

Lew Harris found the immaturity exasperating.

LEW HARRIS

I had a conversation with a long-time friend right in the middle of the flurry. He told me that his son was starting a Web site, and I said that his son could call me for advice. The kid wanted me to invest, so he sent me the prospectus, and I said that I saw some problems because I didn't know what his business model was.

A couple of months later, he called and said that he'd like to talk. We met for breakfast and he proceeded to lecture me on why this was going to work, why he was going to make a fortune, and why I didn't know what I was talking about.

This was a kid who had no background, and I'd been a success in the business world for over *twenty years*. I understood how the money worked on the Web, but I sat there and he lectured me for an hour! That for me was the moment that symbolized the hubris of the time.

The "hubris of the time" extended to retaining employees—seasoned or otherwise. In an atmosphere where, as David Neuman remembers, a graphic designer with six months' experience in the industry would demand (and get) $60,000 to $80,000 a year, inventing incentives to keep the cubes filled became a key to success—or perhaps led to many startups' eventual failure.

"One company would offer yoga and massage and then the next company had to do the same," says Peter Seidler, the former Razorfish chief creative officer. "The demand for talent was really intense."

Lisa Hendricks recalls that when the industry really exploded, "we were getting blackmailed every day. Employees would say with a straight-face: 'If you don't pay me twenty thousand more, I'm going over here.'"

PHILIP "PUD" KAPLAN

The job market was so hot. I was so cocky. When I had a job interview at Razorfish, I sat on the couch and the secretary said, "So-and-so will be right out to see you." Five minutes, he's not there. Ten minutes, he's not there. At fifteen minutes, I just said, "Fuck it, I'm not waiting for this guy." I got up and left.

LEW HARRIS

I hired a woman as an associate editor at E! Online who'd been an intern at *L.A. Magazine*. She was maybe twenty-eight, and she came up with the idea for the live Web cast of the *Evita* premiere. We did another one that she also staged, and she became our live events person. Yahoo! at the time was looking for someone to get them into the movie studios, and they wanted to hire her away for three times what I was paying her. I countered and went up $10,000 from what she was getting from me. It was a lot less than what she would be getting from them, but she really wanted to stay. Yahoo! then doubled her stock options, gave her a signing bonus, added to her salary, and lured her away.

She stayed there for three or four years, and was worth something like $10 million. Then she quit and went around the world. Everyone looked at her as the one who left and did it. How do you keep people in that environment?

HAROLD MANN

I had an employee use the word "loyalty" with me, and he had been with me for only thirteen months! That's when I knew that the Net was doing some serious damage.

SHULI HALLACK

I started as a temp at Rare Medium while I was waiting to go back to take classes. I didn't want to sign on full-time, but they offered me a job. I asked for $46,000, which I thought they'd never give me, but Rare Medium had no problem paying an executive assistant with zero experience a ridiculous sum of money. After that, I said, "Shit, I should have asked for fifty thousand!"

Forty-six thousand dollars for a twenty-two-year-old with no experience? Who wouldn't become jaded in this environment? Or one in which placing a five-minute phone call to hook up two people could yield six-figure thank-you notes?

"I didn't need to invest in Internet stocks," says Bernardo Joselevich, "because people were giving me shares and options for making introductions for them. They were very generous." How generous? "They would give me these shares worth six hundred thousand."

BERNARDO JOSELEVICH

When I established DutyFreeGuide.com, I reserved dozens of URLs that had to do with luxury goods because I felt that they would bring traffic to my Web site. One day, I got a call from a major luxury-goods company saying that they wanted to buy one of the domain names for $100,000. I wasn't really listening, since I was multitasking at the time.

That kind of epitomizes the culture: the fact that someone offers you $100,000 over the phone and you don't even stop what you're doing on the PC! I said, "Let me think about it a bit more. . . how 'bout a hundred fifty thousand?" They said yes, and the only thing I had in my mind was whether I had actually paid for the domain name—because at that time you could reserve the name with Network Solutions and not pay for another month.

Within two hours I had $150,000 in my account. I transferred the domain name, and then immediately went into grieving because I thought that I could have gotten more for it! This was something that I had secured with $70 that I never actually paid, and then I get to sell it with zero effort for $150,000 four weeks later. But everyone—all my friends, family, and myself—thought that I was an idiot for selling it.

When you could get $150,000 for no effort and still be considered an idiot, you knew it was a crazed culture.

STEVEN OVERMAN

Gary Wolf, a writer at *Wired*, sat down at a computer with Louis Rossetto and me to see how many domain names we could buy before anybody else did. We typed in Pop.com, which later got sold to Steven Spielberg, and for a while was part of the *HotWired* family of sites.

I remember the feeling that a name could mean so much someday, and that they were all there for the taking. It was like stumbling across a gold mine and feeling like nobody else is there—you think you own the world. You completely lose all perspective.

PHILIP "PUD" KAPLAN

I put Fucked Company up for sale on eBay because I just decided to do something fun. You see, *The Simpsons* is always on from eight to eight-thirty. And then at nine, *The X-Files* is on. But between eight-thirty and nine, I never have anything to do, so that's when I put my site up for sale. Before I knew it, bids went up to *ten million bucks*, and for the first time, eBay raised the ten-million-dollar ceiling. It turned out to be a hoax, but the insane thing is, ten million didn't seem unreasonable.

PO BRONSON

Six hundred *million* wasn't enough. It was one company after another turning down these enormously large offers, because they thought they were worth more. Sometimes there was something behind it, like that their engineering wouldn't hold up under due diligence, and they wanted to get that fixed first. But wasn't it amazing that they thought $600 million wasn't enough? Like, what would have been enough—a *billion?*

———————

To the rapper Chuck D, it seemed as if nothing was enough for those who logged on to the money-making machinery that the Internet culture had become.

CHUCK D

I was upset when people were just coming for the cash. That was hard for me to deal with. When Russell Simmons came in with 360hiphop.com, it was like, "Oh shit, now the big names are gonna come in and really obscure the purpose." If I had to say, here is the beginning of the end, it was when a lot of those cats started doing it just because it was a gold rush, and I didn't dig that scene so much.

———————

Still, the San Francisco real estate agent Chris Dallas "found the dot-commers to be different from other clients who had money. " Juxtaposed with the opportunism were both a sense of optimism and a genuine passion for the future in which these New Economy leaders were clearly becoming the starring players. Dallas believes this was reflected in his dot-com clients' choice of neighborhoods—not "old-money neighborhoods like Pacific Heights and Knob Hill" but "Noe Valley, the Castro, and the Mission. They really liked a neighborhood feel, a character. Other clients avoided the Mission—they thought it was unsafe—but not the dot-commers. They loved the excitement of the Mission, and they were worth millions of dollars."

"It was this idealistic time like in college when we'd sit around with our friends and get high, saying what we're going to do when we get older," remembers Brad Nye, the cofounder of VIC, an organization that hosted New Media networking events in Los Angeles. "The nature of the conversations was, 'Isn't this amazing what's going on? Look what we're going to *do!* '"

HAROLD MANN

I remember truly being in awe when I walked into Kleiner, Perkins for the first time. It was so exciting! I felt so privileged to go into that office and have the opportunity of meeting with a partner, and listening to him. It's the same feeling I had when we did movie projects, and we'd go in and listen to Steven Spielberg. We'd just listen to him talk—it was that sense of being star-struck. You're almost hovering above yourself and thinking, "Wow, this is the place where things *happen.*"

JEFF GOODELL

I wrote a piece for *The New York Times Magazine* called "The Venture Capitalists in My Bedroom." I grew up in Sunnyvale, which is Ground Zero of the Valley, and we had sold our house after my father died in 1990. One day, I heard from some neighbors that it had been turned into a slum and that it looked terrible, so I decided to write a story about it.

When I went back, there were eight cars in the driveway and parked on the lawn. There were literally four Honda Accords and four Toyota Camrys. I knocked on the door several times and no one answered it. I was about to leave and give up, but I went back that night and knocked again. And this Asian woman opens the door and we start talking.

This house that I had grown up in meant a lot to my family, and we had moved into it when it was brand-new. It was sort of an aerospace, blue-sky neighborhood dream of all working engineers, all 2.5 kids. Everybody making ham radios in their garage. But it had been turned into basically a seedy flophouse for these H1-B [visa] immigrants who had come to Silicon Valley from Taiwan and China to work for the high-tech companies.

At first, I was really sad to see that all this stuff my father had built, like our old kitchen, had been turned into this college dorm kitchen. But eventually, I saw that it was this coming of a new kind of culture. And as I got to know the people who lived in the house, I realized that they really believed in the American Dream, as cliché as it sounds. They really believed that they could make better lives for themselves here, and that they were escaping terrible lives—especially from China—and there was this great spirit to the place.

The Valley was alive in this seedy flophouse that my old house had been turned into. That was a very powerful moment because it showed the complete transformation of the culture: the power of it completely reinventing itself.

CHAPTER FOUR THE PARTIES

Q: What was the party for?
A: Well, what were any of these parties really *for*?
—Harold Mann, Internet consultant

I was negotiating with the CEO of SmartShop.com about a menu for a party. He was literally twenty-two years old. I was trying to explain to him that not everyone ate ham, that they needed to have chicken and maybe some fish on the menu. But he only wanted ham! I said, "Well, one of your investors is Jewish—maybe you should re-think this." So he picked up the other line, called his mother, and said, "Mom, what do you think about this menu?" His *mom*! I had to do a lot of mommying myself. But there was no educating. They were all about, "I want," "Gimme."
—Heather Keenan, San Francisco event planner

The Friday before my official first day at Kibu and hours before the startup's launch party, I was on the phone with my friend Carolyn, a professor in Chicago.

"Launch party?" Carolyn repeated, when I mentioned my plans for the evening. "Sounds like a space mission."

She was only half serious, but to someone from the Old Economy, the Internet seemed like a new frontier, startups the newfangled spacecraft, and launch parties the high-profile sendoffs into cyberspace of those blessed with the Right Stuff.

Or, if she had known the truth, the wrong stuff. Unlike NASA, the New Economy didn't reserve its launch parties for monumental events like moon walks and global space stations. Instead, if your company paid its measly thirty-five bucks for a URL—*boom!*—it got its own swanky celebration. And the splashier the party, the louder the announcement: We have arrived!

"So, it's like a debutante party for Web sites," Carolyn observed, trying to make sense of the concept.

Sort of.

Like a debutante's coming out, launch parties were *the* occasion for start-ups to dress up and present themselves publicly. And like traditional debu-tante soirées, they were an opportunity to show exactly how much money and clout the guest of honor had. Just as each debutante vies to upstage her rivals, so did startups try to outdo the URL in the next loft space. But faced with fierce competition and too much similarity, it didn't take long for com-panies trying to stand out to go from Public Displays of Extravagance to Public Displays of Embarrassment.

In late 1999, for instance, Pixelon, a streaming video site, spent twelve of its thirty million dollars of funding on "iBash '99," a weekend-long Vegas shindig (some say orgy) at the MGM Grand, headlined by The Who and Kiss. Other performers included the Dixie Chicks, Sugar Ray, and Brian Setzer. Not long after, the company's founder, David Stanley (his real name turned out to be Michael Fenne), went on the lam after authorities learned that he was an imposter.

At least Stanley was an original type of New Economy con man and not the by-now common brand of pretender: a brash but innocent kid in over his head, posing as a CEO. Apparently, Stanley was an escaped criminal who'd swindled members of his father's church as well as dozens of senior citizens in Virginia and Tennessee of $1.25 million.

Then in March of 2000, there was Pop.com's party, whose organizers redecorated the bungalow next to where John Belushi died in L.A.'s Chateau Marmont with red balloons, yellow popcorn, and blonde PR girls. No one seemed to care about the macabre setting; the point was to announce the for-mation of a Steven Spielberg–Ron Howard–Jeffrey Katzenberg–Brian Grazer–Paul Allen online entertainment venture. The shameful coda? The company never even *launched*.

Most startups, however, did blast off the launch pad after their glitzy galas. Yet it wouldn't take long for the lights to go out inside and their doors to the real world outside to be fitted with padlocks.

On the phone the afternoon of the Kibu party, my friend Carolyn seemed curious about the startup I was about to join. She knew I was excited by the site's mission: Forget superficial tits-and-ass teens like Christina Aguilera and

Mandy Moore—Kibu, which means "foundation" in Japanese, was to become a foundation or "digital hangout" where teen girls could interact with positive role models.

I'd been told that each of the twenty or so "channels"—ranging from Books to Wellness—would be produced and written by that channel's personality, or "Face," a combination Big Sister–MTV VJ. Eventually, girls would be able to chat online with each Face, and a live version of the site would open as the Kibu Studio in San Francisco's Ghirardelli Square.

But that wouldn't be until the fall. Before then, I explained, we'd have to create content, program the interactivity, secure sponsors, design the site's "look and feel"—

"Great," Carolyn interrupted, "but if you have all that to do in the next few months, why are you throwing yourself a party tonight?" After all, when Carolyn finished her Ph.D., an intensely grueling five-year project, she'd had a small, simple gathering of friends over to celebrate *afterward*. What exactly were we celebrating, she wanted to know, and what was being launched at this, well, *launch* party?

Good question.

Kibu, to its credit, didn't go berserk with its launch party. In an unusual show of restraint, the company threw a low-key get-together at its Redwood City office. No rented concert hall, band, DJ, party planner, party favors, open bar, high-profile sponsor, chi-chi caterer, or celebrities. On the guest list: employees and their significant others, and board members. Period.

This was definitely not a Power Party.

A Power Party didn't necessarily have to make the society pages (though many did), nor even take place on a yacht (ditto). For most, you'd receive a hipper-than-thou, professionally designed invitation. You were asked to RSVP to the e-mail address listed on the "non-transferable" invite, and given instructions on proper attire (often an oxymoron like "dressy casual" or "retro modern chic").

Then you'd show up at, say, Ruby Sky or the Bubble Lounge in San Francisco, the old Barney's warehouse in New York, or Sky Bar in L.A.; fight your way past the limos lingering out front; and stand awkwardly while the doorman, too busy to find your name on his very, very long guest list, waved you by (so much for the exclusive invitation). Inside, you'd enter a room chock-full of Beautiful People drunkenly discoursing on the digital divide or the latest "homerun" business model, and simultaneously handing out oddly shaped business cards, all of which included the suffix *.com*.

Over by the bar, stocked with free-flowing, top-shelf vodkas, home phone numbers were scrawled liberally on branded cocktail napkins offered to the opposite sex, or zapped wirelessly directly into their PDA's. So many dates were entered into Palms, it seemed that as many new relationships as companies were launched at these parties. Bands didn't quit before sunrise, which was okay, because startups had a nocturnal ethos: Come in late, stay all night.

But despite the conventional wisdom that Much Bigger meant More Important, Kibu's mellow launch approach was actually a good sign. The companies that seemed to be succeeding, like Yahoo!, had simple keg-and-chips parties when they introduced a new product. They skipped the glitz and glamour and focused instead on—oh yeah—creating new products.

Still, Carolyn's question was a good one. The issue wasn't whether Kibu deserved a lavish party, but whether it should be having one *at all*.

The first version of the site, a so-called "work-in-progress," was to go live on the Internet at 6 P.M. that evening. Never mind that my official start date with Kibu was on Monday. Kibu's CEO, Judy MacDonald, had assured me that the Faces—although they'd need some "guidance"—had diligently prepared their own content for the launch. But as soon as I walked into the party, I was immediately touted as a "savior."

"We can't write content!" the Faces exclaimed, surrounding me in a circle of anxiety. "We need structure!" they continued. "We're about to launch and have no idea what we're doing!"

This was not what I wanted to hear on launch night. Still, Judy assured me, the site was in good shape: It was cool! It was hip! It was visionary! Girls would love us! They'd tell all their friends! They'd visit the site weekly, then daily, then hourly! We'd provide "fresh" content as fast as they could log on! Our "Faces" would become cyber celebrities! We'd IPO within the year!

Like a dope, I believed her.

A few minutes after 6 P.M., Judy hushed the room full of employees—Central Casting "Heather" look-alikes with coifed hair, high cheekbones, low-cut tops, and manicured nails; a gaggle of their investment-banker and/or venture-capitalist boyfriends who seemed to come straight from the pages of

GQ; and fortyish male board members clad in khaki, who hadn't brought their wives and appeared to be enjoying the scenery.

"It's time for our unveiling," Judy declared, tapping her bottle of Evian with a knife to get everyone's attention. Then, following a speech about what had led up to this momentous, well, *moment*—a part Tony Robbins–, part Horatio Alger–inspired version of the company's beginnings—Judy motioned for an engineer to press the button that would launch Kibu.com into cyberspace.

Silence. All eyes stared at the monitors positioned around the room. More silence. Eager anticipation. Silence now broken by fierce whispering between the engineers and Judy. Then an announcement: Oops. Sorry folks, technical difficulties.

Everyone went back to their mini rice cakes, seemingly unconcerned. More toasts were made, more praise delivered. A full forty-five minutes later, Judy tapped her Evian bottle again. "Take two," she said laughing. The engineer pressed the button, and this time, something appeared on the screen. As the room burst into wild applause, hoots of "Woo-hoo!" echoed off the walls.

"Awesome!" a multiply pierced producer shrieked. "Rad!" "Sweet!" the Faces shot back. Soon the just-out-of-college crowd began clapping and chanting, cheerleader-style, "Kibu, Kibu, Kibu!" and encouraging the others to join in. I worried that they might form a human pyramid. A few actually became teary-eyed.

Turning toward the monitor, I expected something incredible. And what I saw *was* incredible, in the literal sense: not believable. I looked at the screen, then at these euphoric women, then back at the screen. The image I saw wasn't "rad" or "awesome," but pathetic.

Floating within a tiny blue rectangle surrounded by the vast black emptiness of the screen, were three grainy, postage stamp-sized circles, two featuring the photos of attractive young women, the remaining one that of a trendy young man, our Face of Hair. To someone who hadn't received the press kit explaining the "Faces" concept, it made no sense. Nothing was labeled. Heck—there was *no text!* Aside from being confusing, the whole thing looked comically cheesy, like a child's personal Web page. Yet here were these women chirping "Fab!" and squealing "Go Kibukis!"

Once the self-congratulatory cheering died down, Judy came up to me and asked what I thought. "Well," I replied carefully, "how will girls know to click on the Face icon to get to that channel?" I stuck a "just out of curiosity" in there to temper my skepticism. After all, I was new, and maybe I was missing something. "Isn't the opening page a little, um, cryptic?" I asked, before adding another "just out of curiosity."

"That's the point!" Judy explained excitedly. According to her "intuition," teen girls love to "find things" by "randomly clicking" until something pops up. This sounded more like the famous psychological experiment involving rats, levers, food pellets, and Skinner boxes than a new product's selling point, but I let it go and tried randomly clicking on a couple of circles. One led to an error message and the other crashed the computer entirely.

Judy's reply: Don't worry, we'll fix the glitches as we find them. It makes the girls feel like they're building the site along with us if they tell us where the glitches are.

Call me old-fashioned, or just plain Old Economy, but that was the most ass-backward reasoning I'd ever heard. Why launch a product before it's ready or even works? Would an Old Economy company—or any sensible company—launch a half-baked, in-development product? If a new Microsoft product failed to work at the launch party, would everyone be blithely sipping strawberry-kiwi diet Snapples and sharing congratulatory hugs?

Kibu, I soon learned, wasn't the only startup to fête a fledgling failure. With a half dozen parties nightly *each* in New York, Los Angeles, and San Francisco, these unreal bashes both defined and mirrored the startup experience. The no-frills, underground parties in the early days of the Internet soon gave way to extravaganzas costing $200,000 and up, accompanied by celebrity appearances and a more-the-merrier attitude—even if the guests had no idea who your company was (and didn't care).

Of course, not all companies threw bacchanals, and not all startups failed because of their intemperate inaugural celebrations. But rare is the new company today who, like Acteva, invites 3,500 of its "closest friends" (including San Francisco's Mayor Willie Brown, trapeze artists, and go-go dancers) to Treasure Island simply to announce its new name and engage in pig-racing matches.

More than two years after Black Friday, the number of parties hasn't dwindled—they've simply been, as the saying goes, "repurposed." Launch parties have become *un*launch parties. At "Pink Slip" parties for the "unhired," the former woo-hoo spirit has been replaced by that of a wake, and unemployed digerati not-so-jokingly toast to failure rather than funding (and now must actually *pay* for their bar tabs).

Thousands in trendy black T-shirts show up at these networking gatherings in search of jobs, hope, hook-ups, and moral support—a far cry from *Wired*'s rave-like revels of the mid-nineties that Steven Overman attended while working at the magazine.

STEVEN OVERMAN

Wired's parties were the best in the industry. They were buzz-y, people wanted to go, there was an interesting crowd, and they were cheap. More than a thousand people came. This is something *Wired* did right and nobody else figured out. The best party I ever went to for *Wired* cost $15,000, which is nothing for a party of this scale.

In fact, says Overman, before the days of pricey planners and pulchritudinous PR princesses, *Wired* looked to their accounting department to organize their festivities.

STEVEN OVERMAN

We had an incredibly hip accounting department that was a bunch of performance artists and DJs who worked as accountants to make a living, so they could do what they wanted at night. One was a fire eater. The DJs would be people we knew because people who worked at *Wired* were in the burgeoning San Francisco club and music scene. Burning Man people would get involved. It was cheap and super cool and felt underground.

REBECCA EISENBERG

Back in the old days, the biggest party, the Big Ticket, was the *Wired* rave. That's what you wanted to go to in '95 and '96, but even though it doesn't exist anymore, it created a lot of the culture that later permeated the industry when they tried to be hip and cool. Like rave music. If you wanted to show you were cool, you'd play trance and hire a local DJ to spin, but that really came from the *Wired* rave/Burning Man thing.

Nevertheless, house-music "plug-and-play" wasn't always a recipe for a party's success. Heather Keenan, a veteran San Francisco event planner, remembers dot-commers who thought they could appeal to the "rave generation" simply by throwing in some Paul Oakenfold. The result was pathetic, like polka music played at a high school dance.

Marching band music was even lamer.

HEATHER KEENAN

At this indoor rock-climbing party for Simpata.com, they had an oompah band—you know, *oompah, oompah*—and it totally didn't work. I had to go up to the client and say, "Your party is going to be a bomb, let's get them out of here." It was a human resources dot-com, and the theme to the party was "Get rid of the mountain of paper work," so they did all these alpine sorts of things. They actually thought it would be a good idea to have a guy that does that Oktoberfest type of music!

For another party, the theme was Hawaii–Retro–fifties. They insisted on Hawaiian music, so I had to get authentic lap-pedal steel Hawaiian music. Wrong, wrong, wrong. To cover myself, I had a really mainstream, stupid Top 40 DJ inside that they, of course, went *wild* for.

But before both the parties and music went mainstream, Courtney Pulitzer, who founded the Silicon Alley networking events "Cocktails with Courtney," remembers a more organic party environment.

COURTNEY PULITZER

Back in 1995, the parties started out with margaritas at El Teddy's, and WWWAC [World Wide Web's Artists' Consortium] had beers and burgers at Broadway Diner and at Brasserie before it reopened as a hot and trendy spot. Echo, the East Coast hangout that Stacy Horn [author of *Cyberville: Clicks,*

Culture and the Creation of an Online Town] started, was a big spot. People would get together for face-to-faces at the Art Bar and Man Ray, typical New York dark bars where there's some character to the whole atmosphere. No invitations and no guest list. You could easily throw out an open invitation and you didn't have to worry about more than eighty people coming because it was such a small core of people in the industry.

For Ted Werth, the parties hosted by Jupiter Communications, a technology research company; and Pseudo, an online entertainment startup, were emblematic of the early Silicon Alley scene.

TED WERTH

In '94 and '95, you had business people, programmers, models, artists, and freaks show up. You had your CEO of some company taking a bong hit with some East Village model. There was installation art using technology. It's been compared to the Warhol scene. The people there were starting up some of the most interesting companies. Not necessarily the most *successful* ones, but definitely the most *interesting*.

By the time October 1999 rolled around, the parties, not necessarily the companies, became "interesting." The technology journalist Rebecca Eisenberg remembers these affairs with equal parts awe and disbelief.

REBECCA EISENBERG

At TixToGo's party on Treasure Island, they hired Cirque du Soleil dancers and gave away a Porsche! I couldn't believe it! It was an online event startup, and one of the reasons I was there is that I was a finalist in the contest for renaming the company. I came close—I was one of ten finalists—and I almost won the Porsche. My suggestion was "MeatMarket" or something dumb like that. But the name they picked, Acteva, was also really stupid. I thought TixToGo had been a totally fine name to have.

BERNARDO JOSELEVICH

The most interesting and fun party was for Edifice Rex, a company dedicated to building and developing Intranets for select apartment buildings in New York. It was a very incestuous situation. It was owned by one of the largest real estate management companies in New York City. They had a party at the four-thousand-year-old Temple of Dendur in the Metropolitan Museum of Art. That one was incredible—caviar flowing all over the place.

Event party planner Heather Keenan attributes these Caligula-like parties to a lethal combination of too little experience and too much money.

HEATHER KEENAN

Very frequently I was dealing with people fresh out of college, who had no experience whatsoever and were given $500,000 to do a party. They had *no* sense of how to spend this money or what was important, or what the goal was. They'd say things like, "I want a wet bar, and the party is going to last for eight hours, and I want nothing to eat, only drinks!" I'd be like, "We can't really do that, because people will be lying flat on their faces."

It wasn't just the booze and chow that drew revelers—party favors seemed to be almost as important as the events themselves. After all, the point was to be remembered.

"Party favors were a huge deal," says Keenan. "Logo'd Hawaiian shirts, logo'd towels, watches, trips to Bangkok. . . "

COURTNEY PULITZER

At the CarOrder.com parties, they had CarOrder.com big-size remote-control gifts, and custom shirts for each city with the name of the state. You would get big remote-control Jeeps, Corvettes, and other luxury cars with the name of the particular state on the license plate. In New York, they put on New York state license plates. In Los Angeles and San Francisco, they put on California plates. I was impressed with that level of detail.

That level of detail became necessary to distinguish a dot-com party from its competitor's bash at the swanky club across the street.

"I went to a Pseudo party right below Houston on Broadway, and there were people in glass pods shooting videos of each other," says a former journalist for an online business magazine. "But what I remember best was the cereal bar. They had some guy there with fifteen different cereals, and you could get any cereal you wanted. It's like they thought that if they had a cereal bar, their party would be 'different.'"

As attendees became increasingly jaded, the stunts grew more preposterous—and difficult to pull off. Heather Keenan recalls an event she put on for Flipside.com, an online game site owned by Vivendi/Universal.

HEATHER KEENAN

For the Flipside.com event, I had to get an Amish couple. During the Sydney Olympics in 2000, they had a national ad running, which featured an Amish family playing on the Flipside.com site. In the ad, the elders knock on the door, and the family, caught red-handed, leaves a mouse hanging out of the drawer. So, we had the Amish couple welcoming people as they entered. A friend of mine lives in Pennsylvania, and I made her go out and get me authentic costumes. Those were the lengths we had to go to.

COURTNEY PULITZER

The bar got a lot higher, and there was the mentality that having a cool party would help with marketing. Each party was just wilder than the one before it. Razorfish had their annual May Day party, and they always had some bizarre human act going on, like dwarves greeting you at the door. Right after their IPO, they had this huge sheeting that they would wrap around the big pillars in the space. When you entered, there was a big sign that said "www.razorfishsucks.com" because that was the trend that year.

Everyone would get "companynamesucks.com" so their competitor wouldn't have it. They had a moonwalk where you had to crawl through a circular stomach colon. I didn't go in there, but there was a lot of pot smoking and intimate acts going on.

Between Razorfish and Pseudo, there was an unspoken friendly competition. At one Pseudo party, they had naked people in painted cubicles and booths. The people were painted in the design of the background, so it was like a moving painting. Beatnik poetry was going on in another room, and there were henna tattoos. Then Razorfish would have cotton candy, tattoos, and piercing.

With startups vying for attention, one strategy was to secure not just "a" celebrity, but "the" celebrity-of-the-millisecond. No good were what Courtney Pulitzer describes as "has-been celebrities" like "Jim Belushi and the Sacred Hearts Band at the Carorder.com launch party in New York, Gene Hackman at BulldogResearch.com's launch party, or people like Debbie Harry and the Ramones."

"We got a request for Natalie Merchant to perform," says Heather Keenan. "I was not able to fulfill that request, but it was okay, because *nobody* was—whew!"

Apparently, the pop star Elvis Costello, who performed in April 2000 at an AskJeeves party celebrating the rollout of a new business services product, was easier to book than Merchant. AskJeeves declined to disclose the party's price tag, but the site's director of marketing told the *San Francisco Business Times*, "We got a good deal." It may have been a particularly good deal, if there's any validity to the rumors that the tab was heavily weighted in AskJeeves stock options, then priced at $36. By December, the stock had sunk to near the two-dollar mark.

HAROLD MANN

At a party for AskJeeves, we were standing with Rob Wrubel, the CEO. There are all these twenty-something dot-commers listening to Elvis Costello performing, a guy that they only knew as an "old guy." It was sort of surreal, because people were so consumed with what was going on in their businesses, that no one really paid attention. Elvis was merely back-ground music.

For the entrepreneur Marc Greenberg's bride, so was Elton John.

HEATHER KEENAN

This dot-com guy had a million-dollar wedding at Treasure Island, and his surprise for his bride was Elton John. But people weren't blown away *at all*. Elton John signed his piano and that was this guy's gift to his bride. The bride sat there, and she didn't really show any surprise. She just kind of thought it was nice. But this was *Elton John!* It was just so typical.

If even A-list celebrities weren't A-list enough for these parties, the food, drink and location sure had to be. The food was so plentiful, in fact, that according to Live365.com's J. Betty Ray, people "did not buy food because they could go to these parties instead and clean up." She even remembers hearing about a guy who made a commitment between Thanksgiving and Christmas in 1999 not to buy groceries or go to restaurants. "He'd just eat off of launch and holiday parties," she says. "And he actually did it."

HEATHER KEENAN

We kept getting bids from caterers that were outrageous. We'd ask why it costs 150 bucks per person for peanut butter sandwiches, and the caterer would say, "Screw you—I've got four other parties that night."

And location became a problem. First thing in the morning, the phone would ring and someone on the other end would say, "We want to do a party next week," or "We just decided we're going to launch in two weeks, we need a party right away." And I'd be thinking, there is no place! Everything is sold out! The hottest venues were Ruby Sky, City Hall, and Treasure Island, but they got overused to the point that no one wanted to go there anymore.

The requests on bar were also very, very specific. They all wanted only full-premium open bars, and they'd select exactly what vodka and alcohol. They always wanted something interactive—a vodka luge, or a martini bar where they could choose which flavor martini.

COURTNEY PULITZER

There was so much sushi being served that frankly, I got sick of it. During 1999, DoubleClick's Willy Wonka and Enchanted Forest party was memorable for the candy. The ceiling was covered in ivy and there was smoke coming in for the Enchanted Forest, but because it was Halloween, they had an obscene amount of candy, which I'm always a big advocate of.

It wasn't all "sugar" candy, as Boo.com's Cameron Hickey recalls. "There were tons of drugs—Ecstasy, and cocaine was very popular with young hipsters," he says. "A lot of people who think they're hip got into tech."

And a lot of people who think they're hip also get into Hollywood, which is exactly what the dot-com parties began to resemble—from garden-variety cokefests to Playboy mansion-like pairings in grotto settings.

REBECCA EISENBERG

I used to know everyone, everywhere I went, but it really struck me at the Alexa party in 1999 that there were *preppy* people, who I didn't know and I wasn't used to seeing. People were doing coke in the bathroom, and that was totally, totally new to me in this culture. It's not like I never saw anyone do coke before, but when people were doing lines in the bathroom and coming back rubbing their noses, it hit me: This is really mainstream and these people are trying to be like Hollywood or Wall Street. I wasn't used to this approach to the industry.

HEATHER KEENAN

The indoor mountain climbing place for the Simpata.com party was called Mission Rocks, and there were two levels. The company president is giving this speech on the upper level, and downstairs, there's two people in a cave getting it on. It was hysterical! Here's this guy talking about "This is our launch, we're going to do great, all of you have been working so hard." And just as he's saying, "We're a serious, Web-based company, we're not a dot-com," I noticed that the two people screwing were his employees!

Interestingly, one of the industry's most buzz-worthy parties steered clear of Hollywood-style debauchery and replaced its star power with Washington's mega-celeb, Bill (Clinton, not Gates). According to host Andrew Rasiej, the event at Sky Studio in downtown New York attended by the First Couple was dubbed "Silicon Alley 2000: A Salute to the President" and raised $1 million for Hillary Clinton's Senate campaign and the Democratic Senatorial Campaign Committee.

"All the dot-com people showed up" says Rasiej, including Jeff Dachis (Razorfish), Gene DeRose (Jupiter Communications), Paul Francis (Priceline) and Marc Patricoff ([kpe]).

ANDREW RASIEJ

All these senators came and so did all these Silicon Alley VIPs. Clinton looks at the studio's loft and says, "This is pretty nice. I think I'm going to be a dot-com millionaire." The President and senators coming was validation for Silicon Alley. Instead of going to Silicon Valley, they were coming to New York, and there was a certain amount of pride and excitement about that.

But there was also a complete disconnect. The dot-com people and the politicians weren't speaking the same language. Someone used the word "semen" in an analogy about seeding Internet usage, and the whole dinner went silent, since Hillary was there. Dachis spoke for about five minutes in techno-speak and nobody knew what the hell he was talking about.

We were all talking English, but the DNA was completely different. The politicians were only concerned with raising money for their traditional media machines. But for the Silicon Alley people, it was—"Whoa, there's the President of the United States! We see him on *CNN Headline News*, and now he's in the same room as us! We can take a picture with him!"

Like Hollywood premieres and Washington galas, Internet parties also had exclusive guest lists—or so it seemed. In truth, all you had to do was log onto one of several party list Web sites and RSVP, or, for a last-minute crasher, know how to "biz-dev" your way in the door. Never before had such lavish parties been so lavishly attended.

The "go-go '80s" also had their share of garish bashes, notes Damien Cave in *Salon*, "but Wall Street never thought to invite half of Manhattan." He writes of "a whole bevy of party sites that offer lists," including YABA.net, the DrinkExchange, WorkIt, The A-List, and SFGirl.com. But the trendiest online networking communities featuring party listings belonged to Oliver Muoto, cofounder of the software company Epicentric; DutyFreeGuide.com's Bernardo Joselevich; and Courtney Pulitzer.

If these lists were for hipsters, who defined "hip"? "The velvet rope thing is that they let in people who look cool," explains Joselevich. "But coolness in the Internet economy was determined by entirely different parameters than in the Old Economy." Apparently, New York bouncers hadn't been given the 411.

BERNARDO JOSELEVICH

Once I had a venue where the president of Kozmo.com, which at the time was one of the coolest dot-coms in New York, was left waiting at the door for one hour. He didn't look cool enough to the bouncer. This was at a Park Avenue setting, and it was a clash between the Park Avenue culture and Silicon Alley culture. So after that, when I posted parties, I made sure that the promoters understood that the door staff couldn't operate by the normal criteria, because that would bring me embarrassment. Inevitably, they'd leave some millionaire Internet exec waiting outside.

COURTNEY PULITZER

The people who founded the Alley were not "the cool kids" anymore. There was a new, younger, hipper group of people who became cool. The founders are brilliant and can do wonderful work, but they were geeks. They weren't the wittiest people. At one point, the geeks became cool and sexy. Now, they're back in the cubicles.

Feel free to forward this email to your friends in the new-media and venture capital industries.

If you are receiving this email as a forward from a friend and you would like to start getting it directly, pls email me indicating your full name, company and position, to mailto:bernardo@dutyfreeguide.com

INTERNET-INDUSTRY PARTIES & EVENTS THIS WEEK:

3) TODAY Thursday, February 10th. Club Dub Dub Dub (**a get-together for digerati** hosted by George Sachs of BarnesandNoble.com). 6:30pm-10pm @The Gamut (102 E. 25th Street, New York). Free food, drink specials. RSVP: mailto:gsachs@book.com See: http://www.brainstormventuregroup.com/clubdubdubdub.html

4) TODAY Thursday, February 10th. Fashion Week Madness @l'Etoile, 109 E56th street (bet. Park & Lex).10pm. Party for Q Models, one of the country's premiere modeling agencies. **Not strictly new-media but includes new-mediaish crowd.** To RSVP, mailto:remilaba@msn.com or call Remi at 917-821-4730. $10 cover. **Mention at the door that you are on Remi's list to ensure admission.**

5) Reminder only (RSVP deadline passed, first mentioned on my list of 1/26/00) TODAY Thursday, February 10th, 2000. **First Birthday Party of Flooz.com** (http://www.flooz.com). 7-10pm. Ace Gallery, 275 Hudson Street (between Spring & Canal Sts.). Cocktails & Hors D'Oeuvres. mailto:party@flooz.com with your full info, company and position. Space is limited.

9) Saturday, February 12, 2000. Casino 2000, The 13th Annual Night and Winter Ball of the Manhattan Society. Black-tie event to benefit the Multiple Sclerosis Society [**Not a New Media event, but with silicon people well represented among the more than 1,200 professionals in attendance**]. 8:30pm-1am. New York Marriott Marquis Broadway Ballroom 1535 Broadway (between 45th and 46th Streets). http://www.msnyc.org/mansoc/casino.htm or call 212-463-7787 Tickets start at $125.

11) Tuesday, February 15th. **The Downtown Alliance: "Bits, Bites &Bar".** 6pm-8pm @American Park at The Battery, Battery Park opposite 17 State St. Cocktail party with open Bar and Hors d'oeuvres. Free. No need to RSVP. For more info: (212) 835-2755 or mailto:lnovitt@DowntownNY.com

12) Wednesday, February 16th. **Silicon Alley iBreakfast Club. "B-to-B: Building Better Billionaires".** 7:30am-10:30am (note, AM). New York City, Marriott Marquis - 46th & Broadway, 23rd fl. http://www.ibreakfast.com/register.cfm?EID=47 or (800) 273-2832. $60/$50 members ($10 more at door).

14) Wednesday, February 16th. Internet MFG ("**mixer for grownups": a casual monthly mixer for New York new media professionals**). 6:30pm-9:30pm Pageant (upstairs), 109 E 9th street (bet.3rd/4th Aves). Cash bar. No RSVP needed. Hosted by Amy Fried, Recruiter, New Media, Roz Goldfarb Assoc. mailto:amy@rga-joblink.com & Ben Austin, Director of Marketing, Comet Systems mailto:ben@cometsystems.com

16) Wednesday, February 23th. Silicon Alley iBreakfast Club. **"Touched by an Angel".** 7:30am-10:30am (note, AM). New York City, Marriott Marquis - 46th & Broadway, 23rd fl. With some of Wall Street's biggest angel funds. For your chance to pitch: send a 75 word summary of your business plan to mailto:pitch@ibreakfast.com To register: http://www.ibreakfast.com/events.cfm?EID=51 or (800) 273-2832. $60/$50 members ($10 more at door).

17) Wednesday, February 23rd. Cocktails with Courtney. You must RSVP: http://www.cocktailswithcourtney.com

a) **Schmoozing in the UK** and the world: If you want to hang out with Internet industry people in London, every first Tuesday of the month there's http://www.firsttuesday.com Also, email alerts of industry events in many cities worldwide. A good resource for news and tips about the Internet industry around the globe, to find office space abroad and more.

Best,

Bernardo Joselevich
CEO
mailto:bernardo@dutyfreeguide.com
http://www.dutyfreeguide.com

This list is not necessarily sent regularly and I can't assume any responsibility for the accuracy of the information sent or for any of its consequences. In order to unsubscribe please reply with the word "unsubscribe" in the subject.

End. 2/10/2000

"My slogan is 'Bernardo's List: serving the schmoozing classes,'" says Bernardo Joselevich.

At one of the early Super CyberSuds that NYNMA [New York New Media Association] had, a friend of mine said that if he came in there with sticks of dynamite attached to him and challenged five people to tell him what FTP [file transfer protocol] was or this room's gonna blow, they wouldn't be able to do it. WWWAC was considered the New York City group for people down in the trenches. NYNMA was looked down on because they were seen as the slick suits coming in just looking to make a quick buck.

BERNARDO JOSELEVICH

"Bernardo's List" is for people who treat parties as a business practice. Something remarkable about the list is that it's grown to twelve thousand names, and in the good times, I posted over sixty parties a week. Now, I post over forty. If there's not an opportunity for New Media conversation, then I'm not interested. My slogan is "Bernardo's List: Serving the Schmoozing Classes."

The schmoozing classes came out in droves, changing the vibe as dramatically as when Democratic and Republican administrations swap in Washington. In May 1998, when Condé Nast–Advance Magazine Publishing bought *Wired* for $75 million, *Wired* parties went from warehouse raves to posh mediafests.

STEVEN OVERMAN

The year Condé Nast threw the first *Wired* party, I had left the company, but my former *Wired* colleague Kristin Spence crashed it and told me about it. It was about sushi and martinis and guest lists. VIPs and journalists. There was an A-list and B-list, and that really freaked people out. The A-list was MIT Media Lab people and celebrities. Everything had changed.

Especially the notion of inviting folks who had something to do with your business.

"The salespeople were like, 'Yeah, let everyone in, let 'em in, let 'em in,' with the idea of creating a buzz rather than, 'Is this person going to return my business?' which is Old Media," says Heather Keenan. "No one cared if they got their $124 per person."

AUREN HOFFMAN

I went to a party for a magazine called *eCompany*. It was at PacBell Park, which had just opened a few weeks before. You got to run around the bases, and they gave away hotdogs, ice cream sandwiches, the whole deal. In the outfield, they put up a big stage and they had the Barenaked Ladies play. Afterward, they were going to have a private boat party—a big dance party around the Bay on a huge yacht. So, I'm mingling around at the end, and the security guard says, "You have to leave." I asked which way we go out. He asks, "Which way did you come in? Over there"—where I did come in—"or over there"—where all the boats were.

So my friend and I walk over to the boat area, and say to each other, "Yeah! We crashed this exclusive party!" Then we realized that everyone around us was saying the same thing! That was the beauty of these dot-com parties—we were all crashers and had nothing to do with the company whose party it was.

Even for folks attuned to the marketing end of the business—like Michael Feldman, who was director of partner marketing at the sports site Fogdog.com, and David Gilcreast, then a Food.com PR executive—these so-called promotional parties barely registered.

MICHAEL FELDMAN

I'm actually looking at this FortuneCity.com umbrella right now. I have no idea what they do or what they ever did, but they had this big party at F. A. O. Schwartz in San Francisco at the top of the city. They rented the entire thing out and had shrimp bowls everywhere. A live band. Toy-soldier guys dancing. *That* part, I remember.

DAVID GILCREAST

When I first got to San Francisco, there was a launch party literally every day. It became humorous, because you'd be at these parties that people obviously spent over $100,000 on, and you didn't even know what the hell the company did. And no one around you did! But no one gave a damn. We were all just living the life. Free booze. Free food. You'd just try to get in, because if it had "dot-com" at the end of it, you knew it must be a fabulous party.

Some thought the parties were fabulous precisely because everyone was doing the same thing, working the same hours, and riding the same merry-go-round. You didn't have to worry about clumsy cocktail party conversations—"Hi, I'm Jack." "Hi, I'm Jill." Awkward silence. Darting of the eyes. At dot-com parties, the dialogue was practically scripted.

"I don't recall spending a lot of time talking about movies or books or TV or any of the other things," says venture capitalist David Hornik. "We talked about what company was doing what, and who was doing what."

BERNARDO JOSELEVICH

At a normal social party, the exchange is much slower. But in the New Economy, it didn't matter if you were trying to hit on a girl, because everyone had a legitimate reason to talk to everyone else: "Hi, I'm so-and-so. What does your company do? What's your business model? How are you funded? How many people do you have in your office?"

There was this extensive flow of information that would take place in the first five minutes. It was as intense as a T–1 line, but if you went to a normal cocktail party, it was like a 14.4 modem. Everything was very lame. The reason is that people in the Internet economy were crusaders. People enjoyed talking about what they were doing, so there wasn't this strict line between personal and work lives.

LEV CHAPELSKY

Parties were really pickup events. When you had a good company name on your name tag, girls would come up to you, like, "Wow, CarsDirect, I've read about you." And then you'd try to steer the conversation away from that to something more interesting. There'd be intense months when you'd never go outside the business world, and you didn't have time to go to bars or regular social events. So this was our only opportunity to meet people of the opposite sex.

GONG SZETO

If sexual harassment didn't happen in the workplace, it happened at the launch parties. I would see stuff that just blew my mind. You'd have "seasoned executives," guys that left established positions to jump on the bandwagon, and they'd go to these launch parties. All of a sudden they're surrounded by these amazingly beautiful twenty-year-olds and they're like, "Holy shit!" It was really depressing, seeing these accomplished executives turn into meatheads. The *drool*, the *groping*. . .

Sometimes, the midlife crises in one room rivaled the number of sushi trays. But not all older-somethings went for twenty-somethings, and many, like the veteran journalist Alan Citron, wished they hadn't gone at all.

ALAN CITRON

I went to parties, but I remember thinking what's the point? I was already in my late thirties, so I wasn't that excited about free drinks and meeting girls. It seemed like a mentality took hold that you not only had to work eighteen hours a day, but you also had to party and be a really fun person. It was sort of a phony thing, because most of these people weren't fun people, they were workaholics.

For these workaholics who lived to network, the "branded" party was born. Like the annual Oscars or MTV parties, these coveted monthlies became the hottest tickets in town—be it New York's "Cocktails with Courtney" or *The*

Industry Standard's "Rooftop" parties, which originated in San Francisco and later spread to half a dozen cities.

COURTNEY PULITZER

I started the "Cocktails with Courtney" event in September 1998, just to keep up with my core group of friends that I had initially met in the industry and that I had lost touch with because I was running around to all these other parties. I would have it the last Wednesday of every month, and it would be like *Cheers*, a place where everyone knows your name. I figured I'd do it for a year and see what happened. The first one in New York was at Hudson Bar and Books, a place that could hold about thirty. We had over three hundred RSVPs and about a hundred showed up.

For me, it was always about bringing a sense of the 1940s where things were more refined and elegant. I have little branded cocktail napkins, and we always have fabulous hors d'oeuvres. I make an effort to greet everyone who comes. I treat it like the cocktail parties you read about, where the hostess introduces you around to make you feel comfortable—as if you were going to someone's home you knew.

LAURA RICH

The "Rooftop" parties at *The Standard* became this explosive, trendy thing. It was a pretty small rooftop, but there was all this free booze. Top-shelf *everything!* People started showing up as early as four-thirty on Friday and stayed until late. In the beginning, you were getting VCs and CEOs, and then it became middle tier, and by the time the magazine got in trouble, it was the lower-level people

———

To avoid trouble—financial or otherwise—some startups chose to forgo expensive parties and reserve their capital for a time when there would actually be something to celebrate. And even then, the party might be modest.

AUREN HOFFMAN

I told our investors, we will never have one of those dot-com parties. And we *loved* them. We used to have our own employee bonding events at other

The Fresh Air Fund, an independent, non-profit agency, has provided free summer vacations to more than 1.6 million New York City children since 1877. Each summer, more than 10,000 children visit volunteer host families in 13 Northeastern states and Canada, or attend one of five Fresh Air camps. The Fresh Air Fund is launching a special campaign to enhance its educational programs by setting up new computer learning centers at its camps.

The Fresh Air Fund. 1040 Avenue of the Americas. New York, NY 10018

(800) 367-0003 ～ http://www.freshair.org

Silicon Alley's First Black Tie Benefit

on Thursday evening
the second of December
at half past seven o'clock

The Metropolitan Club
One East Sixtieth Street
New York, New York

Cocktails ～ Hors D'oeuvres ～ Silent auction
Gift bags compliments of Corporategear.com

Black Tie
R.s.v.p

OCKTAILS
WITH
COURTNEY

Single Ticket ～ $175
Couple ～ $300
Single Benefactor ～ $250
Couple Benefactor ～ $450

"Cocktails with Courtney" invite. "It was always about bringing a sense of the 1940s where things were more refined and elegant," says Courtney Pulitzer of her monthly events.

people's launches! I would take every new employee out to dinner at these parties. We could have the best sushi and best cut meat, and we would just sit at the side of the party and talk.

ASHLEY POWER

We were launching Goosehead, and I was really excited because we worked so hard, but there wasn't one balloon. There were probably five of us standing around. We were on some little show like ZDTV and I was on a Web cam talking about the launch of my site, and we just sat there and watched it on TV. It was so lame.

JOSH KELLER

We did have a launch party for the first public release of our software, but it wasn't a big deal. It was at a bar in San Francisco called Backflip, and it was just for the employees of UBUBU and their significant others. We didn't think it was worth the money to have a big, expensive launch party. The budget was something like a total of five thousand dollars.

ELIZABETH COLLET

Yahoo! had been up and running as a hobby for a long time, so it just kind of evolved, instead of launching all of a sudden. But we would often do small launch parties for the employees when an update product had shipped that we'd all worked really hard on. They'd bring out a keg and chips and salsa.

The closest Yahoo! got to extravagance was they would throw parties for their big advertisers, but they weren't what you'd call lavish. They were fairly frugal about those things. But you have to remember the little companies who were spending money to have these big, glitzy parties were trying to get their names on a very cluttered radar screen. Yahoo! just wasn't in that situation. Basically, anyone who was on the Internet knew Yahoo!'s brand name, so we didn't need to be doing that.

Yet for every low-key entrepreneur, there seemed to be one whose narcissism wouldn't let him or her go small. Some CEOs, mistaking themselves for royalty, continued to throw stately affairs complete with red carpets, spotlights, security guards donning headsets, period costumes, eleven-piece bands, paparazzi, politicians, music stars, and celebrities.

ANONYMOUS PARTYGOER

I'll give you an example of a party which was held at the Old Federal Reserve. I say "party," but there were *seven hundred* people! When you pulled up to the curb, there was a red carpet going up the marble staircase. There was an eleven-piece swing band, and people in Art Deco period costumes holding long cigarette holders. Very, very Gatsby.

You walked into the room, and you were met on the left by a tray of champagne and on the right by a tray of martinis. You signed in. You walked through a curtain. The designers set it up so all the curtains were on rollers. When the party started, the room was smaller, and as more people arrived, they expanded the room, so it always looked full.

They hired the most expensive caterer, the one who does the opera galas, the symphony. I don't know how many oysters were shucked that day, but many oysters lost their lives. Trays and trays of sushi. And not just the rolls, like you usually see at these parties. I'm talking nigiri sushi, big fat slabs of tuna and yellowtail.

Francis Ford Coppola was going to come but he called to cancel because he was editing. The mayor came. Chris Nolan from the *San Jose Mercury News* wrote a column about it. The CEO made the PR woman sing a song, with the lyrics to Peggy Lee's "Fever" rewritten about the company.

Then there was the big CEO moment. If you stop in the middle of the room, do a one-eighty and look back up, there's a stairway that winds around and goes up to a little balcony. Kind of like the Pope meets Eva Peron. The CEO is standing up on the top, dressed all in black holding a martini glass, and speaking in a very grandiose voice.

So he does a poem that he wrote called "The Little Boat"— "I don't want to stay in the same harbor. I want to go out where the big boats are." You just had to laugh. Anyone who knows this guy could not have taken him seriously. But this company got millions and millions of dollars from Goldman Sachs and Schwab!

LAURA RICH

You didn't even have to get anywhere near the IAM.com party to know what was going on. You just had to look up in the sky at their big spotlight. This was just for some little startup! It was amazing—all the autograph seekers outside, the paparazzi, the crowd. Red carpet and lots of people with lists and headsets.

They were trying to say that they were part of Hollywood, because they were an online talent agency. You walked in and there were all these teen stars. The whole place was really, really decadent. They had a band. Champagne flowing and hors d'oeuvres. This was a little company with no revenue, but they raised a ton of money [a reported $49.6 million from Citicorp Investments and Sierra Ventures, among others].

I was supposed to spend time with the CFO, and this was his first job. He had just gotten out of Stanford Business School and he was so nervous, it was touching. You could tell that this was really overwhelming for him—like he'd been dropped into stardom and he didn't know what to do with it. It also seemed like all the handlers were supposed to make sure that the executives were superstars. It was sort of pathetic.

———————

Pathetic or just plain pricey, the IAM.com party was small potatoes compared to the grandiosity quotient of The Hollywood Stock Exchange's Oscar parties in 1999 and 2000, described by HSX.com's Doug Scott as the "convergence of Hollywood and the digital world."

"What Swifty Lazar did for the literati," says Scott, "we were trying to do for the digerati."

DOUG SCOTT

Based on my frustration of attending studio Oscar parties where I knew nobody, I said, "Fuck it, we're going to throw our own party." So we packaged a nice little event and got the likes of Excite@Home and Pepsi to be the primary sponsors.

The 1999 event was at the House of Blues on Sunset Boulevard with a headline performance by Beck and other performances by Crystal Method and Emergency Broadcast Network. Some of the other sponsors were Absolut, *Playboy*, *Red Herring*, and Chanel. Everywhere I could stick a brand, I stuck a brand. It was a $500,000 event.

It was Silicon Valley digerati meets Young Hollywood meets New York's hip and irreverent. We had Ethan Hawke, Drew Barrymore. The entire night was Webcast by JumpCut. We had over fifty thousand unique streams. I got a little big for my britches the next year, when I was telling the media that my goal was to dethrone Graydon Carter and *Vanity Fair*.

But, in essence, we were Hollywood Stock Exchange, we set the value of people and projects, and we were going to establish ourselves as an *institution*. How do you do that? You own the biggest night of the industry and position yourself with the biggest party! Because of Beck, I got a call the day of the event from Nick Cage's wife, Patricia Arquette, begging me to let her introduce Beck. She shows up with her three girlfriends and she was wearing this hot pink leather outfit with nice cleavage showing. An hour after the Oscars end, Nick shows up in his convertible with Jon Lovitz in his Bentley. All of a sudden, after midnight, I have this hip Hollywood crowd here, and everyone's going crazy on the red carpet! It got a little out of hand.

The atmosphere at HSX was at an all-time high. I mean, Peter Gabriel's calling me directly the day of the event, Billy Idol was calling me directly. The number one guy at Absolut, Michael Bacco, sent me a bucket filled with Absolut. That night I had a pair of diamond studded glasses that Sigourney Weaver had worn to the Oscars which we were auctioning off for the Entertainment Industry Foundation. We also got all this movie memorabilia. It was intense!

Scott walked away with more than a profoundly swollen head. "It gave us a brand on- and off-line," he says of the 1999 Oscar party. That same year, HSX launched a radio show with Infinity Broadcasting, an HSX segment appeared on thirteen episodes of *Access Hollywood*, the company forged syndication relationships for their content with *Entertainment Weekly*, and they closed a $23 million round of venture capital led by Citigroup and NBC. Coincidence? Scott doesn't think so.

The New York–based PR maven Ted Kruckel agrees that parties may have been the best press releases.

TED KRUCKEL

Big events can pay off. I did succeed for my clients, but we had to do some kooky things. For Miadora.com, we had naked models covered in gold and silver paint standing on pedestals handing out free jewelry. The invitation was a metal card with a bar code that we scanned with one of those supermarket checkout things when you arrived. That gave you $100 free on the site, which created a lot of buzz.

For Ashford.com, we took over the pool room at the Four Seasons in New York. We had an Ashford.com diamond, and to promote the giveaway, we got Mrs. Brady, Florence Henderson, to wear it on the *Today* show; Courtney Love at the Golden Globes; Joan Rivers at the Oscars; Faith Hill when she sang the National Anthem at the Super Bowl; and Nancy Kerrigan skating in Rockefeller Center during the *Today* show for Thanksgiving. We videotaped ourselves giving away this diamond, knocking on a woman's door, surprising her. While we were showing the tape at the party at the Four Seasons, Diane Sawyer called to say that she wanted to book the guest for the next day.

So, whether the party cost $75,000 or $150,000, the client got their money's worth.

———————

That party magic might explain why HSX went wild again for their second Oscar bash in 2000.

DOUG SCOTT

Our second Oscar party in March 2000 was called O2K. The theme was "Tech Shui"—technology and feng shui. The presenting sponsor was Toyota. Other sponsors were Excite@Home, MegaChannels, Sun Microsystems, *Movieline* and *Detour* magazines. The event was held again at the House of Blues, and we created a whole Oscar village on Sunset Boulevard and did a historical retrospective of the Academy Awards. We bought out all the shops on the Strip from the House of Blues to the Videotron.

Rob Schneider hosted the event. Moby DJ'd, and Earth, Wind and Fire performed. That whole side garden at House of Blues that never gets used was turned into a Toyota lounge with three big screens projecting driving images with fans blowing through your hair so it felt as if you were driving an MR2 Spider into the mountains. Everything was done in yellow carpets and yellow seats—all funked out. Mark Ronson was DJing outside. It was the first time that anyone had ever built a hundred-foot tent in the lower parking lot at the House of Blues. We had a rock garden, a bamboo garden. The fire chief was in my back pocket—I just kept giving him gift bags for all his men.

The hundred-dollar-plus gift bag was on CNN as its own story. *Good Morning America* did an entire story on the invitation. The party generated about $1.4 to $1.5 million in revenue on a production budget of $1.2 million.

Gary Coleman pulled up in a Lamborghini Coutash convertible limousine with a six-foot-two Amazon woman wearing a UGO.com hat, and we got him on our Webcast saying "UGO's the place to be!" It was like, dot-com all the way!

'NSync showed up and we had problems with all the crowds that surrounded them. We were trying to get them up to the Foundation Room, and we had to deal with some totally crazy security guys who felt that no more people could be let upstairs.

I was like, "Dude, I have 'NSync here. Move."

He goes, "Dude, it's a fire hazard. I'm sorry."

So, I'm like, "Dude, you're a security guard."

He said he couldn't do it, so I told him that he'd be fired in five minutes. Sure enough, I got Arich, the House of Blues general manager, and Arich canned the guy.

It wasn't just egos and parties that became overblown. So did industry conferences. In between COMDEX, Internet World, Streaming Media East, Streaming Media West, Herring on Hollywood, Jupiter's Plug-in, Silicon Alley 2000, and Digital Coast 2000, who had time to work?

ALAN CITRON

There seemed to be people who just did nothing but go to conferences. The thing that struck me was that we'd run into the same people at every show. I'd think to myself that we're spending thousands of dollars to go these events and talk to ourselves. You'd have to ask yourself, "What really has changed from May to June that I need to meet with the same people again?"

MARIA ISABEL GOUVERNEUR

All the Rare Medium creative staff throughout the U.S., London, and Australia met in Dallas for a conference called "Innovate Now." We were in the conference for four days and given any kind of soda, drink, or alcohol you could imagine, but no water! That shocked me—you had to pay for water! We went out every night and drank, and it seemed like everyone managed to have an affair with someone. On the airplane home, everyone was puking and hung over from getting wasted five days in a row. That's how "innovative" we were.

RICHARD TITUS

Razorfish flew all twenty-four hundred employees to Las Vegas. It was a four-day summit for the whole company. We rented out the Mandalay Bay Hotel, and yes, it was a lot of money, but if you're going to fly twenty-four hundred people anywhere, Vegas is probably the cheapest place. It provided an opportunity to have the whole company meet together, but it was a lot of fun, too.

Parties as conferences, conferences as parties. . . had the Marx Brothers come back from the dead for one last movie?

Eventually, these dot-com gatherings had to go. Not go, actually, but morph, as those laid off from the industry came to dwarf the numbers of those who still had jobs with companies that didn't mind stuffing strangers with vodka and caviar. "Unlaunch" events came into vogue, but even those quickly became "branded," most notably with SFGirl.com founder Patty Beron's ultrahip "Pink Slip" parties.

CNET described one of Patty Beron's parties that took place in late 2000: "About half the attendees were job seekers, who were made to wear red dots like finalists at a country fair cook-off. The next biggest crowd was recruiters, wearing green dots, and a smattering of the just-curious types wearing yellow."

"I went to a Pink Slip party at Hush—just *lame*," says Kenny Lin, a former Rare Medium engineer. "It was ex-bartender/waitstaff-turned-Internet-strategists looking for their next gigs as insurance salespeople."

Other online communities, like "Women in Motion," began sending out similar Evites, inviting the paycheck-challenged during the 2001 holiday season to attend a "Chaos" party—a name perhaps more appropriate for the decadent get-togethers of yesterday—featuring, the Evite announced, "special spots dedicated for those seeking jobs and those looking to fill 'em."

Even so, some party givers and goers remain in denial. "With DoubleClick," says Bernardo Joselevich, "it's as if you've entered into a time capsule and it's still 1999. You still feel as if we're in a thriving economy. You don't see the transition from China to plastic dishes, and from ice-sculptured logos and caviar to plastic banners on the wall."

Yet most have sobered up, much to the delight of those who, two short years earlier, watched their colleagues beat the dot-com drum while wondering whether they were missing out on a once-in-a-lifetime parade. Steve Baldwin, the former technology editor at Time Warner's defunct venture Pathfinder, remembers attending a particularly eerie event put on by New York New Media Association, where this transition happened in real-time.

STEVE BALDWIN

I went to an event called Venture Downtown 2001. It was held at great expense at the Grand Hyatt near Grand Central. There were three massive rooms, fully laid out with gigantic screens. They had representatives from the state—Joel Klein from the Justice Department, keynote people—but almost no one was there.

It was a gorgeous gilded ghost town. I would walk across the room and feel guilty for being there. I'm not a VC, I'm not going to give some company fifty million. But downstairs, you'd go to this low-ceiling area, with all these poor people pitching their ideas. They'd approach me, and it was like, "Man, I got fifty dollars in my bank account! You need twenty-five dollars? I'll give you *that*."

In the middle of the conference, Alice O'Rourke, the head of NYNMA, who was hosting this event, was called out for an emergency meeting. The board calls her down, and they must have been shocked to see all the money they're spending to have the grandest, regal time.

She was told that she had to lay off pretty much everyone in NYNMA. *This day.* And this was supposed to be her day of high honor.

LEV CHAPELSKY

People at VIC, this Internet networking organization in L.A., used to wear name tags that said "We're Hiring," and nobody was interested in talking to them because everybody had great jobs. Then suddenly VIC became a layoff lounge because everybody was looking for another job. But no one was hiring, and the nametags turned into "Need a Job."

Heather Keenan wasn't disappointed to see the change.

HEATHER KEENAN

I have to tell you that for event planners, it was one of the most difficult times, with the most difficult people. I'd give a party, and the day before the event, they'd call up and say, "No, I want the waiters to wear *orange* T-shirts and *blue* tennis shoes."

People would offer us stock for our services. I never took it. I was sort of kicking myself for not trading, but now I'm glad I took the cash. Believe me, I earned *every* cent.

CHAPTER FIVE

THE LINGO

All that bullshit-speak was an invention of the marketing and
sales departments of the big Web shops. They'd just use some
stupid-ass word on a pitch because they had to do stuff to
differentiate themselves. Like, you'd have one guy who says,
"I'll make you a Web site." And the next guy says, "I'll make
you a scalable, synergy of convergence with B2B portal appli-
cations." A lot of people will just go with the second guy
because he sounds like he knows what the fuck he's talking
about.

—Philip "Pud" Kaplan, former project manager at
the New York Web design firm Think New Ideas

"By December," my anatomy professor intoned on the first day of classes
at Stanford Medical School in the fall of 1999, "you'll have learned the equivalent of a foreign language."

He wasn't kidding. It was only mid-October, and already, the night before
my midterm, I was surrounded by hundreds of colored index cards translating familiar words like fingers, chest, and cheekbones into medical lingo like
phalanges, *thorax*, and *zygomatic arches*. Thankfully, around nine o'clock, an
Internet consultant friend called and convinced me to take a break at a coffee house in Palo Alto.

"So," Anna sighed, after I spotted her among a sea of caffeinated cell-
phone users, "you wouldn't believe the VC I had to deal with today."

"VC?" I asked, incredulous. I went through my mental list of index cards:
VC. . . ventral cardiac. . . nah, she couldn't be talking about that. She means a

person. But why, I wondered, would a McKinsey consultant have to deal with someone in the Viet Cong?

"Venture capitalist," she explained, as if talking to someone with a learning disability.

The trouble with this particular VC, she said, had to do with his "not getting" that "eyeballs" and "viral marketing" were secondary to "first mover advantage" and "burn rate," and that his entrepreneur's "business model" wasn't the least bit "visionary" because it wasn't "scalable." So even if everyone at that startup worked "24/7," all they'd really be doing was creating a "content portal" like the hundreds already out there.

"And then," my consultant friend continued, working herself into a frenzy, "he says he wants to monetize through e-commerce! *B2C!* I told him if he wanted our buy-in, he'd have to switch to B2B."

Anna waited for a response, but the only words I'd registered were "eyeballs" and "viral"—probably because of my anatomy midterm the next day.

Somehow, I passed the oral exam at Stanford, but soon I was faced with an entirely new language to master. Not only because I joined Kibu six months later; the new jargon extended beyond Silicon Valley, the New York New Media scene, and Hollywood online entertainment. From the evening news to the pages of *Time,* from *Entertainment Weekly's* "What to Surf" column to the racks of New Media magazines that now outnumbered the pornography titles at airport newsstands, the whole country, it seemed, had taken a quickie immersion course in Cyberspeak as a Second Language.

And with my head (*cranium*) buried in medical texts, it felt as if I'd already fallen not a year but a lifetime behind. Blinking into the luminescent sun of the new economic order, whatever the heck that was, I imagined my feelings were similar to those of Japanese soldiers who finally came out of their caves on remote Pacific islands twenty years after World War II was over because they'd never received word to surrender.

But this particular linguistic revolution, like the Internet revolution that spawned it, didn't occur gradually or allow much time to adjust. Before you could utter "dot-communication," everyone from the press to my parents' next-door neighbors began casually spouting the buzzwords and acronyms:

New economy. Old economy. Convergence. Synergy. E-commerce. Killer

App. Beta. B2C. B2B. P2P. O2O. HTML. XML. FTP. PDF. GIF. JPEG. IM. ISP. DSL. Scalable. Eyeballs. Sticky. Portal. Navigation. Page Views. Impressions. Unique Visitors. Hits. Cliff. First Round. Second Round. Vesting Period. Strike Price. 24/7. 404. 411. Viral Marketing. Spam. VC. Buy-in. All Hands. Getting It. Paradigm. Space. Bandwidth. Broadband. Barriers to Entry. Monetize. Incentivize. First to Market. Brick and Mortar. Click and Mortar. IPO. Flip. Time to Exit. Burn Rate.

I hadn't a clue what most of these meant, but fortunately, I discovered that I could fake it far more easily than anatomy, because almost nobody else knew what these words actually meant either. It was as if most of us were at a poker table, all bluffing, all praying no one would call to see our hand.

It's not exactly news that subcultures invent their own languages, both to set themselves apart from the mainstream, and to describe arcane practices that the mainstream wouldn't be interested in anyway. Hollywood, medicine, law, street gangs, and business conglomerates all have their jargon, and in many cases, becoming a true member of these clubs requires initiation through imitation and knowing the password, like little boys with a tree house. "Talk the talk," as the saying goes, and you're in.

And when the mainstream tries to catch on, the results are often hilarious. Who, for example, was smoking what at Coca-Cola when they chose the slogan "A Phat New Bottle"? By the time "dis" went from urban playgrounds to primetime NBC scripts, any self-respecting hip-hopper had already replaced it with a combination of "knucklehead" and "motherfucker" that David Schwimmer would be unlikely to utter on *Friends*.

But Internet revolutionaries often feel a tingle of satisfaction at the fact that few today think about paddles and little white balls when someone says, "I'll ping you back." For the geeks who lived so long on the fringes of *anyone's* acceptance, gaining mainstream recognition for their lingo doesn't seem so bad.

Truth is, much as Net-heads mercilessly mock the middle-aged lawyer who tries to "talk bandwidth," deep down, they know they've pushed a cultural button.

"It's cool," says one San Francisco–based Web designer of the commercialization of her vernacular. "But at the same time, when they talk like that, they sound like"—she pauses, searching for the *mot juste*—"weenies."

Yet the venture capitalist Andrew Anker contends that while "people took this to the extreme," the New Economy wasn't unique in straining to overdo the insider lingo, nor in that jargon's ability to invade everyday communications. "With Wall Street in the eighties," Anker explains, "you started seeing this with marriage announcements that said things like, 'Susan and John are doing an M&A deal, and they're merging their assets.' It was like, gimme a break, this is a bit much."

More than a bit, for many. Words like "revolutionary," "leading," and "visionary" were overused to the point of meaninglessness, and as the line continued to blur between fact and farce, another new term was coined: cyber-gibberish.

In meetings east, west, and in-between, executives bet stock options on a parlor game called "Buzzword Bingo." There was even a nerdy New Economy version of the old game show *To Tell the Truth* in which a panel had to decide who was an imposter and who was what he or she claimed to be. In the new version someone might ask, "Which of the following quotations is made up?"

1. "The CEO of [Web site X].com, an energetic B2B e-business e-solution e-provider, has been forging bold new synergies and formulating exciting new paradigms."
2. "Plug it in, log on to the Terminator portal, and it becomes wireless-enabled. Can we discuss alternate protocols offline before announcing them at the All Hands? Make sure the HTML guys are on this 24/7."

As Regis would say, "Is that your final answer?" Turns out neither is made up. The first was pulled from a technology magazine; the second was uttered by a New Media executive speed-walking along a row of cubicles.

Incomprehensibility became so cool, in fact, that a cryptic sensibility spilled over into the names of startups themselves. "There were companies with silly-sounding names and companies with weird-science names," wrote Alan Citron, then the president-COO of Ticketmaster Multimedia, in *The Industry Standard*. "There were companies with vowel-less names and companies with numeric names. Whatever happened to straightforward, literal-minded names that smack you in the face and say, 'Hey, pal, this is what we do?' Like, say, Ticketmaster Multimedia."

BUZZWORD BINGO

Falling asleep at weekly departmental meetings? Can't stand painfully boring conference calls?
Here is a way to change all that!

How to play: Check off each block when you hear these words during a meeting, seminar, or phone call. When you get five blocks horizontally, vertically, or diagonally, stand up and shout **BULLSHIT!!**

Drill Down	B2B	Space	Incentivize	Scalable
Flip	Burn Rate	24/7	Paradigm	Monetize
Buy-In	Synergy	Visionary	Getting It	Time to Exit
Eyeballs	Sticky	Barriers to Entry	At the End of the Day	Take that Offline
Value Proposition	First to Market	Convergence	Functionality	Leverage

"Buzzword Bingo": discreetly played by dot-commers during many an All Hands.

Citron's conclusion? "Obvious names are another casualty of the digital revolution. Being obtuse, strange, vague, funny, or just plain different is often the whole point. . . thus we have names like Yahoo!, Yoyodyne, Pixel Hype, iXL and Lawnmower"—which had nothing to do with, well, lawnmowers.

Yet despite the gobbledygook, a genuine new lexicon did emerge, one that's both apt and here to stay—at least in the pages of the *Oxford English Dictionary*.

"We started seeing a large amount of vocabulary relating to the Internet and the World Wide Web around 1994—everything took off that year," says Jesse Sheidlower, the first American lexicographer to be appointed a top editor at the *OED*. "You went in the space of a year from no one being on the Web to a lot of people being on the Web. That made all of this new vocabulary necessary."

Even if many misdefined "the Web" itself.

ALEX COHEN

The most egregiously misused phrase was probably "the Web." They would use the word "Web" for "Internet" and "Internet" for "Web," and completely confuse the two. The Internet is not the Web. The Internet is much bigger than the Web.

Whether you thought you were on the "Web" or the "Internet," it was definitely where you wanted to be.

"If it was 'Internet,' " says Total New York's Ted Werth of the term first used in 1982, "it was 'cutting edge.' You could be doing some really boring shit on the Internet, and still call yourself 'cutting edge.' "

Indeed. Soon a fascistic quality emerged to the cool-lingo barometer that seemed to have no basis in reality. Check it, as the dopes liked to say: a cell phone was useful, but not cutting edge. And while a Web phone was virtually useless, it was just so damn cutting edge.

Try this in 1999: "I work in advertising." Ugh. Now this: "I work for DoubleClick and sell rich-media marketing solutions on the Net." Well hello, sailor! Who cared that the majority of the Net's surfers didn't know what the darn thing was? Cathy Brooks remembers defining the Net as "post-Mozilla," and Ted Werth recalls arguing with his friends in the early days over the difference between "Mosaic" and the "World Wide Web."

Mosaic? Mozilla? If you're still scratching your head like Lenny asking George to "tell me 'bout the rabbits" in *Of Mice and Men*, here's an Internet 101 description of those programs: They're both browsers.

"I'll know it when I see it," Supreme Court Justice Thurgood Marshall said in the 1970s when queried as to his definition of smut. Similarly, even though few seemed to be sure of what the Web actually meant, most were willing to say they knew enough to recognize it. Publicist Ted Kruckel waded in with, " 'World Wide Waste of Time.' That's my phrase for the Web or the Internet or the Net, or whatever you want to call it."

MICHAEL KRANTZ

It was funny to see throughout the course of the nineties, that the single word used to connote this new world kept changing. First it was the "information superhighway" or "interactive superstructure." Then, calling it the "infobahn" was the really hot thing.

Although "infobahn" had the shelf-life of a Beanie Baby, "cyberspace," coined by William Gibson in his 1984 novel *Neuromancer*, lasted almost as long as the seemingly eternal IBM Selectric typewriter.

TED WERTH

When streaming began, everything had "cyber" in it. "Cyber" this and "cyber" that. But when "cyber" finally began to lose its cachet and became a cliché, "Webcast" started to pick up. I remember doing a find/replace from "cybercast" to "Webcast" because "cybercast" had become outdated.

JESSE SHEIDLOWER

The *Oxford English Dictionary* tends to be suspicious of words like "cyber"— words that mainly appear in glossaries, even if they've been repeated often. If we have the sense that they're not really being used—they're just being quoted back and forth—then we don't include them.

I think the best example of this is the expression "prairie dogging" which was popularized in Gareth Branwyn's monthly "Jargon Watch" column in *Wired*. It allegedly refers to people working in cubicles and standing up to see what's going on elsewhere in the office.

You find a lot of examples of this term if you search databases. But I don't really believe that anyone has ever seriously used it. It's amusing, it's evocative, and it gets spread, but we tend to stay away from something that doesn't seem to have much genuine currency. The editor working on that term makes this decision. Most of these things aren't widely discussed—either they're clearly in, or clearly there's not enough evidence for them.

Even if your jargon wasn't immortalized in the *OED*, there was still a certain pride in simply coining a phrase.

ALEX COHEN

I coined something called "Internet amnesia." This was the fact that because of the nonnarrative nature of the Net, when you travel from site to site, you never remember where you've been.

KURT ANDERSEN

I unintentionally coined the phrase "digital bubble." I wrote a piece for *The New Yorker* called "The Digital Bubble" that was published in January 1998, well before that phrase had been applied to the New Economy's hysteria and euphoria. There was to me an insane and somewhat irrational overenthusiasm in terms of the market. Which doesn't mean that there was nothing there. But I guess that piece had a "pointing out the emperor's got no clothes" effect, which isn't to say that the emperor was entirely naked. Maybe he was in underwear.

Others who added to the digital lexicon laughed at the newbies attempting to co-opt their lingo.

STEVEN OVERMAN

I can't remember specific words that we at *Wired* introduced. But to the extent we used them, it was in the spirit of fun. We knew that so much of what we were doing was hype because we were an entertainment product, but people who came two or three years into it just didn't get it. They took themselves seriously in a way that we didn't, which really cracked us up.

Andrew Anker and J. Betty Ray "got it"—and enjoyed using tech culture-derived jargon in real life. Simultaneously self-mocking and self-congratulatory, these phrases signaled your entrenchment in the not-so-geeky new geekdom, especially if any of the following rolled off your tongue at an All Hands: *404* (clueless, from error message "404-URL not found"); *mouse potato* (the digital version of "couch potato," usually referring to programmers); *oh-no second* (the realization that you've just made a huge mistake, like accidentally pressing "send" on an unfinished e-mail); *yuppie food stamps* (twenty-dollar bills from ATMs).

ANDREW ANKER

I enjoy using computer or technology metaphors for real life. Like when you say, "Oh, he's got high bandwidth," or "That person's got an IO bust that's not working well." Or you'd hear a lot of, "What's that person's high-order bit?" Those are fun because this is what *Wired* was sort of about. And it's very enjoyable to see this ten years later.

People forget that technologists were the geeks, they were the nerds, the socially inept people you made fun of. That culture was very separate; it was an easy punch line to a joke. Now that the culture is respected, you can say things like "bandwidth" and "bit rate" in normal conversations. And people tend to understand it, or if nothing else they're impressed that *you* understand it.

J. BETTY RAY

I like using words like UI, for user interface: "The *UI* on this door handle is totally confusing." Saying the UI on anything physical is kind of funny. I use that all the time. Also, "I haven't *downloaded* what happened after the events of 9/11." It's definitely its own language with a "we-get-it-and-you-don't" attitude.

———————

Some took advantage of this attitude to establish an internal pecking order, further refining who was in, and how far in they were. "The idea of the 'geek' became a symbol of power," says Jeff Goodell; as a result, tech terms turned into status symbols.

TED WERTH

There was a lot of using lingo to establish who was on the inside and who wasn't. There would be almost a hazing period where you would throw the latest technology at someone and see if he knew it. It was often the established executive who would try that. There were definitely people who were trying too hard.

LARRY GLENN

I worked with a guy whose standard intimidation tactic in a meeting was to just haphazardly put together the latest words and phrases. It worked amazingly well because it would just shut everybody up.

———————

"A unique language gives you an egocentric quality," says the Hollywood producer Peter Guber. "All of us growing up had our own music and our parents didn't like it. Our own clothes and our parents didn't like it. And so every generation also looks to have its own language." It's not surprising that the Net generation, coming off the mellow nineties, chose the ultimate leisurely activity of youth, "surfing," as their metaphor. "When we started using the word 'surf,'" remembers Alex Cohen, "that was something."

Many twenty-somethings don't know, however, that the woman credited with coining the phrase "surfing the Web" in 1992 is a middle-aged former librarian named Jean Armour Polly, a.k.a. "Net Mom." No matter, says Guber, a fellow Baby Boomer of Polly's: "When one talks about the phrase 'surfing the net,' it has a young, hip feeling about it."

But whereas the boomers bonded over, say, free love, revolution, or the counterculture, Gen-Y bonded over money.

"Instead of talking about sex or something," says former Rare Medium chief creative officer Gong Szeto, "I found it fascinating to see all of these young people use 'valuation' every third word."

"A funny thing about the Zeitgeist is that everybody was either an MBA, or talked like one," observes David Neuman. "Investment-banker-speak suddenly became the lingua franca. Twenty-four-year-olds at DEN whose job was to design graphic art for the homepages would be drinking a Coke and smoking a cigarette and talking about whether our business model was valid."

But according to Keen.com's Michael Krantz, the money-speak morphed from ubiquitous to ridiculous. "When it became about money," he says, "no matter what it was, it was suddenly called 'e-commerce.'"

"Everyone talked about being 'first to market,'" says Kal Deutsch, formerly a vice president at HomeGain.com. "eToys.com had to be 'first to market' for toys, and Pets.com 'first to market' for pets." In Deutsch's film spoof *Icevan.com*, a CEO character exclaims, "We have to be 'first to market' in ice!"

"Obviously," says Deutsch, "it rang true for a lot of VCs."

REBECCA EISENBERG

You'd hear people wanting to "leverage the opportunities" and "monetize the customers" and asking "What is your exit strategy?" You'd hear these things over and over again just waiting for a table at a restaurant.

MICHAEL FELDMAN

I was talking with some of my friends from college about the fact that I was working in Silicon Valley. They said, "Oh, can you get me some 'friends and family' shares?" They had no idea what those *were*, but they assumed that everyone just makes money because they get this stock and flip it immediately.

DOUG LEVIN

"Flip"—that word flips me out. Everyone had this concept that they'd be bought by Cisco or Microsoft, that they'd be "flipped." And Cisco and Microsoft certainly did buy some startups, but they were not stupid companies.

ADEO RESSI

I like the term "time to exit." I found that so exemplary of that era. It was something that you would seriously sit in meetings and talk about—"What's the time to exit?" You would have "time-to-exit periods," like seven months, one year—absurdly short periods of time from when an idea was created to when you would sell or IPO.

And everything became a verb. Like I just did with "IPO." You'd hear people saying, "We're gonna IPO next week."

REBECCA EISENBERG

Toward the end of it all, you couldn't go out and not overhear people talking about "return on investments" and "what kind of multiple are you going to see?" I mean, now we laugh, like, "Oh my God—a *multiple*? On your *investment*? Like what the hell?"

"What the hell" was a frequent response to the proliferation of dot-com catchphrases and buzzwords, like the noun "incentive," which was transformed into the verb "to incent," which in turn was transformed into the new verb "incentivize." Or like the phrase "change the world," which Jeff Goodell contends "has been fucked over by so many whores and charlatans, and cheap, money-hungry, two-bit hustlers, that it ceased to have any meaning."

The PR executive Ted Kruckel, who trades in words for a living, puts it another way. "These people with all these words and catchphrases and trendy illogisms, if you will—I came to see that none of them knew what they were talking about. Even though they sounded fancy, it was apparent that their basic understanding of how marketing, PR, and special events worked was at such a lower level than mine. If I could just repeat back to them what they were saying, I was able to get the business."

Deacon Carpenter, a former project manager at Luminant and Digitas, learned this lesson from an early mentor in the fashion business: "You can put a piece of shit in a Chanel suit, but it'll always be a piece of shit. That's perfect for the Internet. You can reinvent the English language and talk about your rich-media this and your banner-ad placement on Yahoo! or Google, but you're still doing online advertising. I don't care what buzz-words you use."

Anyone remember the word "bogus"?

Steve Baldwin, the former technology editor at Pathfinder, sure does.

STEVE BALDWIN

What is "personalization?" It's everything from one-click shopping to My Sports, My News, My Life, My Sex, My Future. It's the ultimate technological manifestation of the global *me*. The Global *I*. Companies spent massive amounts of money on this concept of "personalization" even when it made no sense to "personalize" a product—just because it was the trendy buzzword at the time.

Whenever I hear "personalization," I think: hemorrhaging red ink, cost over-runs, flaky software that doesn't work, and a really good-looking PowerPoint presentation. That's personalization.

TED WERTH

Most people never knew what "hits" meant. Any file that gets called from the server is a hit, but it was the most meaningless number. People began to stack Web pages with tiny GIF images, so if you have 16 images on your home-page, and someone comes to your homepage, you get sixteen hits! There was a time when people were hyping their stuff and getting judged on completely ludicrous and worthless numbers. "Page views" or "impressions" or "unique visitors" all developed out of that.

REBECCA EISENBERG

"Disintermediate" is a word that still drives me crazy. In the more than a hundred columns I wrote at the time, I don't think I used that word once, except maybe to quote someone and make fun of them for saying it. I still don't think it means anything.

DEACON CARPENTER

At Digitas, there was a new group called "tweenagers." I'm still having a hard time understanding that. They're teenagers between the ages of 14 and 17. Well, aren't those just *teen*agers?

Or, I'd be in a meeting, especially with the account managers, and they'd say how great the Web site is going to be, it's going to drive new traffic, and it's going to be "customer-centric." Then you'd have a conversation with them on the side, which they called a "sidebar," and you'd say, "What does customer-centric mean?" They'd say, "I'll send you an e-mail about that," but it would never arrive.

MICHAEL KRANTZ

I don't remember when the term switched from "New Media" to "interactive media." It was by far the best in terms of being descriptive, but then you got anybody who was doing *anything* on a computer talking about how it was "interactive," which is idiotic. I think the word "interactive" quickly ceased to have meaning.

Interactivity did manage, howevver, to mock meaningless jargon with "The Bullshit Generator" (dack.com/web/bullshit.html), an online application that spits out "bullshit-speak" in response to straightforward typed-in phrases. Matt Welch and Dan Adler found it particularly amusing.

MATT WELCH

There was a great moment in February of 2000 when my wife and I went down to San Diego to the *Variety* Interactive Summit. On the opening night, this person is walking around with a video camera interviewing the attendees, and it was fantastic because the next night they played a videotape montage of what they got. And basically every single person said it was like "The Bullshit Generator": "We're just trying to do the backend user of the B2B of B2C space." They edited it all together and it was pure nonsense.

DAN ADLER

I got the biggest kick out of "The Bullshit Generator." You started to listen to people making their pitches, or you'd read executive summaries of business plans, and you could just substitute a couple of words and they'd all read the same. Each ultimately meant as little as the next.

Meaningless phrases and words gave way to meaningless titles. Jerry "chief Yahoo!" Yang may have started the trend, but by the late nineties, Orwellian-sounding monikers like "media evangelist," "minister of reason," "master of logistics," "chief executive officer, reality," and "manager of first impressions" (adding new meaning to the phrase "glorified receptionist") had become the norm in Net culture.

LARRY GLENN

There were actually people called "chief visionary officers." Everyone was trying to appear not just smart, but brilliant—a genius. Everybody was a "visionary."

JOANNE WEAVER

People at Scient had jobs called "chief morale officers," or "CMOs." It was an honorary position in addition to your regular job. They'd organize these parties and rent out some really swank place downtown. They'd put on a rally every month. But in some ways, it was sort of like student government in high school. It was a popularity contest about who was going to motivate people the best.

CAMERON HICKEY

There were so many nonsensical titles. Mine at Boo.com was "Web innovator." But I was actually a twenty-year-old photography major who didn't know shit about the Web.

———————

Even if you could make sense of the farcical lingo, some phrases were as overused as "alternative" in music, "independent" in film, and "is the new black" in fashion.

"Everything was 'awesome,' even when it wasn't," says Rare Medium's former designer Maria Isabel Gouverneur. "You heard that all the time. So if something really *was* awesome, there wasn't a word to describe it." Nicholas Hall of StartupFailures.com found a word to describe the excessive gibberish: "nuts."

NICHOLAS HALL

"Internet time" was used so much that it created a paranoia. It was that unrealistic "24/7" crap. Like people weren't going crazy enough, and missing out on life enough already?

DAVID GILCREAST

"Scalable" was at the end of every sentence and the beginning of every conversation. It was all about how "scalable" these ideas were. Food.com was no different. "Scalable" was the idea that while it's small now, the upside and the growth potential are enormous. What people forgot is that in order to have the ability to scale, you have to have the demand. I think people really overestimated what people were willing to do on the Internet. Most ideas weren't "scalable" at all.

AUREN HOFFMAN

The most common word for about a year in 1999 was "bandwidth"—as in, "I don't have the bandwidth to do this." Or, "I don't have the cash bandwidth to do this." I remember we had an adviser meeting with our investors, and at this big pow-wow, one of our VPs counted the number of times that an investor said "bandwidth." It turned out to be *forty-five* times.

DAN ROACH

"Paradigm" was a word I heard way too much. I used to meet people all the time who were "paradigm shifters." I would sit down with someone and go through their seemingly generic business where they're, say, transporting something online. They'd give their pitch, and say, "Well, here's how we're going to shift the paradigm of such-and-such." I mean, I *know* what a paradigm shift is, and it was never what they were describing.

MARIA ISABEL GOUVERNEUR

"Innovating" was used on a regular basis. People decided they were innovating just because they were part of the Internet party. They didn't know you had to actually *innovate* something to use the word.

The constant barrage of these words in everyday conversation made them contagious—even to veteran journalists Alan Citron and Kurt Andersen.

ALAN CITRON

I was a reporter at the *Los Angeles Times* for thirteen years, so I had a sensitivity to language, but I did find myself falling into using dot-com words because it was the easiest way to make people understand you. When we did the road show for Ticketmaster/Citysearch, I completely drifted into that tech-speak about how our site was "sticky" and we were the ultimate "B2C." I had the whole glossary down.

KURT ANDERSEN

I found myself using this language unironically, just as a matter of course—phrases such as "this space" that probably just a few months earlier I would have found ridiculous.

———

Whereas Andersen's "space" refers to "this category," Ted Kruckel had a bone to pick with a different "space" usage.

TED KRUCKEL

People always bragged about their "space." They never called their offices "offices"—it was always their "space." They were like, "It's free-form for the flow of ideas." I was like, "It's a *loft*, okay? We've had them around for a while."

———

Industry insiders were divided not only over what to say—loft or space, Web or Internet, visionary or revolutionary—but also whether they liked what was being said. Some relished the new lingo, logging on to Buzzwhack.com and picking up words like "meta-ignorance" ("not knowing what you don't know"). Others believed that the Buzzwhack listings further fueled the industry's meta-ignorance.

Thumbs up or thumbs down on a particular piece of cyberspeak? Internet consultant Harold Mann and PayMyBills.com's former marketing director Tom Lazaroff agree about as much as Ebert and Roeper.

{HATE}

HAROLD MANN

Words like "monetize" bugged me. "Monetize" was the most misused term because it presumed that by saying "We're going to monetize these people," they'd all of a sudden open their checkbooks. But companies were unable to "monetize" 99 percent of the people they were talking to, and that ended up costing them a lot of Aeron chairs.

{LOVE}

TOM LAZAROFF

I loved "monetize the eyeballs." That phrase was the mantra, man!

{HATE}

PETER HEINECKE

The most annoying fallacy was "land grab"—grabbing the real estate. It turned out they were grabbing the swampland.

{LOVE}

HAROLD MANN

I found the term "land grab" distasteful at first, but in hindsight, I found it prophetic. It seemed so opportunistic, because it was all, "We're just doing a land grab," meaning we're just trying to be the first player in that category. But as it turned out, you only get one eBay. eBay became the Kleenex of its sector because it had the chance to. If it wasn't eBay, it would have been something else that came first. There was nothing about eBay's brand name or technology that guaranteed its position in history. So I came to find the term "land grab" to be an apt expression.

{HATE}

REBECCA EISENBERG

I feel like puking every time someone says, "B2B" or "B2C."

{LOVE}

AUREN HOFFMAN

Two of my favorites from 2000:
  B2C: Back to Consulting
  B2B: Back to Banking

Love the lingo or hate it, the attorneys David Hornik and David Epstein contend that mastering it was a necessary stepping-stone to moving ahead in the industry.

DAVID HORNIK

The truth is, I think the new lingo helped me. One of the reasons that young attorneys were able to progress quickly during that time is that we were better able to adopt the vernacular than older people. The more you could speak the way the entrepreneurs were speaking, the more accepted you were.

DAVID EPSTEIN

There's a strong movement within law to "talk in English" so your clients know what you mean. But with the Internet you didn't want to use plain English; you wanted to sound intelligent. Like using the word "interstitial," rather than saying a "pop-up." Or using the word "stickiness."

Clients really liked hearing you use this lingo because it made them feel like you "get it." That was another big one, "get it." It also became a great rationalization if you didn't win a client. Then it was always, "They didn't 'get it.' Oh, okay, it's them, not us." We used language to make us believe what we wanted to believe.

Like believing that you had a business plan, even if you didn't. Or believing that you were working toward a "higher purpose," even if you were more concerned with the millions you hoped to make along the way. Sometimes, notes the journalist Laura Rich, the language "was like religion."

JOANNE WEAVER

Christopher Lockhead, our very exuberant, bald Canadian VP of marketing, would do a workshop called "Innovations and Communications" during our Spark orientation classes. He would be totally outrageous, screaming—a huge *Austin Powers* thing. In the early days of Scient, someone had chanted,

"We're on Fire!" So that caught on as a catchphrase, and they kind of institutionalized that during Spark.

Everyone was taught, "We're on Fire!" and we'd always chant it at our rallies. We also had a cheer where we'd rev our right arm up like we're pitching a softball, and we'd go, "Goooooooooooo Scient!!" It was our own special language. But when the company got much bigger, it had an empty ring to it. It was like, these people are employee number 1500 and 1501, they have no idea how this phrase started. You'd hear new people shouting this from Spark down the hall, and it had a lifeless feel to it.

Nothing had more of a lifeless feel than Old Economy abbreviations. Often, one could easily guess the meaning of these dated word soups—BCC (blind carbon copy), FYI (for your information), and the ever-popular TGIF (Thank God it's Friday)—without being a Scrabble champion. New Economy acronyms and initials, on the other hand, presented a far greater challenge, and many a wordsmith had to humble him- or herself and ask a question.

Question: What does Yahoo! stand for?
Answer: Yet Another Hierarchical Officious Oracle.

AWGTHTGTTSA	Are We Going to Have to Go through this Shit Again
DKDC	Don't Know, Don't Care
FOAF	Friend of a Friend
GTGP	Got to Go Pee
PMFJI	Pardon Me for Jumping In
TANSTAAFL	There Ain't No Such Thing as A Free Lunch
TIC	Tongue in Cheek
WE	Whatever
WITFITS	What in the Fuck is this Shit?
YYSSW	Yeah Yeah Sure Sure Whatever

Dot-com Alphabet Soup.

CATHY BROOKS

You know what PCMCIA stands for? "People can't memorize computer industry acronyms."

JESSE SHEIDLOWER

It's hard to put all the abbreviations in the *Oxford English Dictionary*. We tend to put in those that have currency. Things like LOL [laugh out loud], AFAIK [as far as I know], IMHO [in my humble opinion], RTFM [read the fucking manual]—these are all going in. PERL, the programming language, is often said to be an acronym, but, in fact, is not. There are a lot of extremely obscure ones that we keep out, but if they become popular enough, we'll put them in.

If abbreviations were difficult to decipher, sometimes entire phrases needed a translation. Or maybe just a good ol' dose of truth.

"At PK Interactive," says Philip "Pud" Kaplan, "we never said that we 'synergized new paradigms to create next-generation destinations.' We said we made Web sites. That was pretty refreshing to our clients."

Like many of their peers, Steve Baldwin and the Silicon Alley attorney Steven Masur saw right through the boardroom bullshit.

STEVE BALDWIN

You had to do some decrypting. On job boards, you'd see "a fast-paced, dynamic, exciting work group." That translates as "chaos, you probably don't have a private phone, and you'll have to report to four different people in four different time zones."

STEVEN MASUR

"Monetize the value proposition" is a euphemism for "I have a really fucking stupid idea and I have no idea of how to make a penny off it."

Ultimately, this euphemistic doublespeak couldn't keep revenue-challenged companies from going belly up. But in an ironic twist—some would say it was justice—the dot-com downfall resulted in doomsday definitions for words previously coined on sunny days.

"Filing" now meant "filing for Chapter 11 bankruptcy," not "filing to go public." "Doing another round" referred to the next "round of layoffs" rather than the next "round of financing." "P2P" now meant "Path to Profitability" instead of "Peer to Peer," while "B2B" more often was used for "back to basics" or "back to B-school" rather than "business to business."

Yet despite the Internet's confusing, meaningless, overused, and often ludicrous linguistic legacy, for some, the new language had an oddly poetic ring to it.

MICHAEL FELDMAN

I was described in an article as being "uninstalled" recently. I thought that was more clever than being called "unemployed" or even "unhired."

JENNIFER MUSILLO

I thought "click and mortar " was such a great play on words.

STEVEN OVERMAN

I remember learning the word "meme," which was originally coined in 1976 by the biologist Richard Dawkins. Kristen Spence, at *Wired*, explained it to me because it was being used a lot there. A meme is an idea that can be spread like a virus. A meme right now is the idea that smallpox is a greater threat than anthrax to our nation. I thought it was a beautiful word.

LARRY GLENN

I liked the term "bleeding edge," which came from the VC world. The concept was that the first person with an idea got shot, just as the first person out of the foxhole got shot. So investing in bleeding-edge technology became a very high-risk thing to do. You don't know what's going to happen. It's perfect!

JEFF GOODELL

The original Steve Jobs idea of putting a computer on a desktop and bringing power to the people was a really powerful idea, before it became an excuse to market you a lot of shit. So the phrase that keeps popping up as the most elegant piece of technology-spawned poetry is Steve Jobs's phrase "the computer as a bicycle for the mind." It's the only piece of poetry that has come out of the technology industry.

CHAPTER SIX

THE SPIN

I always liken what happened to people who went to work at startups to what happens when a ring gets put on a bride's finger. Instant lobotomy. They lost all objectivity, especially when it came to marketing themselves.

—Ted Kruckel, president of the boutique marketing and PR firm, Ted, Inc.

Before the slick ad spreads appeared in *Seventeen* magazine; before Judy MacDonald, Molly Lynch, and three of the Faces smiled smugly while hocking stylish Slates clothing in the pages of *Rolling Stone*; before the daily national press queries began pouring in to Kibu's spokeswoman, Kristi Dyer—the company spent $10,000 on a one-day retreat to solve its most pressing problem. Like its teenage target audience, Kibu was undergoing a major identity crisis.

This was a serious predicament: Unable to boil its essence down to a few consistent buzzwords, Kibu couldn't describe itself to the press. Heck, Kibu couldn't describe itself to *itself*. Who or what was Kibu? Was it really, as the cofounders claimed, a "digital lifestyle brand"? And if so, what *was* a digital lifestyle brand? Did it target thirteen-year-olds (the period-obsessed) or eighteen-year-olds (the penis-obsessed)? Was it an online interactive magazine, an empowering community for teen girls, or a flashy retail space and marketing survey tool simply *disguised* as an empowering community for teen girls?

And how could we make the cryptic name Kibu familiar to American teens when our competitors included the catchy ChickClick.com and the Jennifer Aniston–sponsored teen site Voxxy ("That's XX for female chromosomes," reported E! Online)?

With $22 million at stake, these were no trivial musings. Kibu desperately needed that Old Economy stalwart, a definable brand—and fast. So Judy hired a Portland-based consulting group, On Your Feet, to help us create one.

On Your Feet is that curious breed of consultancy that uses New Economy gimmicks (improvisational comedy) yet comes armed with an impressive list of Old Economy clients (Southwest Airlines, Audi). But as Ruth Shalit, a New York advertising executive and journalist, noted in *Salon*:

> The pairing of On Your Feet and Kibu.com did not, at first blush, seem particularly auspicious. . . . The people at Audi know what their brand is—they make a high-end car—and so they can afford to play around with it. Pulling out scarves, juggling beanbags, playing wacky group games and generally getting all funky and outside-the-boxy might be useful in shaking up ossified ideas and stirring creativity. But Kibu's brand-identity problems seemed more fundamental. It didn't seem to need an improv comedy session as much as an old-fashioned, logocentric management consultant.

Nevertheless, on the morning we met On Your Feet's enthusiastic leader, Gary Hirsch, in a large conference room with a view of San Francisco's picturesque Marina, he told us to take off our shoes (mostly Prada slide-ons), turn off our cell phones (bleeps followed by whiny groans), and get ready to improvise.

"In the fast-paced, competitive Internet world, you need to be able to think on your feet—no pun intended," our leader said, pointing at his "On Your Feet" T-shirt and laughing alone at his self-referential joke.

Then, after looking around the room and announcing, "Boy, it's an estrogen fest in here!" Hirsch got down to business. "You have some contradictions in your brand," he explained.

This was encouraging to me, as I didn't realize Kibu *had* a brand. "So," Hirsch continued, scanning the semicircle of fifty or so mostly trendy young women, several of whom were filing their fingernails or fixing their lipstick while gazing into tiny mirrors, "how would you describe your company?"

"An estrogen fest?" I offered.

Ignoring me, Hirsch cheerily repeated the question. Reflexively people began calling out the so-called Five Pillars that Kibu's marketing department had ingrained into new employees: "Fun!" "Fresh!" "Knowledgeable!" "Uninhibited!" "Inspired!" We also knew to answer any queries about our business plan with the neato but nonsensical "integrated online marketing," another catchphrase that someone yelled out.

"Great, fabulous," Hirsch replied. "Can anyone define these terms?"

The room went back to nail filing and lipstick fixing. A few people gazed longingly at their turned-off cell phones.

For the rest of the day, among other seemingly useless exercises, we circled the room with our eyes closed (to see what it's like being blind?); paced while talking rapidly to ourselves (to see what it's like being psychotic?); made cat, dog, and monkey noises (point also unclear, although I did learn how to anthropomorphize ape sounds as "Ooo! Eeee! Oooo!"); came up with "content" through a free-association gimmick called "Word at a Time" (which generated such brilliant prose as, "When your dude isn't home, scream 'Hey, Loser!' " or, as an antidote to teen depression, "I would go to the bathtub and sleep"); and played something called the Bunny Game.

Shalit was there to observe the proceedings:

After the Bunny Game has run its course, we have a discussion about what it all meant.

"Was that easy?" Hirsch asks. "Was it hard?"

"It was *hard*," says Lynn, the Face of Homework.

"I was trying to anticipate, trying to plan, trying to win, win, win," says Alison, the Face of Sex and Relationships. "But when you did that, you got eliminated."

"What did you have to do to play this game?" Hirsch asks.

"You had to be the bunny," someone says.

"Okay," Hirsch says. In large block letters he writes, "Be the Bunny." "Anything else?"

"You had to focus," says the Face of Homework, thoughtfully. "You couldn't focus on other things. Like, 'Oh, what a cute shirt.' "

"Okay," Hirsch says again. "Focus. That's good. Anything else?"

"It's about being in the moment," says Emily, the Face of Money. "It's like, if you're going to show up to work anyway, you might as well really get into it?"

"Exactly," Hirsch says. "What we're talking about is commitment. If you're going to be the bunny—BE THE BUNNY. Whatever that means to you."

It didn't mean much to me, or anyone else for that matter. No wonder Kibu left the retreat ten thousand dollars poorer and still clueless as to its brand.

Fortunately, although Kibu had neither a brand nor much of a product, it managed to produce a bevy of press releases lending the illusion of both. In media coverage from *Time* to *Fortune* to *Daily Variety*, Kibu was touted as a hot teen site whose slogan was "Girls Who Get It." (Which almost led to an embarrassing blunder: Just before posting "Girls Who Get Some" on the give-away portion of the site, our male Face of Hair pointed out the unfortunate double entendre.)

On May 29, 2000, in an article entitled "Hot Teen Site Kibu.com Bucking Startup Odds," the *Chicago Tribune* ran a Reuters story about consumer Web sites going out of favor—and out of business. The article asked, "So how do you explain Kibu.com, a late entrant into the crowded field of teen Web sites that launched in early May with $22 million from some of the biggest names in Silicon Valley investing?"

Citing a Teen Research Unlimited study claiming that U.S. teens spent $153 billion in 1999, with teen girls topping $60 billion, the article goes on to list other teen sites aiming to capitalize on this demographic before explaining why Kibu would be different.

"After researching what 13-to–18-year-old girls like to do online, co-founders [Judy] MacDonald and Molly Lynch decided to offer something akin to a TV network, with 20 different channels of programming on such topics as fashion and relationships. Each is hosted by young adults the company calls 'faces,' who act as a cross between an older sister and an MTV VJ."

We didn't have much of a Web site, but we sure had great buzz: a sexy Idea Story, glitzy backers, a "visionary" concept (who cares if it would never come to fruition), and the semblance of sponsors (the article listed two, implying several more forthcoming).

Bolstering the high-profile media coverage and leveraging the "Girls Who Get It" tag line, Kibu also began a grassroots campaign, which consisted of getting teams of teen girls around the country to write our slogan in chalk on sidewalks; asking them to chant "Kibu" in the street like perky drill team leaders; and, as a reward (shamelessly taking advantage of many teenagers' dreams of being a "star"), posting their pictures on our site.

"Kibu Girl Ashley in Seattle!" read the caption under a picture of a blonde fourteen-year-old decked out in a Kibu hat, Kibu T-shirt, and Kibu backpack. Another read: "Kibu Pals MacKenzie and Veronica in Houston!" Our site became not so much a "digital hangout" to create community for teen girls but a "digital press release" used to boondoggle them.

After all, you'd never know from these rah-rah photos, much less from the glowing press coverage, that teen girls who didn't receive "free stuff" in exchange for their public endorsements were decidedly less enthusiastic than the Ashleys and Veronicas pictured on our site. When our VP of marketing finally convinced Judy to do some *concrete* market research (as opposed to relying on what Judy liked to call her "intuition"), Kibu hired the KP-backed firm Vividence™ to get the scoop. According to their extensive study, conducted in June of 2000:

- Only 65 percent of testers are satisfied with their experience on Kibu (vs. Vividence client average of 73 percent);
- 29 percent of users are *unlikely* to return to Kibu in the next month (vs. Vividence client average of 9 percent);
- Vast majority of testers can't decipher/don't notice icons or links (so much for Judy's theory of girls "loving to find things by trial and error").

Under the "Verbatim Comments" section, here's what some of the girls tested had to say:

- "I think this is an uninteresting dull site without much to offer."
- "Apparently, this site takes me to be a fool."
- "I can't use any of this stuff. It's boring and irrelevant to my life as a teenager."
- "If you are a rather superficial person. . . this is a great site for you. Translation: If you are one of those girls who wants to be popular and perfect and tries everything to get there, WOO-HOO FOR YOU! But for those of us who form our opinions

based upon what we like, not what is popular, this has no real benefit other than to kill time."

- "These people don't really have anything interesting to say. It's kind of like their own personal ramblings, which in some cases could be interesting, but not here."

Hmm.

Even teen girls picked up on the site's insularity, homogeneity, and lame product—but Kibu wasn't the only startup plagued by these demons. In fact, perhaps some weren't demons at all, but assets: without this level of denial and self-involvement, how could anyone orchestrate a successful media campaign for such a wide range of deficient products?

Or nonexistent ones.

"There were massive numbers of embarrassing press releases," says the marketing executive Ted Kruckel. "There was a time when every single dot-com company, in their press releases, would call themselves 'the premiere' this or that. And it was like, 'You just launched, you don't *do* anything yet!' "

According to Doug Scott, the former VP of sales and marketing at Hollywood Stock Exchange, the pressure to spend money on advertising "whether your site was up or not" outweighed potential humiliation. "The attitude," he says, "was build a brand. It was the Amazon attitude."

But did this advertise-now-produce-product-later strategy work? Apparently not. I still have my Kibu hat, Kibu T-shirt, Kibu incense, and enough deposition-sized folders filled with Kibu press to indicate I was arguing a landmark case before the Supreme Court, not working for a startup that gave away "Girls Who Get It" lipstick. But "Girls Who Got It" is the farewell message that appears when I type in the site's URL.

Don't let your mascara run, Kibu Girls: You're not alone.

———————

Recently, Jesse and I were driving and saw three consecutive billboards for Modo, Pets.com, and eToys. All three companies are out of business. No matter—they continue to flaunt their in-your-face, cooler-than-thou brands from the digital graveyard.

Thing is, we had to admit that we *liked* these ads. Internet ads tended to be gimmicky, sure, but they had an edge, a wink-wink irreverence. They spiced up magazines, radio, billboards, TV, skywriting, even *bananas*. ("How much vitamin C do you need a day?" asked a banana sticker for the search engine AskJeeves. To find out, naturally, the banana owner was instructed to go directly to their site.)

And don't forget those groovy "bagvertisements" sold by SmartBags at a rate of $25,000 for 200,000 bags. I can still picture *Red Herring*'s "Get hooked on *Red Herring*" paper bag, with the giant fish hook dangling in the doomed fish's gullet (a sign of things to come?).

Some companies, of course, didn't use ads at all, but survived on "viral marketing" or cyber-style word-of-mouth as pioneered by Hotmail and copied by virtually every other consumer-oriented dot-com and brick-and-mortar shop since. Yet many did, and huge companies like DoubleClick and 24/7 Media were built solely around online advertising and marketing. Even traditional ad agencies such as Omnicom, Saatchi, and Grey created immense New Media departments—and, crooning the chorus of the moment ("IPO!"), planned on spinning them off and taking them public.

Then, as IPOs went M.I.A., good ol' reliable Budweiser and Coca-Cola appeared on the back covers of your favorite newsstand magazines. The infamous Pets.com "pet sock"—gone. In January 2000, seventeen Internet companies spent an average of $2.2 million *each* on thirty-second Super Bowl spots. A year later, seven of those went out of business or had been acquired.

Not E*Trade, however, whose thirty-second spot during the 2000 game featured a dancing chimpanzee and proclaimed, "Well, we just wasted two million dollars. What are you doing with *your* money?"

Prophetic, perhaps, but only for the company's fellow Super Bowl advertisers. The following year, E*Trade mocked its dead digital brethren with the same chimp riding through a ghost town littered with the graves of what twelve months earlier might have been considered bona fide businesses, like Tieclasp.com and Pimentoloaf.com. By 2002, advertisers displayed a post-bubble, post–September 11 cautiousness, and a mere three Internet companies—HotJobs.com, Monster.com, and Yahoo!—joined E*Trade during the NFC-AFC clash.

Prime-time TV may have lost its feasibility, but as late as October 25, 2001, the *New York Times* proclaimed that "all is not bleak at companies that sell Internet advertising." Reporting that iVillage, the high-profile Web site for women, increased its ad sales 19 percent in the third quarter, the *Times* pointed to the startup's strategy of employing new forms of advertising, such as "bigger ads with sound and motion," and "television-style commercials on some of its pages."

As 2001 came to a close, *Time* magazine touted the unorthodox ad strategy of Ted Meisel, the thirty-eight-year-old CEO of Overture (formerly named GoTo.com). "Overture invites advertisers to bid for placement in its search results, with the higher bidders getting the top spots," the magazine said, adding that the company had just reported its first profitable quarter.

Then in January 2002, the *New York Times* declared, "Start-Ups No Longer Shout from the Rooftops," citing LocalAlert, a New York–based startup that sends bulletins to subscribers on their cell phones, as a prime example of the sea change in New Economy spin. Cofounded by Spencer Waxman—whose previous startup, the high-profile online payment company Flooz, spent $43 million to put its pitchwoman Whoopi Goldberg's mug on buses nationwide—LocalAlert had chosen a decidedly low-tech, and low-cost, promotion strategy: handing out fliers on the street.

Yet whereas today, after the dot-com shakeout, the debate revolves around which kinds of advertising are most effective, less than ten years ago a more fundamental question was being discussed in a conference room at the *Wired* headquarters.

"At *HotWired*, there was this debate: Should there even *be* advertising on the Web?" recalls the former executive assistant Steven Overman. "That went on and on, and someone in the room asked, 'Why do we need to put advertising up? Why can't it just be a self-supporting ecosystem?' So I raised my hand and said, 'Because someone has to pay our salaries.'"

Indeed, to Bernardo Joselevich's surprise, many were happy to pay handsomely for Internet advertising.

BERNARDO JOSELEVICH

In January 1996, my future boss at HotelGuide.com told me to meet her on the island of Madeira, in the middle of the Atlantic. She wanted to teach me how to sell Internet ads. So I'm at this posh hotel, and she's pulling out these pre-formatted contracts that I was supposed to sell to hotels. All I knew about luxury hotels was that the senior executives spent all their time terrified that a roach would show up in a soup bowl or their lobby. The Internet seemed so far-fetched. But she was showing me this contract, and going, "Here's the box where you can check off the $23,000 Internet ad package."

When I got back home, I made five appointments with major hotels on the same day because I was so sure that I'd be shown the door in no time, and the whole thing would end with a nice vacation in Madeira. To my amazement, I closed three deals and made $6,000 in commissions that morning. I had never made such easy money so quickly! I was totally shocked. If I had won the lottery, at least I would have suspected it was *possible*—otherwise I wouldn't have bought the ticket. But people buying Internet ads? No way.

In 1996, I sold $500,000 in Internet advertising for hotels alone. It seemed irrelevant to ask whether it was a fad or not. When you're flying around, pulling out your laptop, and people are just giving you money, all the existential questions dissipate.

Joselevich hadn't, in fact, stumbled upon a magical formula for minting money via the Internet. In the grand tradition of American business, he was simply providing a service that customers had never needed before—and then convincing them they couldn't do without it. Yes, a luxury hotel needed luxury sheets. But Internet advertising? Yes, that too.

Laura Rich wasn't so sure.

LAURA RICH

When I was about twenty-five, I was covering magazine advertising at *Inside Media*. That was in 1995, so advertisers had just started building really elaborate Web sites. Our columnist, Jane Weaver, left and suggested that I take over the column. I was a bit reluctant because I thought this Net thing was a fad. I thought it was all crazy for advertisers to build these elaborate Web sites. At the time, it was just these big, huge brochures and some had features like games. I mean, why would you want to go to the Stoli or Absolut site and play games? I was reviewing advertisers' Web sites, and I guess I made an okay columnist, because I bashed most things.

Universally bashed, however, were what became known as "banner ads." These "468X60s" were the thirty-second TV spot, one-page print ad, or outdoor billboard of the Internet Age. With one advantage. According to Doug Scott, "Unlike TV, print, or outdoor—where three million cars might drive by a billboard, yet no one knows the return on that billboard relative to action—this was a media form that people could actually quantify."

True, but perhaps this data was Too Much Information. Ridiculed for their low click-through rates (most sources report a measly 0.2 percent to 0.5 percent), these annoying GIFs—like the one with the seemingly Ritalin-deficient monkey obsessively playing a shell game—gave way to equally headache-inducing superstitials, interstitials, pop-ups, pop-unders, and eye-blasters.

The Internet Advertising Bureau lists more than a dozen other ad units, including the half banner, vertical banner, skyscraper, rectangle, and microbutton.

In its defense, however, *Wired's* Steven Overman says that the much maligned ad banner came from people "just trying to figure this Web thing out."

STEVEN OVERMAN

We prototyped what an ad on the Web would be. The first idea was an ad page, like in a magazine, but how would you get there: a button? text link? And then someone in the room said, "Yeah, a button. We'll just call it an ad button." But that didn't sound very good, so someone else said, "Well, maybe we could call it a flag." They're on the whiteboard drawing a long rectangular thing and nobody liked the way "flag" sounded, so somebody else said, *"Banner!* It's an ad banner." And you could feel everybody go, "Ah, that's it."

To celebrate selling the first ad banner to Zima, we had a party and they donated tons of the stuff. It was horrible and everybody was gagging on Zima. When you think about where the industry has ended up, maybe there was something portentous about this undrinkable swill being the first product that was advertised with a banner.

ANDREW ANKER

Over the summer of 1994, we developed this idea for *HotWired*: the ad banner. There was no advertising on the Web before us, so we had 100 percent of the market share in 1994. It was early in 1995 that Starwave and CNET started to have ad banners, and by late 1995, the Yahoos and the Infoseeks came around.

We came up with two concepts. One was we knew that this was an important medium, so we only talked to big Fortune 500 advertisers. The second was that *Wired* was the first magazine to have tech and consumer advertising. No one had ever placed an Armani ad next to one for a new Unix work station before, and we wanted to have that same mix on *HotWired*. AT&T was the first to sign on. And then we had Sprint, MCI, IBM. On the consumer side, we had Club Med, Volvo, Zima.

In some ways, it was easier for us to sell because we were *Wired*. We had the ability to tell them, "Look, we won't make you feel dumb. We know this medium. We're the people working to create it." So I think we got a lot of people more comfortable because we had that Net credibility.

While the online sales community was out evangelizing the power of Web advertising to the likes of Zima, Volvo, and Club Med, online PR flacks had an equally difficult task—translating megabytes into sound bites for the major media outlets. Cathy Brooks—then a technology neophyte—became one of the early interpreters.

CATHY BROOKS

I went into PR mostly by talking to people at my gym, which was near the ad district in San Francisco. I had absolutely no intention of going into technology. I blindly walked into an interview at a PR firm and said, "Look, I can take any job and do it, but all I know about computers is that there's a computer, a screen, and you don't have to use white-out." Three weeks later, I was at my first COMDEX, the national computer trade show, in Las Vegas. I was kind of thrown into the fire headfirst.

Back then, there was a feeling that we were doing something different that the outside world didn't understand. Especially for me, being in a position of working with these brilliant technologists and explaining to the media—in English—what they did.

As much as we like it and think in Silicon Valley that this stuff is pervasive, there's a whole world out there that could give a shit. These people use computers, and know that they're in homes and schools, and you can't spit without a tailwind and not hit technology in today's day and age. It's in your supermarket, it's how you buy your clothes. It's probably how you plan your vacations. But people don't really care about relational databases unless it's relevant to their lives.

So I'd say to these tech types, "Tell me in English, if I'm looking at my computer, why do I give a flying frog's fat ass about what this thing does?" Because the *New York Times* does not care about Oracle databases unless you can explain the end-user benefit: I care because my hospital is using this technology, and this is how my doctor will process my information, and this is how I can learn more about my health on my own.

My mother was a litmus test: If she didn't get it, it needed to be explained in plainer English.

DOUG SCOTT

I was managing all of Hollywood Stock Exchange's PR. The *New York Times* was doing a huge Sunday full-page article on the company, and I had built a really good relationship with the writer. She said, "Look I'm going to send you the article to read, which is unheard of." When I got it, there were no quotes from the CEO, David Herman. He freaked out on me and said that I was an egotist and that this was all about me, me, me. How dare I do something like this! He thought that he should be the focal point of the article.

So I called the reporter back and changed all my quotes to his name. I said, "I don't know why you didn't include any quotes from David Herman, but these quotes need to be attributed to him." And she said, "Because I didn't understand a word that he was saying. He was talking in such an elevated manner that I didn't understand what the hell your *business* was."

––––––––––

Forget the business. Many working in the media didn't understand what the Web was, or at least what it could do for their clients—forcing Internet pioneers to struggle for recognition as a viable marketing entity.

"The publicists saw the Web as outer space," says Lew Harris of his press encounters while editor of E! Online.

Both Harris and the former music manager Lisa Hendricks recall having to persuade celebrities, musicians, and their representatives to take advantage of online publicity. Hendricks says she offered to bring artists online, but the labels' first response was, "Well, what are you going to pay me for that?" She remembers "trying to convince them that this was free promotion and marketing, and a way to get directly to their audience. No one really got that."

LEW HARRIS

Personal publicists had no idea at all what was going on with the Internet. Celine Dion had an album coming out and she wasn't quite huge yet, so I called her publicist. I said, "We want to do these things called Star Boards, where we'll put her name up and ask users to send in questions. She answers, sends them back and we'll post the answers."

It was kind of fun, and she could get close to the fans. Her publicist said, "Sure, that sounds great." So we collected the questions, sent them over, and we never heard back. I called the publicist and asked what was going on. She said, "Oh, she's on tour, she can't do it." This happened with four or five celebrities in a row.

Just before we launched, HBO's *Arliss* was starting up, and we called to do a feature on them. We did the interview, and the night before it's supposed to run, they sent us a contract. It said that the only way we could use their content and images was if we put ads for HBO on every page of the story. They'd *never* do this with a print publication! I had to call them up and say, "You know, you're crazy. I'll pull the story. It's *free publicity* for you."

––––––––––

Even Harris's own company took a while to catch on.

LEW HARRIS

The second we hit one million page views at E! Online, that finally got people's attention. And, in a funny way, that's when E!, our cable network, said, "Why don't you *do* anything for us?" We were set up to do original content that was nonpromotional. No one cared before the first million page views. They thought, "Aren't you guys cool, look what you're doing." But when we hit a million pages, it was, "Well, you should be promoting us." That's when the light bulb went off that we could really promote them on the Web.

At least E! Online had an offline brand to lend it some credibility. Most startups lacked a built-in name brand, and they did their darnedest to create one.

So what if "Do you Yahoo!?" could just as likely have meant, "Do you jerk off to photos of underage girls online?" rather than its intended "Do you search for information on the Web?" As with "I'll Google her" or "Just Ask Jeeves," the goofy Yahoo! name caught on overnight.

"Amazon, obviously, was the best," says Jerry Blanton, a branding strategist. " 'We don't want to get Amazoned' became part of the vernacular. 'Getting Amazoned' meant a big player coming in and taking over your particular niche."

ELIZABETH COLLET

When I first got the job at Yahoo!, I'd be on airplanes a lot and when people asked who I worked for, I'd say, "I work for Yahoo!." Then everyone would say, "Oh my gosh, the chocolate drink! I know that company." And I'd say, "No, it's Yahoo! It's on the Internet," and people would look at you completely blankly. People thought we were a division of Coca-Cola. We thought it was so funny that we'd keep Yoohoo bottles in the lobby, but really, we wanted our brand to be recognized. It was nice when people would say, "Oh yeah, I know Yahoo!—the Internet company."

Still, the brand name meant something. At one point, we got sued for trademark violation by Miss Marble Texas Yahoo Cake. She had a bakery and was famous for her Texas Yahoo Cake. They never told us exactly what they had to spend to keep the name, but I'm fairly sure we wrote her a large check.

DAVE BARTIS

Doug Liman's idea was that to brand yourself, you should make up a word like "Yahoo!". The initials NBC, of course, came from radio, National Broadcasting Company. But there was no real legacy for what we were doing, and we didn't want to call it College TV Network. We kept struggling with the words "film," "TV" and "network," and my thinking on it was we need to make up a word, but I didn't want it to be random. We were playing with the concept of information delivered as bits or bytes or packages. "Nibbles" was a treat of entertainment. And "box" came out of when TV was started.

The concept of Nibblebox just made us laugh. One of our early slogans was "Byte-Sized Entertainment." Warner's actually held the copyright for a campaign they did for *You've Got Mail*, so then we came up with "Entertainment Bytes." The whole thing started to work as a theme. Our logo was an "e" for "entertainment" with a bite taken out of it.

ASHLEY POWER

I guess Goosehead is an odd name, but we were moving and I tripped over a goose statue in the yard and broke the head off. I vaguely remember my mother screaming, "You broke the goose head!" That's how the name came about. You know how hard it is trying to name a Web site—you just get so desperate.

CATHY BROOKS

We were trying to brand ourselves, and we needed a name. It was a meeting when we all drank an extensive amount of sake, and one of the people wanted to put the word "red" before any name we came up with. She wanted our logo to be red because she thinks she looks good in red.

We had thrown around about twenty things that were very red, and finally I said, "Why don't we say something about San Francisco?" So someone said, "Why don't we do something about the bridge?" And that first woman said, "How about *Red* Bridge?" So I turned my head and kind of spat at her: "Red Bridge, Blue Bridge, One Bridge, Two Bridge. What the hell is this— Doctor Seuss?"

Then someone said, "Wait, wait, wait. Say that again!" I said, "What, 'Doctor Seuss'?" No, no, no. "Oh," I said, "You mean, 'Red Bridge, Blue Bridge,

"Our logo was an 'e' for 'entertainment' with a bite taken out," explains Nibblebox.com's cofounder Dave Bartis.

One Bridge, Two Bridge'?" They said, "That's it! Two Bridge. That's what we do. We bridge information. And we're in between the Golden Gate Bridge and the Bay Bridge."

So we settled on Two Bridge. But I don't think anyone else had a clue what it meant.

That wasn't the only problem. In addition to distinguishing themselves from canned carbonated chocolate milk drinks, startups also had to stand apart from competitors in their own field.

"Pets.com was a great brand," says Jerry Blanton. "They did everything right—they didn't fidget and switch ad direction every two minutes, and their ads were really brilliant." Yet they failed. Why? "The pet people killed themselves because all their names were the same," Blanton believes. "You advertised one, you advertised them all."

In other cases, the similarity was intentional, as when *Red Herring* tried to associate its brand with successful Old Media imprints like *Rolling Stone* and *Premiere* magazines by subliminally—or not so subliminally—copying their logos.

DOUG SCOTT

Basically, *Red Herring* was branded as the racing form for technology. When I was an executive at the magazine in 1993, we built that reputation up. Our first issue had Jaron Lanier—the guy who coined the term "virtual reality"—

on the cover. The logo was a spitting image of the *Rolling Stone* logo. But several months later we got a letter from *Rolling Stone*'s publisher, Jan Wenner, complimenting us on the magazine, but also saying that we'd ripped off his font, which they own the rights to, so we had to change the logo. From there we ripped off *Premiere*'s logo. We just iterated our logo one more time.

———————

R*ed Herring*'s brand-swindling aside, the magazine earned a solid reputation by focusing on one specific sector—smart, in-depth analyses of the VC scene and the technology market. Other Internet companies changed their business models more often than they altered their exit strategies—and it became increasingly difficult for these companies' marketers to keep up with the messaging.

Ted Kruckel, whose New York boutique PR firm took on "three or four of the biggest launches in the Net," recalls an even greater challenge: educating his uninformed New Economy clients.

TED KRUCKEL

It was never clear what they actually wanted us to do. For example, they would always talk about B2B messaging, yet they would ask about getting press in consumer outlets like *Wired*. I would be like, "No, no, no, those are B2C. Business-to-*consumer*, not business-to-*business*. Consumers read those publications. Business-to-business magazines are places like *AdWeek*. And they would be like, "Oh yeah, that too."

———————

These clients may have seemed confused, but that didn't dissuade ad agencies from taking their money. Some startups, like the ill-managed Modo, which sold a wristwatch-like gewgaw chock full of restaurant listings, burned through $27 million in funding in just ten months before it folded—having allowed the Portland-based agency Wieden & Kennedy to spend half of the startup's capital on flashy, big-city billboards and print advertisements. The result? A campaign that CNET.com described as "asking consumers to buy a $99 wireless *TimeOut* magazine in a city where the *Village Voice* was free."

Misguided Modo wasn't alone in its profligacy with venture capital. "More than Pets.com, the company, it was the Pets.com sock that was funded by VCs," says Doug Levin, a former Microsoft senior executive. "It was created for millions of dollars by some advertising firm where guys wore black and used the word 'cool.' Like, 'It would be really *cool* if we had a talking sock.' And now, after the fact, the company's dead and those socks are selling on eBay for twenty-five dollars."

"One thing that does stick in my mind is how the agencies always made the clients pay upfront," says the Ziff-Davis ad executive Jennifer Musillo. "That says a lot about what they thought of their clients—and how much faith they put in the success of their campaigns."

Even in-house advertising departments seemed amazingly absurd. Matthew Klauschie, then a young video editor at DEN, found the gaffes hilarious.

MATTHEW KLAUSCHIE

At DEN, the marketing was being run so poorly, and not just because they were spending a lot of money. I mean, this controversy's going down where our founder's being charged with homosexual pedophilia, everyone knows about it, it's public knowledge, and it's embarrassing. And then they come out with this slogan for their next campaign: "DEN, Spank Your Mind." And the whole theme is "Spank"! It was, "Spank" everything!

LEV CHAPELSKY

When I was the head of advertising for CarsDirect.com, we started out conservatively because we were afraid to spend money too quickly. But Bill Gross, the CEO of our incubator company, IdeaLab, ripped into us like there was no tomorrow. He said, "What the fuck do you guys think you're doing? That money is in the bank to spend, now get out there and spend it!"

So we did everything: network prime-time TV, radio, online, magazines, newspapers. The *Wall Street Journal, Business Week, Newsweek*—the most expensive print you could possibly buy. Everywhere you could spend money, we were spending it.

The Pets.com "spokespuppet" lives on, even if
the company it made famous doesn't.

Those who did business with these spend-it-all-now ad agencies and startups, on the other hand, seemed to be the unwitting Masters of this New
Universe, whose typical day was simply to sit by the phone and wait for an
order.

Kevin Wendle recalls picking up an issue of *The Industry Standard* "so thick
that I didn't even want to read it. I didn't even want to take it to the beach
with me. I thought, 'How could any rational ad exec think about putting an
ad in this magazine packed with distractions?' "

The same went for PR. It didn't take long for press overload—dubbed
"PR by the Pound" by Rare Medium's Gong Szeto—to afflict dot-commers. Szeto remembers his company sending out daily press releases
announcing. . . well, he wasn't always sure what.

"You just checked your email messages, and there was your scoop," says
The Industry Standard's Laura Rich.

To break through the clutter, companies needed to come up with more
creative marketing methods, ranging from trucks cruising Interstate 101

between San Francisco and Silicon Valley to a date with a former Disney executive turned dot-com CEO.

"Everyone was always looking for the homerun from a marketing standpoint," says Tom Lazaroff, who was the marketing director of PayMyBills.com. "There was this expectation that if you'd just do this one thing—be it a great publicity stunt or the right promotional offer—the floodgates would open and people would pour in."

ANDREW BRENNER

I was in an interview for a job, and the CEO had a model truck from the trucking company J. B. Hunt with the company logo on it. I said, "Oh, that's a really cute truck. Why do you have it?" He said that J. B. Hunt was pitching him to buy ads on trucks out here because all of the billboard space along the 101 was completely booked up for the next five years. So this was just a way to have ad space on the prime highway paved with gold in Silicon Valley.

ELIZABETH KALODNER

When I first got to SocialNet, I said to everyone, "I have two goals for the company: One is to make everyone a lot of money, and the other is to get myself married."

So someone came up with this promotional idea: "Win a Date with Our CEO and Make Her Mother Happy." The idea was to showcase our matching system. We picked twelve finalists, three in each of the four time zones.

It really was an effort to get ourselves on the map, and you couldn't spend enough advertising dollars to do it if you were just one more startup company. But if you were lucky enough to have a PR idea that could break through, that could make the difference.

So I went on all these dates and ended up dating one of the West Coast winners for five months. And the PR really worked—*Good Morning America* sent their film crew to Boise. We were also on *Extra!, Inside Edition,* CNN, and *To Tell the Truth*—which I did with my mom. Our registration went up 42 percent. I didn't get married, but it helped the company enormously.

Some tried to shout above the din with irreverence but instead got attention for perceived controversy.

TOM LAZAROFF

PayMyBills had the original "hurry up and get it out there" campaign, which was sort of the teaser campaign—the Howard Stern stuff. Then we had a month to put together a message. We came up with some unfortunate truths about life that were related to bills, with the idea that despite whatever those bad things were, we would be there to pay your bills.

We used humor like: "Men rate personality third; we'll pay your plastic surgery bills," or: "Tiny green monkeys are eating your toes; we'll pay your psychologist bills." But somebody is always offended by something. One slogan was something about, "Your undergraduate degree will be completely useless; we'll pay your tuition bill anyway." So some parents' group said this was undermining our need for education. The story ran on the San Jose news saying that the dot-coms are trying to get publicity by being controversial.

Others relied on a "viral marketing" or digital word-of-mouth approach. Dan Myrick of Haxan Films remembers when his *Blair Witch* Web site went from 10,000 to 8 million hits without a dime spent on advertising. It's a screen capture he says he'd show to his grandkids, both as a source of pride and a cautionary tale. "You don't need a fifty-million-dollar ad campaign," he insists.

DAN MYRICK

We didn't use ads or do anything on purpose. John Pierson had a show called *Split Screen* on the Independent Film Channel, so Gregg Hale, the producer, and I put together this short little trailer for *The Blair Witch Project* to raise money for the movie. It was a fake little trailer that we shot as an investment tape, but John dug it and put it on his show.

Next thing we knew, on John's Grainy Pictures Web site, this discussion just blew up about the trailer. For weeks, his discussion board was dominated by who Haxan Films was, what the trailer was all about, and did these guys have a Web site? We had a huge spike in our hit counts, and from that point on, we thought, "Holy Moley! The Web is this amazing advertising vehicle!" People emailed their friends about it, and it just exploded.

Getting the word out helps, but not until there's something tangible to promote. Yet many startups with little more than a newly registered URL cried "Web site!" prematurely. Worried that their competitors might be "first to market," they went ahead and pitched their products without—oops—*product*.

CATHY BROOKS

I worked for a company that had an idea of how to make it easier to integrate information within an individual company using the Web. Like, using the Intranet. Brilliant idea, brilliant idea!

We hand-picked a couple of media for the release and did a big launch at an elite industry conference. Front-page coverage. All the trades. Bunch of the business trades. All the analysts thought it was a great idea. The plan was to pull the plug for a couple of months. Go quiet. Then say, "Okay, we told you what we were going to do. Now, here are the real-world examples of this in action." But what the company failed to tell me was, all the customers that they had been talking about weren't actually in implementation!

So, we go dark for a little bit. And now it's time for me to go back to *Newsweek, Business Week,* and all the trades, and say, "Here's this story for you, this one for you"—so we'd have eight different customer stories and every media outlet would have a different one. Normally, we'd be likely to get half. But I didn't get any, because, frankly, there was nothing to say.

DOUG SCOTT

When I first got out to HSX in L.A., the cofounders, Michael Herman and Max Keiser, had taken out billboards on Sunset Boulevard that said "HOLLYWOOD STOCK EXCHANGE: www.hsx.com." But you'd go to that URL and it said, "Coming Soon." So here they are, spending hundreds of thousands of dollars pointing people to a Web site that was "Coming Soon"! These are two former investment bankers riding the wave of the Net craze.

Whether they were former bankers, former B-school boy wonders, or former sports stars (remember John Elway's failed MVP.com, cofounded with Michael Jordan and Wayne Gretzky?), company honchos often pressured their publicists to promote a site's personalities over its products. For some, it was more important to make the *Silicon Alley Reporter*'s "100 List" than to run a successful business.

But when the press did focus on the star and not the startup, just how effective was it? Depends on whom you ask.

TED KRUCKEL

I got lots of beauty editors to write up BeautyJungle.com. The site worked really well, and they had good consumer packaging that shipped on time. But that wasn't what the founders wanted in the press. They kept urging me to get profiles on *them*, the people behind the company.

In all honesty, these people were not media savvy, they were not ready for prime-time TV. They were not ready to be on camera and be interviewed. It was kind of a dream fantasy that they would become famous, and the site would be about their vision. Whereas if they had allowed me to push lipsticks and hair-care products that were exclusive to them, we could have kept going. But they wanted something much grander written about them.

And I just thought they needed to sell lipstick like crazy.

JEFF GOODELL

When Netscape was sort of coming around, Marc Andreessen, who was then around twenty-three, became this great poster boy for this whole revolution that they thought for about thirty seconds was going to destabilize Microsoft. The Netscape PR apparatus put him out in front while Jim Clark and others involved were in the background and didn't want the attention focused on them. But Marc was always out there with that famous photo of him picking his toenails on the cover of *Time*.

I think that kind of backfired for him a little bit. The story was really the company, but in the pitch, it was all about the poster boy.

ASHLEY POWER

ABC's *Primetime Downtown* did a piece on me, and that was huge. They came to my house the moment I woke up at six in the morning—while I was drying my hair getting ready for school—and followed me around for the day.

That definitely affected traffic on Goosehead. Our servers shut down. My stepdad was on the phone with the guy watching our servers, and he said, "Okay, it's going to air right now," and then all you heard was the guy screaming, "Oh, shit!" Our systems couldn't handle it. But it was great! Of course, then you have a newbie flood, which all the people on the message boards can't stand. They start crazy threads that make no sense.

JOSH KELLER

Right after I graduated from Harvard Business School, I was contacted by Betsy Morris, who was writing an article for *Fortune* ["MBA's Get .Com Fever"]. While I was driving from Boston to San Francisco to start UBUBU, she interviewed me, told me when the article was coming out, and that was that.

Then I got a call from the photo editor of *Fortune*, and he said, "We understand that you're traveling, but we'll fly a photographer anywhere you want, because we want a photo of you for the article." I didn't know it was for the *cover*. I said, "Well, okay, but I don't know where we're going to be the next day." I told him that the only place we know we're going to be is the Lake Tahoe area on such and such a date, because we had a friend who had a house there. So I suggested that we meet there, and they got really excited because that's gold rush territory.

You'd think a *Fortune* cover would have a great effect on a new company, but it didn't lead to much in terms of dollars and cents. There were no huge spikes in Web traffic and hits. It had some kind of reaction in the investing arena and from potential partners—like, "Yeah, I've heard of you guys. . . . Don't know from where, but I've heard about you guys"—but in the end, the biggest payoff I got was surprising my parents. It was a bit outside the realm of doing well in school or scoring a goal in soccer league.

Whether providing fodder for the family album or increasing site traffic, journalists wielded great power.

"It definitely gave you a haughty feeling all of a sudden," says Laura Rich of her experience as a columnist for *The Industry Standard.*

"Publicists really courted us," agrees the journalist Rebecca Eisenberg, remembering how "fun" it was to be a pundit for the *San Francisco Examiner* and CBS MarketWatch. "As Carl Steadman"—cofounder of suck.com and a former columnist for *The Industry Standard*—"said, we became microstars. "

PO BRONSON

I had written a piece about the company Epinions in *The New York Times Magazine* in the summer of 1999. It was about how some nine weeks earlier, they had been valued at $24 million. The week after my piece ran, they did another round, and they were valued at $84 million. Of course, since their previous valuation, they had added twenty-five people, but people would say to me, "You wrote this piece and suddenly added $60 million to their valuation for a company that's just at Round One!"

That was really eye-opening. I had wanted to give them attention, because I believed in what they had done. I thought that everyone rushing off to do the next AutoParts.com was just going to cash in, and I didn't respect it. But I was shocked that my article had that sort of effect. I realized I had to be really careful about who I'd talk about because, if I didn't watch out, I could make a lot of money for people I didn't like.

LAURA RICH

I wrote this story about an online entertainment company, Icebox.com. It wasn't a bad story, but I think that having a good story in the *Standard* meant so much, that having one not-so-great was like the worst thing in the world. So the company became really resentful of me. They felt like they had given me so much access, and been so helpful to me, and I'd slammed them.

I don't think that was the case. I just sort of questioned their business model. I backed it up with other people in the industry, and threw some numbers in there about how viable their business was. That's one of the things that we tried to do at the *Standard*, but a lot of other reporters got caught up in the excitement and didn't really question the business models.

———————————

Rebecca Eisenberg was one who did.

REBECCA EISENBERG

A pretty successful PR agent used to have dinners to accommodate her Internet clients, and I went to one. But I warned her beforehand, "My take of the industry is often cynical and you know that." And she said, "Yes, I know, you're not going to be pitched, you'll just meet them."

So I ended up writing about that dinner, really making fun of those CEOs. One of them said something really dumb about hype and another said something really stupid about his business and the industry. One had a real estate–oriented site, and another had an online storage company.

This publicist got really, really mad at me. I said, "Listen, I warned you. This is the kind of stuff I write." But she was really mad at me, and I think she probably still is.

———————————

Other publicists, like Ted Kruckel, believe that journalists were justified in refusing to shill for the new industry.

TED KRUCKEL

It was a double-edged sword, because every time you tried to place a story about one of your companies, a third of the journalists were trying to write negative stories about what a dumb idea or bad business you had. And often they had good reasons to write that.

The *Wall Street Journal* was writing an article on one of my clients, Ashford.com, a jewelry e-commerce site. So they ordered a diamond, and it arrived with a major flaw in it, one that their independent jeweler described as a scar. Well, if someone's buying an engagement ring, and it's described as having a *scar* in it, that's a bad thing! How else can you spin that?

In the Old Economy, many believed Andy Warhol's dictum that "the best publicity is the worst publicity." Not so in the New Economy, where, as Kruckel witnessed, "press outreach could have a negative impact"—if the site was picked up on a reporter's radar at all. "Sites were either hot or not," adds Kruckel. "Some ideas just could not get arrested."

Many of the ideas that couldn't get arrested eventually failed, leaving unemployed dot-commers searching for a new gig. But even as companies went under, spin survived, as demonstrated by this Peace Corps campaign targeting the newly "unhired."

DENNIS MCMAHON, PEACE CORPS SPOKESMAN

The Peace Corps did several ads that targeted people in the Internet scene. Initially we took out a couple of ads in a San Francisco independent weekly newspaper. One ad read: "Dot-com dot-gone? Now it's time to network in the real world. Peace Corps."

We have a minimal budget. We can't go crazy with billboards, but we probably received a thousandfold more exposure from the media attention generated from those ads than from the ads themselves. The *Wall Street Journal* picked up on the story, and NPR called us, as did *Time* magazine, the *New York Times*, and the *Washington Post*. We could never even hope to pay for that sort of advertising.

Then we got bus ads. Because we're a nonprofit, we made an arrangement with the company that does the transit advertising in the Bay Area and they agreed to put up our ads. So we had a bunch of three-by-eight-foot banners printed for buses that said: "Upgrade your memories, download the world." We thought it was a theme that would catch people who were computer-savvy.

And it worked.

CHAPTER SEVEN

THE
MISMANAGEMENT

We had no management. Every time I would come up with
an idea, I would really hit a wall. I answered to myself
most of the time. Looking at the org chart, a guy was
above me, but they would just tell me that we worked
together. I mean, all I said the whole time I worked there
was how much I wished someone would take me under
their wing and, like, teach me. You know?

—Twenty-five-year-old former producer at Disney's Go.com

I'm guessing we will look back at DEN ten years from
now as a symbol of an era that will then seem unreal—
when any[one]. . . could put together a staff of syco-
phants and plotters, and be rewarded by investors with
$65 million to waste on 12 months of Webcasting, all
because people back then placed monster bets on business buzzwords rather than on the people or products
pretending to operate by them. I was fortunate to have
the opportunity to see what Rome must have looked like
as it burned.

—Matt Welch, *Online Journalism Review,* May 25, 2000

It wasn't just the nonlaunch launch party and the "Be the Bunny" offsite, or
the fact that in my first week of work I had to fire two people I'd just met.
In truth, I'd already detected hints that Kibu was being run Forrest
Gump–style, at best.

To name a few:

1. Although I was hired as head of the site's content division, Kibu didn't bother checking my references before offering me the position. Not one. Nor had they checked the references of the fifty-plus employees already there. (Which, I guess, makes sense if you consider that the hipsters paid lawyer-like salaries to produce and write content for their channels had either worked in completely unrelated jobs or had never had one before. I mean, whom *could* Kibu call as references, their mothers?)

2. I learned at my interview that Kibu's current editor had suddenly decided to leave the company because "the teen-girl thing was never for him." I didn't ask why he had chosen to join a teen-girl Web site in the first place. Then, just as I was told that the CEO's "management style" was about "totally open communication," I was asked to keep the editor information a secret. (Again, I didn't ask why.)

3. Molly Lynch, the company's cofounder, whose most recent position had been secretary to one of our principal investors, had mentioned during our interview that she was done working long hours. "I'm tired by five," she said. "I want a life." Far as I knew, the founders of other startups were sleeping under their desks and working ninety-hour weeks. If you wanted to rest, you didn't launch a new company—you went to Hawaii. (Which is exactly what she did for much of the time I was at Kibu.)

In any other context, given signs of this magnitude—not subtle every-workplace-has-its-quirks signs, but flashing-billboard-in-Times-Square signs—I would have turned on my heels and run like Olympian Marion Jones. But this wasn't any other context—this was the millennial gold rush, where "rules were to be broken" and "paradigms were shifting." So I approached these red flags the way virtually every other hopeful did: I ignored them.

Meantime, I gushed to friends about how I couldn't wait to start my new job. I can only explain these sentiments with two words: Jim Jones. It was like everyone in the startup world—from entrepreneurs to board members to investors to employees—had become embroiled in a Jonestown-style mass delusion that led to none of us questioning what was in the Kool-Aid. So, what might have seemed like glaring caveats in my Old Economy Hollywood jobs seemed like nothing more than idiosyncrasies of the startup culture.

And I was willing to imbibe not just because everyone else had, but because there was no reason to doubt the flock. I'd never worked at an

Internet company, or a startup of any kind, so I wasn't about to walk into this brand-new environment with the smugness of a know-it-all. These people drove cars with sticker prices of more than $60,000. They thought nothing of spending $30 on lunch each day. Judy, our CEO, had started a company that sold to Mattel for mega-millions; Valley legend Jim Clark sat on our board; and the venture-capital firm Kleiner, Perkins had given Kibu a big-bucks blessing. Who was I to question their wisdom?

So I didn't panic when, my first day on the job, I learned that Kibu's "confidential" business model was revealed to be nothing more than a string of nifty-sounding phrases. The buzzwords used to describe our business plan were "integrated online marketing," but no one seemed able to explain what this meant in practice. According to Judy, it had something to do with girls getting redeemable points for responding to surveys furnished by our sponsors. Never mind that we had neither the sponsors nor the girls to make this work, nor the goods to be redeemed. Even if we did, "integrated online marketing" couldn't support the business. Apparently, we would also be making money through e-commerce.

Only problem was, we didn't have any products to sell. As far as I could tell, the sole product Kibu produced—and quite successfully, thanks to our savvy publicist—were reams of splashy press releases promising both a unique Web community and a revenue stream that didn't exist. It was genius: These dispatches created a media blitzkrieg, and, along with the public, we began to believe our own hype.

Which is why I also wasn't particularly worried when, my second day on the job, I attended the weekly All Hands—a companywide staff meeting that was supposed to ensure that each department, like Marketing, knew what the others, like Editorial and Business Affairs, were doing but instead consisted of singing "Happy Birthday" (no one broke thirty); complimenting a staffer on her "hot" red leather pants; sharing "your most embarrassing story" (strangely, most had to do with wraparound skirts falling off at inopportune moments); and, for no apparent reason (no deal closed, no significant jump in numbers), applauding ourselves for how great we were.

No matter what someone said ("It's Tuesday"; "That's Shannon's sushi"), it was always followed by high-pitched squeals and whistles, with an occasionally shouted, "Right on, team!" According to Judy, "the culture" was as important as the product.

The culture was so important, in fact, that Judy distributed a hand-out to all new employees, a Cliff's Notes version of "Kibu culture":

- Always assume the best intentions.
- Communicate directly.
- No factions.
- No scapegoats or favorites.
- Get through the issue and learn.
- Blame is a waste of time.
- Define the holy grail, the true north.
- Extreme pragmatism along the way.
- No entitlement.
- No whining.
- Sanity is important—let's be balanced.
- Confidence + humility.

Granted, this memo sounded more Oprah in tone than Jack Welch, but as a blueprint of company culture—and, presumably, its management style—at least it made Kibu seem like a pleasant place to work.

I was surprised, then, that the editorial meeting I called the next day turned out to be not another love-fest but the most difficult meeting I'd ever run—and this includes the time I volunteered to lead a group of troubled teens in prison. After some introductory remarks, I handed out proposed deadlines and production schedules for each channel, which were met not with appreciation or relief ("We need structure!" the Faces had beseeched at the launch party), but with dead silence and blank stares. The only noise in the room came from a dropped metal hair clip that the Face of Adventure was using to braid the Face of Books's hair.

Finally, the Face of School (whose sole qualification for this job appeared to be that she'd once gone to school herself—albeit as a self-described C student) asked, "What does an editor *do?*" I explained that I would help the Faces brainstorm, generate ideas, and refine their pieces, but it soon became apparent that the Faces thought I'd come in and write their copy *for them*. Each Face seemed to have the same agenda (how can I do less work now that the new editor's here?) which, of course, conflicted with every other Face's agenda of doing less work (if I do less work, some other Face who also wants to do less work will have to pick up the slack and do more). Tears were shed. Voices were raised. Whines resounded.

So much for "Kibu culture."

Still, I told myself, everything will be okay. After all, we'd just launched; people were understandably anxious. I figured that, with some reassurance, everyone would realize they could write adequate copy ("3-Channel Makeover" wasn't exactly *The New Yorker*) and gradually calm down. I decided to meet with each Face individually to address their concerns and offer some guidance.

But first, I wanted to check in with Judy, who preemptively declared that she didn't like to get "bogged down with details." (I later observed that her attention span lasted exactly three sentences, unless she was in the presence of a board member, an investor, or a cute guy.) I gave her the broad strokes: We don't have the budget, manpower, or sponsors to support twenty channels. I suggested the eventual possibility of consolidating some channels, like folding Advice into Relationships; and discarding others that seemed doomed to unprofitability, like Animals (most seventeen-year-old girls have lost interest in downloadable puppy stickers).

"Okay, you can let them go," Judy replied, eyes drifting with inattention. I mentioned that maybe she should be the one to have that conversation since, well, I'd literally just met these people, nor had I hired them, but she was adamant that I do the firing. "I'll be there for support if you want," was the best she could offer.

"And they're not being fired," she corrected me on the way out. "They're being *unhired*." Apparently, "firing" was also bad for "Kibu culture."

The Face of Animals took her unhiring gracefully (she had a day job at the local zoo), but the Face of Advice, a just-out-of-grad-school psychology Ph.D., immediately burst into tears. This was followed by pleading ("The girls *need* me!"), hysteria (hiccupy sobbing), threats ("I want my image taken off the site immediately!"), and, although I'm no therapist, what seemed like suicidal ideation ("This job meant *everything* to me. It was *my life!*"). Judy offered her tissues; I wanted to offer her a plane ticket to McLean. (I also immediately canceled her upcoming story, "How to Deal with Rejection.")

When I called a couple of days later to tie up loose ends and see how she was doing, our former Face of Advice wailed, "I still can't believe I'm being fired!"

"Oh, no," I assured her gently. "You're not being fired. You're just being, you know, *unhired*." It didn't sound that strange at the time.

The Kool-Aid finally began wearing off after I met with the remaining Faces to discuss their respective channels. To be fair, all of the Faces were incredibly nice, well-meaning, and talented people, but by no fault of their own, most had been hired to perform a job for which they simply weren't qualified.

Over the next few weeks, I learned that the Face of Horoscopes (who happened to be the CEO's cousin) didn't "believe in astrology"; the Face of Fashion (who drove a Porsche) kept forgetting that teen girls shop at The Gap, not Gucci; the Face of Wellness (an earnest Martha Stewart-like ophthalmologist) was interested exclusively in sharing healthy recipes (when I suggested that her content could be a bit more "fresh," she thought I was asking her to post a salad recipe); the Face of Beauty used the word "luscious" so incessantly (luscious lipstick, luscious liner, luscious lids) that when I did a search for "luscious" and left the "replace with" space blank, the word count in her 150-word piece went down by 30; and the Face of Guys (a Backstreet Boys doppelgänger and the Face of Hair's twenty-year-old brother) called me "uptight" because I wouldn't let him wax poetic about the hot chicks featured in his favorite magazine, *Maxim*, on a site aiming to provide "insight" and "inspiration" to teen girls.

At the end of my first month, I attended *Fortune* magazine's extravagant party at San Francisco's Ruby Sky in honor of what its editors called "cool companies." Thanks to our ubiquitous media coverage, Kibu had been included in this category. I schmoozed the room and spouted the buzzwords from our press releases (*Fun! Fresh! Knowledgeable! Uninhibited! Inspired!*). I talked about how our Faces were serving as role models for teen girls across the country and how our site, unlike all those shallow digital *CosmoGirl!* clones, was giving young women a unique voice in cyberspace. Then I drove home and stayed up until three A.M. editing pieces on glitter nail polish, seamless bras, and why unscented hair gels are better than pomades.

Something had to change.

———————

Apparently, our CEO needed a change, too. At the next All Hands meeting, Judy announced that burnout should be prevented before it makes you crabby, and that she'd therefore decided to chill out on a beach in Hawaii. By coincidence, Molly Lynch was already on the tropical island, as was our Face of Fashion. (At a later All Hands we were treated to photos of the three bikini-clad women perched on stools at a ritzy hotel's beachfront bar, laughing with a beefy pro football player and sipping giant mimosas.)

In any event, now that our bosses were M.I.A., certain patterns became clear for the first time. For instance, the people at the company who could do no wrong were either relatives or friends of the CEO. Analogous to Bill Clinton's infamous "Friends of Bill," or "FOBs," these groupies became known as the "Friends of Judy" or "FOJs." Included in this posse were her sister, her brother-in-law, her cousin, her former hairdresser and *his* brother, her department-store makeup-counter artist, and a model she'd befriended on an airplane.

My other observation, however, was that everyone at Kibu looked the same (black capris, snug Lycra tops, wedgy sandals, perfect bodies), acted the same (kiss-kiss, rah-rah enthusiastic), talked the same ("Rockin'!" "Right on!" "You go, girl!" "LOVE it!"), and had the same interests (the perfect G-string). They all sported lavender toenail polish and used a hair-straightening device called a Flat Iron to make their locks look like Jennifer Aniston's on *Friends.* Even the interns, cutesy local high school girls paid to do nothing more than flirt with the hormonal Face of Guys, appeared to have just stepped off the set of *Beverly Hills 90210* or *Dawson's Creek.* I, on the other hand, worked eighty-hour weeks, developed stress acne, stopped exercising, and let my curly hair air-dry as I returned an onslaught of calls on the way to work each morning.

And so it became increasingly difficult to separate out the world of our audience from the world of our business. "My boyfriend was in town, and we hadn't slept together in a while," one Face replied matter-of-factly when asked why she'd missed several deadlines in a row, leaving me to write her copy overnight. Another Face called me a "bitch" to a fellow Face because I didn't authorize an expense that wasn't, well, business-related ("If my photo's gonna be up on the site, I have to get regular facials," she asserted). When I asked one Face to rework a paragraph, she sulked for days and accused me of "liking the other Faces better."

Soon two cliques formed, composed of those who tried to keep the business on track ("the studious kids," a small management team), and those who just wanted to have fun ("the popular kids," almost everyone else). I began having vivid memories of high school, and if there's one lesson I learned from that adolescent arena, it was that if you wanted to exert any power at all, you had to belong to the popular crowd.

I called an emergency meeting with the Face of Hair.

The effects of the Flat Iron were instantaneous, allowing me to look like a clone of my Kibu kin. The Faces complimented me on my sleek new tresses. They said "Hi" to me in the Excite@Home cafeteria and invited me to parties. They gave me eye shadow and blush samples as tokens of our truce. They joked around with me and confided their boyfriend and imaginary cellulite problems.

When I started dating someone new, the Face of Relationships gave me a "highly recommended" instructional video that had been circulating in the office, a hand-job bacchanal featuring the well-endowed "Matt" and "Steve" and entitled *An Intimate Guide to Male Genital Massage*. Most important, the Faces showed up for many of their story meetings, pretended to appreciate my suggestions, and turned in their work pretty close to deadline.

I was beginning to think that there might be hope for Kibu after all.

Until, that is, Judy returned tanned and rested from Hawaii. The Faces were doing their best, but Kibu still needed a major overhaul. Although we called ourselves an online community, engineering informed me that *any* interactivity (message boards, chat) was months away; Production said that the redesign (we didn't even have a *navigation bar*) had been delayed again; our site constantly crashed on Macs, resulting in angry emails from the large percentage of teen girls who used them; the Face of the Kibu Studio, a multi-million-dollar live space in San Francisco's Ghirardelli Square due to open within weeks, was having anxiety attacks because she had no idea what the other Faces would be doing there when (and if) teens arrived; our target audience age changed daily from thirteen to eighteen; we were hemorrhaging money like hemophiliacs with a paper cut ("Treat the Faces like 'talent,'" Judy insisted, which only added to their diva-dom); my suggestions on how to attract "eyeballs" and therefore sponsors were deemed "not as big a priority right now as establishing the culture"; and despite the On Your Feet offsite, no one had ever decided what our business actually *was*: a Community, a Destination, a Portal, a Multimedia Enterprise, a Content Provider, or a Digital Lifestyle Brand.

When I raised these issues with Judy (I had carefully planned how to present my case in exactly three sentences), her response was to label me "negative." If there was one thing she couldn't abide, she said, it was people who weren't "team players." Work had to be "fun," and as a result, making people "happy" trumped our small management team's concerns (including the one that our condescending product conflicted with Kibu's mission statement of empowering teen girls). In particular, she said, the teen girls she spoke to thought our Face of Guys was "delicious" and I should therefore let him do whatever he wants.

Picking up some Kibu-branded tea bags strewn about the office and emblazoned with inspirational girl-power slogans like "sheology" and "girlosophy," I asked if she felt comfortable letting our Face of Guys advise a teen-girl audience that it's okay for a guy in a committed, exclusive relationship to kiss another girl, because that's not really cheating. (In our editorial meeting, I'd asked if it was likewise okay for a girl in a committed, exclusive relationship to kiss another guy, to which our Face of Guys responded with an outraged, "NO WAY!")

"He's our most popular Face," Judy repeated. "Let him do whatever he wants." In fact, she declared, let *all* of the Faces do exactly what they want. "Bond with them," she urged me. "It's in the interest of Kibu culture."

Because Kibu culture also espoused "totally open communication," within minutes word got out that the Faces could write whatever they pleased, and that their editor had been told to take a backseat. By the end of the day, I'd been kicked out of the proverbial 90210 beach house. I should have remembered that when you were in the popular crowd in high school, having an alternative opinion was tantamount to heresy.

That night, I went home and, instead of editing, finally watched the male genital massage video with my boyfriend. When the feathered-haired, white-tuxedoed narrator repeatedly referred to a ten-foot-high replica of the male genital organ as a "magic wand," I remarked to my boyfriend that unless Kibu's management did a reality check—and fast—it would take a real live magic wand to make the company viable.

At our next All Hands, two men, purportedly there to "observe," appeared around the conference table. One was Kibu's first—and belated—VP of finance (whose "most embarrassing story" had something do to with accidentally calling a friend's new bride the ex-girlfriend's name at their wedding), and the other was one of our investors (who glanced impatiently at his watch and seemed wholly unamused by our time-consuming "most embarrassing story" ritual).

Although "Girls Who Get It" was Kibu's slogan, it seemed that these two outsiders might be the ones truly "getting it." I spoke with our finance guy,

who was able to convince Judy that budgets needed to go into effect immediately—Kibu culture be damned. Corporate credit cards were collected.
Employees had to account for time out of the office and meet project deadlines. Our overpaid Face of Wellness could no longer hire an intern to write
her copy at an hourly rate while she spent the afternoon at Tae Bo classes.

Judy even agreed to let the management team run an offsite meeting to
address the Big Issues (role of the Faces, target audience, business model,
engineering needs, what Kibu *is*, exactly) that she'd dismissed out of hand
weeks before. Kibu was in crisis mode, but at least our energies were being
focused in the right direction. Sure, we had virtually no sponsors, no users,
no business plan, and our lavish live studio space was about to open, but if we
stayed the course, it seemed like Kibu might have at least the *chance* to succeed.

And then, astonishingly, Judy eloped in Bali.

Corporate mismanagement, as the Black Panther leader Huey Newton
opined in the 1960s about street violence, "is as American as cherry pie." Take
Henry Ford's disastrous planning and production of the Edsel in the 1950s; or
Westinghouse's imperfect original formula for commercial electric current,
which was at first deemed safe enough only to fry prisoners strapped in an
execution chair.

Unlike the New Economy's house-of-cards architecture, however, temporarily shamed companies like Ford and Westinghouse were built on a
bedrock of stable resources that allowed their blunders to pass into the midst
of historical footnotes. Not so the scores of doomed startups.

The Young Turks dominating the New Economy failed to usher in a so-
called New World Order owing not to a lack of ambition but, perhaps,
too much. Some viewed these bright kids as visionaries; others, however,
like the more cynical-minded J. Betty Ray, saw them simply as "dot-com
yuppie scum." An adolescent sense of entitlement coupled with a laugh-
able lack of adult experience inexorably led to arrogance, waste, and
strategic blunders.

Sometimes their attempts at revolution morphed into absurdities hiding behind rationalizations. How else to justify the excesses of the man-

agers at the fashion startup Boo.com, which began by spending hundreds of thousands of dollars on travel and renting hideously expensive board-rooms in ultraswanky hotels? "Change-of-scenery meetings," was the official explanation.

Yet for all the talk of "creating new management paradigms," some sta-ples of poor business practices remained as clichéd as the Man in the Gray Flannel Suit. "There was a ridiculous level of nepotism in manage-ment," says Chris Ewald, a Web consultant who served as CTO of Balduccis.com. "People were brought in not because they were the most qualified, but because of their relationships with others in the company. It was, 'Hire people and *then* figure out what to do with them.'" At the online entertainment site DEN, former employees claim that hiring was also based on who knew whom, often in the biblical sense.

Kibu may have earned the *Wall Street Journal's* dubious title of "poster child for mismanaged Web startups," but Kibu, Boo, and DEN aren't isolated examples of what has since become known as "myth management." There's a reason that "Silicon Valley"—a mentality more than a location—was dubbed "Silly Valley." Hundreds of people really did walk into what was supposed to be a cool new job, only to find on their first day of work that their boss had been fired the night before and that nobody had bothered to tell the new hire, let alone find a promised replacement. Ever.

How could this happen? Fledgling Internet companies felt they had to ramp up at orbital speed, and ultra hip humanities graduates usually without any technical or management skills made up the hiring pool. "It was just, 'Come on in, we'll give you some ridiculous title!'" remembers Brad Nye, founder of VIC, the once-popular networking organization for Los Angeles dot-commers.

In previous years, English and psychology majors would have picked the "Do not pass Go; head directly to medical, business, or law school to make yourself marketable" card. But suddenly, these twenty-two-year-olds were *immediately* marketable. Even high school students, like Ashley Power, the Goosehead.com founder, could become company presidents.

Never mind that many knew more about *Macbeth* than management. Almost everyone abided by the twin mottos of "We'll just figure it out as we go along" and "Don't trust anyone over thirty." Gut and intuition were valued almost as much as stock options, while proven methodology was viewed with suspicion.

"I saw it as a younger generation tugging at an older one and saying, 'Much needs to change.' We didn't feel we needed to learn from our elders," says twenty-four-year-old Shuli Hallack. "But you can't give young people everything, like free lunches, raises, and games. They'll think they know it all and they'll get spoiled. In fact, it's just like the movie *The Last Emperor.*"

Or like the film business in general, where hopefuls with thin résumés and wide smiles show up expecting to run the show. But David Neuman, the former DEN CEO, feels that some young dot-com managers took entitlement and arrogance to another level entirely.

DAVID NEUMAN

The entertainment business is full of young people who rise to high positions very quickly, but the attitude in the Internet economy was different. Instead of somebody who was ready to pay their dues, work hard, kiss ass, salute their superiors, and do everything they could to succeed in the company, you had a different mentality: "If you don't recognize my brilliance at twenty-five, then you're an idiot."

When DEN started I was thirty-seven. I understood the overachieving young executive, and I did what I could to mentor a lot of the young managers we had in our company. Some of them were really open to that, and some were contemptuous of it, really. There was a swagger and arrogance that was unique at that time, because their reality was different. They were saying to themselves, "Well, Marc Andreessen has never had to deal with this, so neither should I."

RICHARD TITUS

At Razorfish, we hired a certain type of person. People on the outside like to say that it was guys with blue hair or girls who were really good-looking, but that wasn't the case. We hired really, really smart people. We expected you to be not just smart, but the arrogant kid at school who always knows the answers, but never raises his hand or cooperates. The rebel in the back who throws rocks.

It was very successful for a while, but the problem was that we built the company with mavericks. You're talking about operational issues, and you have a company filled with really smart mavericks who, as long as they're all going in the same direction, they'll do fine. But the minute they stop going in the same direction, they're going to fail.

ELIZABETH COLLET

Most of these twenty-year-old kids didn't have the combined skill set of an interesting idea, the ability to pull it off from a fundraising perspective, and the ability to be good managers of a big company. The ones who did well were the ones that let the gray-haired manager be the CEO. Our cofounders, Jerry Yang and Dave Filo, immediately stepped aside and said, "We aren't running this business. We're going to hire someone," and in this case it was Tim Koogle as CEO and Jeff Mallett as COO.

Jerry and Dave were freed up to be the spiritual leaders. Dave spent all his time programming. And Jerry was the opposite: the public spokesperson, the poster boy traveling all around the world doing conferences. The egos of the young entrepreneurs who say, "I came up with the idea so therefore I'm going to run it"—that's just hubris.

LAURA RICH

With my *Industry Standard* column, I always wrote about these young kid founders who would get replaced by people with more experience. But it was a shock to them, *every single time.* And I was like, "Don't you read my column?!" Writers, senior editors, and reporters—we were always saying, "Where's your management? Why isn't your management reading our stories?" Because we were showing how it was all very predictable. It became a formula: The kid founder got his money, then got replaced. It was such a pattern.

Despite this rampant denial, a few rookies were painfully aware of their inexperience. Maria Isabel Gouverneur, an economics major, "didn't expect to be hired" as a designer at Rare Medium. "I didn't have any Internet experience," she says, "but I had one interview, and was hired right away."

SANG LEE

The most humorous thing was watching some of the people that I worked with at Rare Medium pretend to know more than they did. I knew what my limitations were, but I'd see some of these people with art history backgrounds trying to answer questions from prospective clients about whether they could do X, Y or Z, or whether they thought it was a good idea to invest money in A, B, or C. They didn't understand the implications of getting into these businesses, but they were paid a lot for their "expertise."

AUREN HOFFMAN

At Kyber Systems, we had no idea how to hire. We had just graduated, and we were hiring students at fifteen dollars per hour. One night, we had a project due at nine A.M., and two of our employees flaked out on us because they had *midterms!* I had never coded before in my life, so my partner sat me down and put two computers next to each other. He coded on one and he taught me how to code on the other. We were barely able to get the product out. We never should have had our entire staff made up of students. But we were young and we didn't know any better.

Still, many believe that youth actually fueled, not derailed, the industry. What the tyro managers lacked in business experience they made up for in the energy to pull all-nighters, the willingness to take risks, and, most important, a fresh perspective. They hadn't been burned out or fucked over yet. They had already made the transition from paper to bytes in college or high school. And they were precisely the demographic that the media and business world's most coveted.

"In the beginning I would just laugh at the Internet kids," says Alan Citron, "but as soon as they became millionaires and billionaires, you had to take them more seriously." Some, like Rare Medium's Gong Szeto, feel that the forty-somethings, Luddites and gold-diggers alike, were partly to blame for the rampant "myth management."

GONG SZETO

It was amazing to see seasoned executives get overwhelmed by the speed and vigor at which this thing moved. Sure, there are all kinds of stories of young, energetic entrepreneurs mismanaging people, but the same thing happened to these forty-year-olds. When you first meet them, they walk in with a swagger. And when they resign or are fired, they're walking out with their tails between their legs.

LYNN HARRIS

You had kids who were bossing around grownups, but you also had a lot of grownups from other realms coming in to take over the Internet who couldn't use e-mail. These people didn't know what they were doing. I'll wager that while there were flaws in the youthful leadership, they definitely had grown up with some semblance of computers and the Internet, and that's not something to be underestimated.

MATTHEW KLAUSCHIE

The guy I reported to at DEN was in his late forties. He was one of the older guys, a real character. There was a hierarchy, but they tried to play it off like, "We want everybody's input," which wasn't really true. There were higher-ups who didn't want input from the younger employees, or weren't willing to pay attention.

When I was first starting, they asked me to go through all the content, watch everything on the site, and write my reviews of everything. So I was like, shit, this sucks. It just *sucked*. The content was terrible, and the production values were pretty poor, so I wrote down all my thoughts. I mean, our demographic was like the people who were working there—literally, teenagers and early twenty-year-olds.

But nobody paid attention, so after like a month, I got the e-mail address-es for the board of directors and producers, and I wrote that we should have a survey that all employees take, and we should have an open brainstorm on how we can make this content better. One of the main producers, who was kind of an MTV hotshot, came to me and said, "Oh man, you're making a lot of friends around here. You better be careful, man, you may not have your job for very long."

All these older producers are coming up and saying, "We're just starting off, it takes time for these things, we want you to see some of the new stuff we're working on." But I pushed for the survey, they asked me to write it, and I e-mailed it. Then I tried for two months to get them to deliver it to all the employees, but they never did. And the content continued to suck.

———————

Young or old, hip or wonk—the result was often corporate boneheadedness. It was as if each company chose from a menu called "How to Destroy a Company" when they received their funding. Panic only exacerbated the descent. Traffic's down? *Hire a new head of online marketing.* Fast-forward three weeks: Traffic's still down? *Fire the new head of content and hire another.* You can't find anyone? What about Jimmy in engineering? *He seems bright—hire him!*

Adeo Ressi sadly recalls his experience of selling his Web shop, Methodfive, to a competitor, Xceed: "This was part of my personal naiveté because I actually believed that Xceed was going to do what they said. And then to go into the harsh world of what the Internet had become: unprofitable companies and terrible management. One individual at Xceed switched the sales management process and organization—they literally changed every-thing—six times in four months! There was a new management, new process, and new ideas in less than a three-week cycle. You can't do that. Your clients expect certain deliverables. If you keep changing it on them, they go away."

CarsDirect.com's Lev Chapelsky shared Ressi's frustration at watching company managers concoct their corporate strategies on the fly.

LEV CHAPELSKY

Bill Gross, the CEO of our incubator company, felt he had the right to change his mind and do complete turnarounds without cause. He wanted to stick in a new CEO, and I don't know where the pressure came from, because

Scott Paynard, the CarsDirect CEO, was his wunderkind. Then all of a sudden, Bill Gross was like, "Whatever Scott's doing, eliminate it."

When the new CEO came in, he brought in all his investment banking and management consulting buddies. Bill's position was, "This guy 'gets it.'" That was the primary qualification for people working in the Internet space, but there was no definition for "getting it." You had to be able to talk the talk and walk the walk, but this guy didn't "get it"—he didn't understand who people at our company were, what they were doing, or why they were doing it.

The designer Nicholas Goldsmith and the publicist Ted Kruckel realized that you didn't have to be in-house at a startup to get a taste of the "whoops, scratch that" management style.

NICHOLAS GOLDSMITH

When Boo.com started, they had no facilities manager and didn't know how much equipment space they would need. So somebody would come on board and say one thing, and then in three weeks, he was gone. Then somebody else would come on board and say something completely different: "Oh no, the server room needs to be bigger, you need to walk around it on all sides." Finally, we ended up building a larger room than what was required because it kept getting bigger and bigger!

TED KRUCKEL

Every single company that I represented screwed up the announcement date. They'd say, "We'll launch October third," then, "We'll launch October twentieth." And they'd miss that, too. I was like, "Stop doing that!" and each company would say the same thing: "You don't understand our business. This company is driven and we won't miss the date." But they would. Each and every time. Finally, I'd say, "Oh, but you *will* miss the date. Don't you understand that you're *incompetent?*"

The incompetence extended beyond senseless strategy changes to misplaced priorities.

DAN ADLER

One problem is the notion of having a great technology, and *then* searching for some application for it. That's certainly the backward way to do it. The way to do it is to search for something that people need or want, and then find them a way to get it.

A bunch of people were running around saying, "Isn't that great? A million people can watch our stream simultaneously." Well, a million people can watch a stream on a cable network simultaneously, too. And they don't have to worry about latency or a tiny window. They can sit on their butt in front of a TV. If they're not getting more premiums, like interactivity, then it's not really a good technology. There was so much excitement about the fact that you *could* do it, that people lost sight of the fact that this may not be something that you *want* or *need* to do.

CAMERON HICKEY

At Boo.com, the cofounder, Kajsa Leander, spent so much time focusing on what Miss Boo would look like. She would speed back and forth from London to New York to decide what hairstyle she would have, or what top she should wear. They were spending tens of thousands of dollars on an animated avatar that they thought would enhance our brand, but we didn't even have a *database* that worked. The information in our database is bad, the Web site can't process orders, nothing functions properly, but they only cared about this animated cartoon avatar.

SHULI HALLACK

In the summer of 2000, we got out of an All Hands meeting and two laptops were missing. We couldn't check the security tape, because they stole that too, since it was sitting at the reception on the way out. Only then did the management think to *lock* the security tape in the server room. Then they finally got a really expensive alarm system. Of course, it was never armed because the facilities manager from New Jersey was the only person who knew how to turn it on, and never did. She's gone now and, since nobody knows the code, it never gets turned on. That's sort of how things were run at Rare Medium: we spent all this money and energy on the wrong things.

CHRIS EWALD

People entirely missed the point. In one meeting, we were building models for a Web site. We were whiteboard brainstorming on how to visually present the models, and one of the lawyers actually *copyrighted* the whiteboard. He got up, drew a "c" with a circle around it, signed his name, and said, "I'm copyrighting this." We were all stunned. It was so absurd. After that, it became clear that the project was going nowhere.

DOUGLAS SCOTT

Our cofounder, David Herman, had brought in Josh Katz of VH–1 at $15,000 a month to design a $70,000 fuzzy media kit. Just ridiculous shit is going on. Stan Weil is brought in from the cable business to be our executive VP of sales. This is a guy that Ted Turner had put out to pasture. But for some reason, we hired a sixty-five-year-old sales guy who knew *nothing* about the dot-com space. He didn't feel as if he had to sell because he was an executive vice president. So, he's building a fat-ass department with a VP and two directors. It's like, *"Hello!"*

No wonder Web startups got a bad reputation when it came to accountability—or lack thereof. Food.com's David Gilcreast believes that "too much access to the capital market" may have contributed to this lax attitude. "Management didn't really have to answer to anything that they implemented," he says.

DAVID GILCREAST

If a startup did something wrong or if something didn't work, they could just blame it on the market at the time. Or, if it was a misdirected idea, they'd say, "If we get more funding we'll figure it out." Funding was so accessible that they thought they could just pour more money into their companies. The rationale was, "Everyone's making this up as they go along, so we have to be prepared to make mistakes and figure it out."

But those who worked in this environment found the flaky "figure-it-out-later" principle particularly exasperating.

TOM LAZAROFF

One of my original concerns coming to PayMyBills was, What is our revenue model? Bill Gross would say over and over again, "Don't worry about revenue, just get the eyeballs and we'll figure out how to monetize them later." I wish I had a dollar for every time I heard it.

To me, that idea was so foreign. In the first two rounds, it was all IdeaLab money, and they're the ones saying to "Go free"— offer the service for free. Bill asked, "What does it matter if you're getting $7.95 from these customers?" and I said, "Well, actually, it does matter."

If you're telling customers you'll do their finances for free, anybody who has half a brain has to say, "What's the catch here?" In January of 2000, we had a limited offer that anyone who signed up would get the service free for two years. Like I suspected, a lot of people signed up, but almost nobody actually used it.

CATHY BROOKS

In PR, you didn't get started with a client until you had some basic questions answered: Do you have anyone using the product right now? I don't care if it's in final-beta, but this needs to be in real-world use, not in a test lab. Do you have any customers?

Do you have any revenue, or what is your planned timeline for becoming profitable or breaking even? How much money did you take from the VC community? The more of their own money that they put into the product and the R&D, the more likely that the company would be around.

Not a lot of startups had answers to these questions. I found out most didn't even *ask* them in the first place.

DAVID NEUMAN

Very early on in DEN's history, Marc Collins-Rector was out to grow an AOL- or Yahoo!-level company. I remember asking, "Gee, what if we grew this gradually? I would be perfectly happy after a couple of years if we had a $100 million business, a chance to get the product right."

And his point of view was, if you go at that pace, you will be passed by. The Internet economy, blah-blah-biggest-fastest, and if we don't pour money into getting that marketing and brand position early on, we'll be wiped out.

LYNN HARRIS

In the world of Web content there was a sense of just get the content/brand/space and we'll figure it out later. It's like when you're running to get a space in Central Park for the free opera: just mark the space with a blanket, and we'll figure out the picnic later. That's an inept analogy because the picnics are always fine. But the sense of getting the space and not thinking about what will actually work, or what architecture will support the idea, or what content people want? That's what tripped things up.

Possibly the most egregiously visible form of ineptitude was the massive amount of cash thrown away on seemingly nothing. Ask any business school professor—from Harvard to Stanford to an instructor who teaches correspondence courses advertised on the back of matchbook covers—and you'll hear the following: Startup companies are supposed to be frugal. Modest expense accounts. Coach air travel. Bic pens.

But ask many New Economy players for a startup business credo, and they might have replied: profligacy in lieu of profitability. Which may explain how Boo.com managed to burn through $185 million in a little over a year, only to sell its remaining assets for pennies on the dollar.

Matt Welch, writing in the *Online Journalism Review*, recalled his experience as a consultant at DEN. "Whenever I stepped outside of my extremely narrow working group (me and the guy who brought me in), any spending or hiring number I suggested was almost automatically doubled, followed by comments such as: 'Spend the money! It's not yours, after all, and they've got tons of it!' "

The annals of wastefulness are legion.

DAVID NEUMAN

In the summer of 1999, DEN's burn rate was $5 million a month, and I remember making the observation that we never had more than four months' worth of cash in the bank to sustain us. Some of us had heartburn on a daily basis.

Marc called the executive management team around the conference table, talking about the burn rate, and he said, "I want that burn rate up to ten million a month within sixty days." All of us looked at each other with eyes widening. What in the world?

I pulled Marc aside later and said, "Explain to me why this is a rational course of action." And he just looked at me and said, "David, if you want to ask for a lot of money, you've got to need a lot of money." I thought, "Oh, boy."

JIM MEDALIA

I was at one of these VC get-togethers in New York, and I was talking to a VC about JustBalls. I said that we were making just under 30 percent margins, and that we'd be profitable within a year if things continued. She looked at me and said, "What would anyone want to be profitable for?" It was one of these telling moments of the kind of extreme that things went to. The investment community wasn't interested in profitability.

PHILIP "PUD" KAPLAN

When I was at Think New Ideas, we had to build a new Web site for Avon. We did it in about three months with two full-time guys. There was a programmer on the project because even though I was a programmer by trade, I worked as a project manager for the company.

They billed one million dollars for the site! I just laughed when I heard that. I was making like $55,000 at the time. It was such bullshit. I remember being in so many meetings when Avon would ask for something that was really basic, that would take me like an hour to do on my own. It was my job to price stuff, so I figured an hour for a programmer is about $150 or whatever.

But then the senior manager on top of me would say, "Well, you have to add an hour of your time and an hour of a database guy's time and blah blah blah," and by the time we were done with it, it would seriously cost tens of thousands of dollars. And the client would okay it! They just didn't know. They thought of the Internet as a big magical black box.

This would literally happen weekly—that we charged a company $35,000 for something that took a day to do.

KENNY LIN

I realized earlier this week why we were charging millions and millions for projects—we produced an unbelievable amount of paperwork. Every meeting was replete with agendas, project schedules, and documents for every participant. E-mails were printed out and inserted into binders. We spent half a day throwing away binders of stuff from former colleagues. For a company in the digital economy, we seemed overly reliant on paper and laser printers.

CHRIS KINNEAR

From my perspective, the biggest waste of money wasn't the stuff around the eToys office, it was all these new site initiatives. We'd all of a sudden feel like we should get into the hobby market, and create a whole new store. But instead of building something small in a traditional business sense, we just did flat-out, straight development every time. We built a summer shop and spent $100,000 on a photo shoot for it. Well, how many toys are you going to need to sell to offset *that*?

Some companies crossed the line from monetary mayhem to outlandish scandals worthy of last week's episode of *America's Most Wanted*. The hype, youth, and wealth of the industry made the New Economy's outrageous tales of employee harassment, blatant theft, and felonious behavior seem almost as juicy as watching Michael Milken and his toupée being led off to jail.

The most talked about Silicon Babylon scandal was the one involving DEN, the infamous Netcaster generously funded by deep-pocketed investors—including Microsoft, Dell, and the then high-flying energy company Enron (hmm)—sought to capture the Gen-Y market through delivery of "webisodes" (read: cheesy online television). It's bad enough that the company's obscene executive salaries made it the butt of a host of dot-com jokes. Even worse, just weeks after DEN filed for a $75 million IPO, the company's cofounder and chairman resigned after settling a civil lawsuit filed in federal district court in which it was alleged that he had been doing more than baby-sitting with a junior-high-school-age boy. Meantime, employees were thought to be misappropriating enough goods to fill a Neiman-Marcus catalogue. DEN eventually closed its doors on May 17, 2000, having burned through more than $65 million.

DEN's CEO David Newman reportedly received a $1.5 million salary and $1 million signing bonus.

DAVID NEUMAN

There were a ridiculous number of stories about salaries at DEN. I was brought in with a huge salary that was widely published. But these salaries eventually all got trimmed. Within a year, I radically reduced my salary a couple of times, because it was a problem for the business and I wanted us to succeed. I took it down to 15 percent of what it was when I started. Those things never got reported because they don't fit with the stories that sell books or magazines—stories about excess and mismanagement.

BOB MAKELA

Neuman's version was that so much of what was reported in the *Los Angeles Times* was wrong. But there was no doubt that there was weird, freaky stuff going on. When there's an eighteen-year-old kid, who looks like he's thirteen, driving up in a Mazaratti or Lamborghini type of car, and he's the number three guy in the company, and he's this feminine, hairless boy cruising around—I mean, c'mon.

When we were shooting bathroom scenes for *Frat Rats*, I remember one of the execs asking me, "Can you get more shots of the guy's ass when they're coming out of the shower?" The intent to reach a homosexual audience was never stated, but when this goes on and most of the top guys are gay, you can only wonder if part of this is servicing their fantasies.

MATTHEW KLAUSCHIE

A week after I got to DEN, my friend told me right off the bat, "You know, the founder of this company is a pedophile." But the pay was good, and I was desperate. I didn't know what I was going to do when I got out of school. It was just this big unspoken understanding that the founder was a whacko, and two of his boyfriends were in upper management. One of them was probably nineteen at the time. They were never in the office—they were figureheads. They got their paychecks and didn't seem to have too much to do with the daily operations.

———————

Scandals and corruption, of course, were by no means limited to DEN; they flourished at untold numbers of startups—and the most questionable conduct often started at the top.

DAVID GILCREAST

When I interviewed for Food.com, I met with upper management people and then had to meet with Jim Brimhall, who essentially ran the company. The weird thing was that his name was nowhere on the Web site. I didn't even know that he existed until I found out that I had to interview with him.

He requested that we meet at a bar, of all places. He didn't really explain what he did in his past life, but he alluded to the fact that he'd made a lot of money in the financial markets in the eighties. He really laid it on: "Come join this company and I will make you a millionaire." Those were his exact words. "We're going public very soon. Come on board and you'll be rich within the year."

He was ousted from the company a couple months after I arrived. Turns out this guy started the company, secured financing—and he was a *felon!* He had a multiple-count indictment for fraud, which is why they didn't have him on the Web site or in any of the press releases. He'd been hooked up with some con men in Vegas. This guy was a real scumbag. He managed to re-create himself as a dot-com entrepreneur, which I thought was kind of indicative of the whole business.

After a story was done in *The Industry Standard*, Accel Partners, one of the backers in the company, got rid of this guy. He was very bitter and I think he sued. In fact, he went off and started a competitor company that did the exact same thing, because he was so pissed that he got pushed out. But it's like, you're a convicted *felon*, okay?

PETER HEINECKE

In one company I worked with, the CEO really thought that this large pod of money his company had been given was his to spend. He would transfer it out of the company bank account to himself, and submit anything on his expense report—to the extent it *was* an expense report. Helicopter rides, stereo equipment, all of this sort of stuff.

Before the board stopped him, he was about to buy Blackberries and hand them out to everybody on the team. Not that they really needed them—he just thought they'd be cool to have. It took a while for the board to figure out what the hell was going on. There was a real shortage of seasoned controllers and financial people around.

With CEOs looting the till and barely bothering to wipe off their fingerprints, and company operatives hiding their ties to organized crime, it was natural that an atmosphere of lawlessness filtered down to the grunts. So it seemed like no big deal for an employee to have sex with a colleague—on another colleague's desk.

DEACON CARPENTER

There was an account manager and a producer working in the same office with me at Luminant. They were working on the same account, and they absolutely hated each other. Every day, the account manager would give the producer a hard time. Absolutely the worst: "You didn't do this. You didn't do that. Don't you know what you're *doing?*"

I left one night at eleven-thirty P.M., after putting out yet another fire. I came in at seven-thirty A.M., and my entire desk was a mess. It looked like an earthquake had hit. Well, apparently, they got into such a fight the night before that she slapped him. I got this from my assistant who was at the office at the time. The account manager started yelling and they ended up shagging up on my desk. They fucked on my desk! She's in her thirties and he's twenty-something. They stopped fighting after that.

Add up all the bad behavior, strategic incompetence, managerial inexperience, sense of self-entitlement, and the misbegotten belief that the wheel was being reinvented, and what do you have besides shattered companies, lost fortunes, and a smattering of jail time? A world where even the most buttoned-down corporations like Disney and Time Warner seemed unable to distinguish between the reasonable and the absurd.

FORMER PRODUCER AT DISNEY'S GO.COM

One of the last-ditch efforts to make money was so anti-Disney, but we did it anyway. In the last few weeks, Disney sold all of the search results for words that would be considered "profanity" to a porn site. If you searched for the word "fuck" or "cunt," you would get a page that said, "We don't host these sorts of pages, but if you want to go to this porn site, click here." They didn't tell anyone about it, but all of a sudden it just happened.

STEVE BALDWIN

The first day at Pathfinder, we were lectured by the brass and big guns. Walter Isaacson, head of CNN now, was the head of Time Warner's New Media at the time, and he briefed us as if we were being briefed by the President.

We had a full day of orientation. A big whiteboard. Everyone was wearing suits and looking great. It was like, "Gentlemen, the task ahead is not to be underestimated." It was like Patton. "We do not know the course. That is for you to determine, but we will not fail. This is Time Warner."

I thought my old job at Ziff-Davis was intense, but at Pathfinder, we'd have Monday morning meetings, Wednesday All Hands meetings, emergency meetings, ad hoc department meetings, and people would constantly pop into your office for a meeting. It was all about meetings!

Naturally, we had to confer, to strategize, because they had eighty different magazines, all these record companies, New York One, the cable people. And everyone went to us. "Hey, Atlantic Records needs a Web site!" "The people at *Progressive Farmer* need a site!" I didn't even know that Time Warner *had* a farming magazine! All of a sudden, we gotta build this page for them. It was like, "They're flying these guys in from *Progressive Farmer*. We gotta come up with a plan. Now." So, we're all running around like mad.

I was overseeing this sad collection of Time Warner tech e-zines. Very nerdy. We'd get daily news feeds from *Interactive Week, MIT Technology Review*, and *Interactive Age.* I had to format it, put it up, change the text, and then lobby for a placement on the homepage. After my meetings ended at three P.M., I had to start working. I had to fix the whole site. But it was schizo, because half the organization was just nine to five. And that's also the only time you could get Walter on the phone, before he went back to Long Island or wherever.

From five P.M. until whenever, I had to get the stuff up on the Web. It was like, "It's gotta be updated every day." Well, good luck with this kind of management! It was a sign of what would become a company totally out of control.

This chaotic atmosphere, Baldwin believes, contributed to the notorious "O. J. Simpson blunder."

STEVE BALDWIN

At Pathfinder we had this huge site called "O.J. Central." It was the most popular site during the O.J. Simpson trial. People were there at all hours, and on the date of the O.J. verdict, we knew that the world would be

Pathfinder's "O.J.'s Guilty": Mix-up amidst the dot-com chaos.

watching. So we had the tech team across the street in this underground bombproof shelter, and we're all sitting there watching the TV: What's it going to be—innocent or guilty?

We had two GIFs: "Innocent.gif" and "Guilty.gif." We're all waiting, leaning over these cube walls, and finally the word comes out—"NOT GUILTY!" So, our art director charged with giving the "Go" code shouts into the phone, "NOT GUILTY! GO! GO!"

Someone grabs a file from the folder, fires the slingshot, and BLAMO! The Web page is updated. But it's the *wrong* file! I'm the first guy to see the homepage, so I hit RELOAD and yell, "Look! Look!"

The art director looks up and all the blood drains from his face. He reaches for the phone and screams, "It's the wrong file!" It took maybe fifteen seconds to get the right file up, but no one had anticipated the browser cache. Within an hour, someone had made a copy of our fantastic error. There were mirror sites around the world. E-mails went out. It was like Dewey vs. Truman. It was the greatest mistake in the history of New Media!

The next sound you heard was the phone ringing in the editor's corner office. It was Walter Isaacson, and the editor disappeared. He wasn't fired, but there was a long investigation and no one ever figured out what happened. The file could have been misnamed, or the phone could have blanked out when he said "not."

But what tweaked the Time Warner brass more than anything was that by six P.M, Rupert Murdoch, our archenemy, had that mistaken "Guilty" graphic on Fox's homepage.

Mistakes can happen at any company, obviously, but when the management's all over the place, I kind of felt like we had it coming.

CHAPTER EIGHT THE IPO

Question: Do you ever do the math in your head?
Answer: To keep myself alive, I've stopped that.
　—Jeff Goodell, who left Apple four months
　　before its IPO to deal blackjack in Lake Tahoe

"Did you hear about the IPO?". . . "There was an offsite
today. . . I think they discussed the IPO.". . . "What will you
do with the money?". . . "I'm gonna buy 365 leather jackets,
one for each day of the year.". . . "You can't wear leather in
summer!"
　—Snippets of conversation overheard
　　while walking through the Kibu cube farm

Even after the tectonic market correction in the spring of 2000, the most
gossiped-about grist for Kibu's rumor mill involved plans for the company's
initial public offering. Inside the Kibu office space, "initial public offering"
became a three-word combo more thrilling than the biggie triplet, "You lost
weight."

Few at the company, including me, understood the nitty-gritty details of
how an IPO actually worked, or precisely what it meant for our bank statements, but that didn't stop most Kibu Girls from secretly dreaming about an
IPO as feverishly as about a ten-carat Tiffany engagement ring. Post-April,
our digital clocks ticked anxiously, making it painfully clear that we were no
nubile Netizens on the Internet timetable. Whatever this "IPO thing" was we
wanted one, and we wanted it before the bubble burst entirely.

Like perennial bridesmaids browsing the *New York Times* Sunday wedding
announcements, we watched with dismay as the IPOs hogging headlines

belonged to other startups. And while we waited longingly for our board members to propose, the environment at Kibu became decidedly less sisterly.

On the surface, of course, we professed loyalty to our noble mission of empowering teen girls. We cheered passionately at All Hands meetings, invoking mixed metaphors of staying afloat and running races. We nodded solemnly about "adjusting market conditions" and the need to be patient. We vowed to hang in for the long haul, even though, given our company's profligate spending habits, it seemed we would barely have enough money for the short haul.

Yet much as we vilified the greedy girls at other startups-turned-public companies who came in for the quick bucks (those sluts!), we looked around the smiling semicircle at each All Hands and secretly wondered, "How much equity does *she* have?" When the team chant ended and we shuffled back to our cubicles, sisterly sentiment gave way to sibling rivalry, resulting in a flurry of furious hush-hush speculation about who'd received the most stock shares. Or options. As the Face of Hair once remarked, "Like, who can tell the difference?"

Call 'em what you want. I refused to disclose how many I had, not because of the number, but because I'd been such a chump. In negotiating my contract with Judy and Molly, I'd taken $20,000 less in salary in exchange for doubling my option package. And here's the most humiliating part: *I fought for this!* But as early as my first month on the job, I realized that—market conditions or no market conditions—Kibu didn't have a chance of making it to the Nasdaq altar. And as for being acquired? Our ungainly site was damaged goods. So, my worthless stash remained a secret.

Or so I thought.

In fact, the status of the staff's salaries and stock options were as common knowledge among our Kibu clan as cup sizes and condom use. When one of our art directors remarked after a particularly grueling day: "It'll all be worth it, Lori. Think of your seventy thousand stock options," I gave her a questioning look. How did she know?

"C'mon, everyone knows you'll be richer than practically any of us here," she added without explanation. "You know, after the IPO?"

"Ah, IPO, IPshmo," I replied.

This was not, to say the least, a popular sentiment at Kibu.

The company's post-grads may have grown up in the era of New Math, but apparently no one taught them the Old Math, in which 70,000 times zero still equals zero. So while Kibu's more mindful VPs increasingly realized they held nothing more than pipedream employment contracts, the rest of the staff saw stock certificates as valuable as a Publisher's Clearinghouse bonanza through their then fashionable rose-colored glasses.

Apparently, our board members preferred clear lenses with sensible frames. In October of 2000, instead of Kibu's IPO making headlines, the press gleefully announced that board members Jim Clark and Tom Jermoluk had pulled their investment, because, as the columnist Chris Nolan reported in Upside.com, the two backers "had decided Kibu didn't have enough of a business plan to make it viable or take it public."

Forget the fact that this business plan–challenged startup was fortunate enough to get funded in the first place. Even then, Nolan continued, "Other investors were shocked by the decision." Molly sent out a mass e-mail offering, in lieu of clarification, a sentimental comment on this "very long, very emotional story that we'll share in person"—no doubt over catered tofu sushi rolls. One miffed insider, talking as if Kibu had accepted a setup from con men, asked Nolan, "Who would take money from these guys again?"

Um. . . *me?*

And so would anyone in search of backers who put more, well, *stock* into building a viable business than in taking a floundering startup public only to see it fizzle, as many did.

Like WebVan, the once celebrated online grocery service which filed for a $345 million public offering in August 1999, only two months after it began selling product in San Francisco, its first market. By July 2001, it had shut down operations and filed for Chapter 11 bankruptcy after burning through $1.2 *billion* in capital—hardly recovered by the mere $3 million the dead dot-com raised from its public auction. (Plastic tote bins went for $3, delivery trucks sold for $35,000, and a promotional VW Beetle changed hands for $15,500.)

Which isn't to say I didn't fall prey to the silicon siren song early on. After all, it wasn't the six-figure salary that had lured me away from Stanford Medical School. I'd had that in Hollywood and happily said buh-bye. It was those pesky stock options! I didn't realize back then that startup options were often tantamount to getting net rather than gross points on a movie deal: It's money that neither you nor your great-great-grandchildren will live to see.

Yet even Hollywood was seduced by the sonorous initials I-P-O. "We believed that Hollywood Stock Exchange was going to make us millionaires," says Doug Scott of the company whose seed investors, "a Who's Who of Hollywood," included the former CAA "superagent" Michael Ovitz. But like Kibu, HSX never made it to Internet's version of what *Bull Durham's* Crash Davis called "The Show."

Still, sitting in the stands while farm teams like TheGlobe.com made the big leagues in 1998—setting a then record for the largest first-day gain of an IPO by rising more than 900 percent before closing up 606 percent—many wanted in on the action, and felt envious of those who might partake.

Jesse remembers the day in early 2000 when he decided to contact his ex-girlfriend after being out of touch for almost a year. He called Workman Publishing, the specialty East Village publishing house where she had been toiling away when they last spoke.

"Sorry," the receptionist told him matter-of-factly, "she doesn't work here anymore. She's over at Rare Medium."

Immediately, Jesse logged onto Google to look up Rare Medium. "Please," he thought to himself while clicking through the search results. "Please God, don't let her be one of those people who become instant millionaires off Internet stock options."

He decided to call the Web shop and find out. After a conversation ranging from, "Yes, I still have your Gomez CD" to "No, she and I are just friends," Jesse popped the question. "So, uh, did they give you any stock options?"

Yes, in fact, they had. And though the stock had been at 5 on her first day at Rare Medium, it was now at. . . 90.

Gulp.

After more prying, Jesse calculated his ex-girlfriend's paper wealth to be worth $756,000. He wanted to shoot himself. Or get back together with her. He chose the latter, although by the end of 2001, the stock was selling for under a dollar and the company had sold its Internet services business.

Sang Lee, then a young producer at Rare Medium, certainly didn't see what was coming. "When we went to ninety-six dollars," he says, "I was already thinking about whether I should buy a house in Greenwich or take a loft down-town."

As this so-called "irrational exuberance" inexorably led to understandable despondency, worthless stock certificates recovered some value on eBay. Like Dr. Frankenstein's creation coming back to haunt him, the very medium that spawned the IPO mania became ground zero for collectors of what now pass for Internet memorabilia. One stock certificate from WebVan sold for $530, a far cry from the 6 cents that the company closed at the Friday before it filed for bankruptcy. But will this piece of nostalgia hold its value, or will it go the way of the company's stock?

Nostalgia, it is said, is a form of depression. Not, however, for those lucky few who jumped in and out of the golden IPO pool at the exact right moment. But while those who never played the game can let out a collective "Whew," others, like Jeff Goodell, opted out too early, back in the days when IPO sounded as alien as a UFO.

On eBay, one WebVan certificate sold for $530. Before the company filed for bankruptcy, the stock had fallen to a mere six cents.

JEFF GOODELL

I got out four months before the IPO at Apple in 1980. My manager came to me and said that I should think about sticking around, that Apple had a big future. I was like, "Gimme a break. This is a company of guys building these whacko machines that are going to be holding Grandma's recipes."

I dumped it and ran off to Lake Tahoe to deal blackjack, which I thought was much cooler. Of course, I go back a year later and everyone's got their BMW motorcycles in the parking lot and their sailboats. At the time, Apple was the first real IPO. No one had any idea what IPOs really were or dreamed about the big money that came along with them. It was just unheard of.

That had all changed by the time *Wired* filed to go public at a $450 million valuation in June 1996. The IPO—soon aborted—was followed by another aborted IPO in October at a reduced, but still inflated, valuation of $250 million to $290 million. Attempting to salvage the IPO, *Wired* repriced the initial asking price from the $12-to-$14 range to the $8-to-$10 range. Still, not enough demand.

To add to their public embarrassment, according to *Salon,* just ten days before *Wired* officially botched its plans, cofounder Louis Rossetto sent out an e-mail to "Wired Ones," his three hundred-plus *Wired* employees, reassuring the troops that the flurry of "shoddy, if not malicious" ink in publications ranging from the *Los Angeles Times* to *Business Week* was nothing more than bullshit atop baloney. The e-mail continued: "The takeaway is that media envy and ignorance are rampant (no surprise). That *Wired* is on track to conclude its IPO and execute its business plan. And that in the end, as F. Scott Fitzgerald put it, success is the best revenge."

As it turns out, the recipients of this e-mail—some of whom had mistakenly remained in *Wired's* online address book—were the ones who got the best revenge. The WELL contributor Gerard van der Leun shared it with the online community, alarming potential investors that Rossetto's companywide missive might run afoul of the SEC's "quiet period" rule.

Andrew Anker adds another blunder to the list. "If *Wired* made a mistake at that time, it's that they gave people too much of a sense as to what their equity might be worth," says the former *Wired* Digital CEO. "When we didn't go public, and their equity wasn't worth anything, it became much harder to retain people because you'd disappointed them."

Steven Overman, Rossetto's executive assistant at the time, remembers the beleaguered bunker mentality inside *Wired*:

STEVEN OVERMAN

When I first heard the acronym "IPO," I didn't know what it meant. John Plunkett was the creative director of *Wired* with Barb Kuhr, and they said that if we're a public company, we'll be under the scrutiny of investors, we'll need to make quarterly earnings, and it will be very bad. He was very nervous.

But Louis wanted to do an IPO, and was incredibly determined to make this happen. He wanted to build this thing big. He wanted a media company that had TV and radio and albums and books, and he was treating the IPO as a real funding mechanism. A lot of people just did IPOs to get rich quick, but Louis had a vision.

The mood in the office before the IPO was awful. I don't think people were excited about it. People didn't "do" options back then like they do now. I got to see the list of who got what, and it actually came down to, "Well, this editor got here two days after this editor, but she does more. Give her the options."

I remember not knowing if my option grant was a good number or a bad number. Nobody knew what the fuck it meant. I was told that what I got in relation to others was good, but the gut feeling was that people were getting screwed.

There'd been a remarkable culture in place at the magazine, and this threatened it. There was almost a war between Jane Metcalfe, the cofounder, and the engineers around IPO time over who owned the intellectual property. Everyone at *Wired* joined believing they were part of a mission. Later, everyone at a dot-com used that language, but anybody in marketing making $75,000 doesn't know what a mission is! Being on a mission means making $20,000 in San Francisco. Part of why we had this missionary zeal at *Wired* was because we were underpaid.

So people were willing to bring their intellectual property to the greater cause, but then suddenly Jane is saying that *Wired* co-owns it. And that made people go, "Wait a minute." People were young and naïve. I was older than most people in the office, and I was twenty-six.

The announcement of the IPO had the reverse effect of incentivizing employees. It may have incented some of the managers, but it created rivalries in the trenches. Jane said, "Don't go out and buy the Lexus yet,"

and I was thinking, "What's a Lexus?" There was a gleefulness in management presentations that this was going to be happening, and the rest of the
room was sitting there like, "Uh, what does this mean?"

Louis wanted to design the prospectus and it was beautiful, but it
pissed off the investment bankers because it was slowing things down.
Some people say that's the reason the IPO failed. I totally disagree. If
Louis wasn't so anal about design, *Wired* never would have happened.
Whatever came out that had to do with *Wired*—whether it was direct
mail, or a cheap flier on a telephone poll—it had to be consistent with
our brand.

My opinion is that the IPO was flawed from the beginning, because the
valuation was way too high. But if Goldman Sachs comes to you and says
your company is worth $400 million, are you going to say, "No, make it
less"?

Not if you saw the Web browser pioneer Netscape go public on August 9,
1995, an event that CNET cofounder Kevin Wendle describes as "the
moment the world changed." After Morgan Stanley priced the startup at $28
per share, up from the original $12-to-$14 range, the stock opened at $71
before closing at $58.25.

CNET and Yahoo! also make the roster of closely watched early entrants
on the IPO block.

KEVIN WENDLE

What was remarkable for us at CNET is that we were a year older than
Netscape, and we were in a related business. We were both technology companies, but Netscape was a software company, and we were a media company. We felt like time was on our side, and we would soon have a chance to
dip in on that.

When we went public in July 1996, we were priced at 16, the stock went
to 21, and then went to 12 and sat at 12 for a while. There were a lot of
naysayers who thought that it would go from 12 to zero.

It wasn't until I left the company in 1998 that the frenzy began. [CNET's stock price eventually peaked at $79 on December 17, 1999.] In fact, it was bizarre because I had just retired from this startup, was taking a year off, and was getting calls every week from family members, neighbors, former school-mates, or friends of friends who wanted to start an Internet company. I thought it was a lot of lunacy. Far as I was concerned, it was inevitable that 99 percent of these ideas were going to get flushed.

ELIZABETH COLLET

I came on right before Yahoo! did an IPO in April 1996. I remember watch-ing the stock run up and drift back down the first day. I got options at a price equivalent to sixty cents in today's currency. There's obviously been a lot of appreciation since then. By the time spring of 2000 came along, it was in the two hundreds.

———————

During the euphoria, it seemed like every stock had hit $200—or more. In December 1998, Merrill Lynch analyst Henry Blodget became the industry's Kreskin by predicting that Amazon.com's stock would hit $400 within twelve months. It achieved that mark in a matter of weeks. The Nasdaq peaked at 5,132.5 on March 10, 2000, when it was worth $6.7 trillion. Brocade and Broadcom replaced Coca-Cola and Caterpillar as portfolio must-haves, although more people could probably recite their Nasdaq symbols (BRCD and BRCM) than their means of business (storage and semiconductors).

Teenagers found new icons in TheStreet.com's Jim Cramer and Morgan Stanley's Internet analyst Mary Meeker. Drunk barflies yelled, "Cisco rocks!" as they watched the CNBC ticker with the same passion that made them cheer "Yankees rule!" while scanning the ESPN ticker in years past.

"It was pretty insane," recalls Michael Feldman, who says that even already-rich celebrities, attempting to pull rank, would ask companies for 'friends and family' shares. "Barbra Streisand called us up at Fogdog," says Feldman. "And I had friends at other startups who said celebrities called them up, too."

Year	Celebrity	Web site	Role	Status
1998	William Shatner	Priceline.com	Spokesperson for equity	Still in business
1999	Francis Ford Coppola	Ebags.com	Spokesperson for equity	Still in business
1999	Cindy Crawford	Babystyle.com	Board member and spokesperson for equity	Still in business
1999	John Elway	MVP.com	Founder of company	Company went out of business (sold most of its assets to CBSSportsline.com)
1999	Wayne Gretzky	MVP.com	Director/spokesperson for equity	
1999	Michael Jordan	MVP.com	Director/spokesperson for equity	
1999	Stan Lee	AtomShockwave	Content for cash (Shockwave bought $5 mil of Stan Lee Media stock)	Still in business (but exclusive relationship with SL over)
1999	Sophia Loren	Giftcertificates.com	Spokesperson for equity	Still in business
1999	Alanis Morissette	Mp3.com	Tour sponsorship for equity	Still in business (but Morissette has sold most of her shares)
1999	Christopher Reeve	Healthextras.com	Endorsement for equity (plus donation to Reeve's foundation)	Still in business
1999	RuPaul	WebEx.com	Spokesperson for equity	Still in business
1999	Matt Stone & Trey Parker (*South Park* creators)	AtomShockwave	Content for cash and equity	Still in business (but episodes have yet to air)
1999	Tracey Ullman	Purpleskirt.com	Chairwoman and partner	Still in business
2000	Pamela Anderson	PamTV.com	Founder	Company went out of business
2000	Stephen Baldwin	HSX.com	Spokesperson for equity	Company sold to
2000	James L. Brooks	AtomShockwave	Content for undisclosed details	Still in business (but Brooks' episodes have yet to air)
2000	Tim Burton	AtomShockwave	Content for undisclosed details	Still in business (Burton's web series "Stainboy" is still live)
2000	Larry David (*Seinfeld* co-creator)	Icebox.com	Content for equity	Company went out of business, has since been resurrected as a pay-per-view site. David produced one episode of his show, "Paula Principle."
2000	Ellen DeGeneres	Z.com	Content for equity	Company went out of business
2000	Whoopi Goldberg	Flooz.com	Spokesperson for equity	Company went out of business
2000	Melanie Griffith	OneWorld Live	Co-founder and Investor	Still in business
2000	Michael Jackson	HollywoodTicket	Co-founder and Investor	Company went out of business
2000	Shaquille O'Neal	Dunk.net	Principal backer	Company went out of business
2000	Chris Rock	Z.com	Content for equity	Company went out of business
2000	Britney Spears	Sweet16.com	Spokesperson for equity	Still in business
2000	Patrick Stewart	UBUBU	Spokesperson for equity	Still in business

Even already-rich celebrities tried to get in on the action.

Entire companies got caught up in the commotion, as Joanne Weaver recalls of the giddy weeks before Scient's IPO.

JOANNE WEAVER

The CEO, CFO, COO, and investor relations person were on the road pitching to try to get funding for the IPO. There was a guy by the name of Chas Watkins, a rather infamous figure at Scient. He was employee number four, and made sure everyone knew it. But he's a really great character, really sarcastic.

So he and I decided to write an anonymous installment on our office e-mail that we called "Shallow Esophagus," based on Deep Throat. The investor relations person, Caroline Leakan, would send us stories from the road in response to our questions—How are the guys doing? What's the vibe? Are they getting along? Who'd they visit today? What's the response?

We'd make up stories and send them to All Scient Global under the name Shallow Esophagus. It was real tongue-in-cheek, and people got a kick out of it. We made fun of the situation, but we also told people what was going on. It made the leaders accessible.

Scient went public in a $60 million IPO on May 14, 1999, before merging with another Web shop, iXL. But by mid-2001, the stock had fallen to less than the price of a gumball. Scient was on a long list of Web shops to go public that included Rare Medium, Xceed, Viant, Sapient, MarchFirst, and Razorfish.

RICHARD TITUS

When we sold Tag media, our Web shop, to Razorfish, I became the company's hundredth employee. They told me they might go public, but they weren't sure. I laughed. I refused more stock because I thought, "Why would a services company go public? You have no assets. There's no multiple. Why would anyone buy your stock? It's a Web shop!"

They thought I was a fool, but they were happy to give me the cash. We made an agreement after the successful IPO to replace some of the cash with stock. But up until the day we went public I didn't really believe

---

The History of Shallow Esophagus
by Joanne and Chas

"Close your eyes (but keep one open to read) and picture this: In May of 1999, the Scient leadership team---Eric, Bob, Steve, and Bill---toured the United States on a Roadshow to spread the Scient gospel and garner as many funds as possible for Scient's imminent IPO. As each day of the Roadshow passed, a new email from a mysterious sender using the alias "Shallow Esophogus" appeared in the inboxes of Scient colleagues everywhere, causing people to scratch their heads, wonder who was doing this, and, if Shallow Esophogus got his way, perhaps even put a smile on their faces. The stories contained in these emails would give a rundown of the day's events, where the LT had traveled, how they were faring on the road, and were almost never based on actual facts. On the day of Scient's IPO, Scient wasn't the only thing to become public: Shallow Esophogus' true identity was likewise brought to the masses. It turned out there were actually TWO digestive tracts working in harmony: Chas Watkins and Joanne Weaver, who took turns each day to write the Roadshow installments with information fed to them by then-director of investor relations, Caroline Leakan. We hope you enjoy this little trip down memory lane (or this little Scient history lesson) as much as we enjoyed writing it. Allow them to take you back to a small, familial, and just plain silly Scient, and may their kookiness and irreverence remind you that Scient, of all places, is the place where you can be just that."

Edited Selection of "Shallow Esophagus" emails

From:RoadShow
Sent:Tuesday, May 04, 1999 8:49 AM
To:All Scient
Subject:...and their off
Day One.
...The Breakfast
...The event was FULL of the institutional types...........ur sorry I mean institutional investor types. Sorry, don't want you to get the wrong idea about the people attending. FULL is a GOOD thing. Just in case you are not that quick on the uptake! ...
I
will
be
back
Shallow Esophagus
****
Quote of the Day
"So you're asking yourself how are we going to scale this puppy!"
Bob Howe using some top notch MBA metaphors to convince institutional investors that Scient is a, soon to be,
 Legendary company.
****
-----Original Message-----
From:RoadShow
Sent:Wednesday, May 05, 1999 10:36 AM
To:All Scient
Subject:IPO Roadshow: Day 2: LA Story, Scient Style
......
As the boys drift off into a dreamy wonderland, a lone nightingale sings the melody "Good Night Sweetheart" and they wonder if they're dreaming or actually hearing the words in the distance: Good night Scient/No time to slow/Good night Scient/Dream of an IPO/I hate to publicly trade ya but I really must let go/Good night Scient /Good night......
They fall asleep smiling and envisioning the heavenly nectar of sweet success.
FADE TO BLACK
--until next time
Shallow Esophagus
-----Original Message-----
From: RoadShow
Sent: Thursday, May 06, 1999 11:13 AM
To: All Scient
Subject: Can you say "Oversubscribed"
...Some real news today; my spies have been working hard. OK they are all over Denver today. I'd list the places but the list looks like something like
SILLY INVESTMENT COMPANY
BIG INVESTMENT COMPANY
BURGER INVESTMENT COMPANY
WEGOTCASH INVESTMENT COMPANY.
So what's the point.
...***************
As always I try to keep the best for last and the latest buzz word is "oversubscribed." Am I counting wrong or is this only day 4! Will they bother to complete the tour?

(continues)

"We made fun of the situation, but we also told people what was going on," says Joanne Weaver, the former Scient receptionist, of the "shallow esophagus" missives chronicling her company's roadshow in the days before their successful IPO.

-----Original Message-----
From:RoadShow
Sent:Thursday, May 13, 1999 5:18 PM
To:All Scient
Subject:Day ???: The Final Installment
Note to readers: SE felt a bit verbose and overly silly today, so if you want to skip the flowery story stuff, scroll down to the script in green and that will give you the IPO story. And for the slackers, hope you enjoy the read.
Look forward to seeing you tomorrow at party time!!!!
C-Day (the Day Before D-Day)
or
A Silly Little Story for Scient Before the Storm
….Bob and Eric, the trusted leaders of Scient, had a top secret meeting in Andromeda with the other decision makers of the company. The decision to go public was swift, quick, and no holds barred. A sample of their top secret conversation:
"So, like, what do you want to do?"
"I dunno. What do you wanna do?"
"Like, let's go public, maybe."
"OK, let's do it."
"OK, when?"
"Um, I dunno. When do you want to do it?"
"How about Friday?"
"OK, Friday works for me."
"Break for lunch!!!!"
The banker selection process was equally as stringent (rumor has is that it was a dartboard with the bankers' names on it, but the spies of Shallow Esophagus, the hidden informer, say that it involved a game of Twister and the loser got to pick the bank, a small consolation prize considering he had to hop around all day with his foot wrapped behind his head), and finally, with 4 weeks left in the running before Public Day, the S1, chock full of legal mumbo jumbo (so thick you could stand a fork in it), returned back from the Sam the Legal Butcher's office and no one recognized it.)
Bob got down on his knees and sobbed. Chris Lockhead slammed his hands down on the table. In a rare display of humor and catty snide style, he sneered, "Why don't we just say on the cover of the Prospectus, 'Our bankers have advised us that we cannot make forward looking statements, but we ARE a forward looking company, serving forward-looking clients in a forward-looking market'?" Although he probably would have been backed by most of his coworkers, the forward-looking lawyers gave him a forward-looking eyebrow raise and that was that.
………..
Alice approached a guy in a 10 of Hearts suit. "Hey, nice Gucci blazer. What's going on?"
The card replied, "The Queen is about to arrive to give her blessing to Scient!"
Immediately, a hush fell over the crowd and everybody fell to their knees, looking down. Trumpets blared.
The Queen strolled regally down the palace front staircase, a chocolate labrador puppy nipping at her heels. She wore her blond hair cut short, and her royal purple robe sported a "J.Crew" label inside.
"Kneel to Her Royal Highness, the Queen of Hearts! Known by her friends as Beth!"
The townsfolk dared not look up. Alice stared at her, quizzically. The Queen approached her and looked her up and down.
"Where do you come from." The Queen said, dryly.
"I come from County Cornwall, to the west."
"Off with her public funding!!!" The Queen yelled.
"B--But wait, I'm Alice and---"
"Don't say another word! Throw her to the lawyers! I won't hear her any more!"
Two burly looking men approached her and seized her by the arms.
"But wait! You've got it all wrong! I come bringing news of the IPO!"
The Queen put up her hand for the men to wait. They weakened their grip. "Oh?"
"Yes! I do! And it's gonna be great!"
"OH....?"
"Yeah, there's gonna be Twister and aliens in the wall and ticker stuff all over the place and lightbulbs flashing and lots and lots of champagne!"
"Did you say......champagne?"
"Yes!"
In one swift motion, the Queen ripped off her purple robe, revealing a red sequined bellbottom pantsuit and 6" high red platform shoes. "Well, then, LET'S BOOGIE ON DOWN!!!!!!!!"
The crowd erupted in screams of joy. Donna Summers blared from the overhead speakers and confetti flew through the air. Alice was raised on top of her former captors shoulders and went swimming through the crowd, everyone congratulating her and thanking her. A huge SCIENT banner unfurled at the palace gates and the kingdom thrived for years to come.
Alice awoke when her sister nudged her awake. "Alice! Come on, now! It's time to go now!"
Had it all been a dream? Alice rubbed her eyes, completely and utterly disappointed. Did Scient make its dreams of going public? She slowly got to her feet and dragged her feet the whole way to the street to catch a cab.
A black and white checkered cab pulled up. Sitting behind the wheel was----could it be???--the White Rabbit, munching on a carrot stick.
"Hop in, babes. It's gonna be a wild ride."
<FADE TO BLACK>

that we'd see much of a spike. Maybe a little bounce. [Razorfish stock, priced at $16, opened on April 27, 1999 at $35 and climbed to $38.75 its first day.]

My wife and I considered it Monopoly money. We would exercise our options from time to time, and go on trips or buy things. It was like winning the lottery over and over again. I saw some of my peers leverage themselves to death, buying cars, houses, extra apartments, motorcycles, but my wife and I lived in the same apartment. We slowly liquidated money on a managed level over the next two years. And priced down. I recently sold my last few thousand shares for less than six thousand dollars. They were once worth more than a million.

———

Peter Seidler, the former chief creative officer at Razorfish, shares his colleague's skepticism regarding the wisdom of Web shops entering the public market.

PETER SEIDLER

I don't believe any of these client-services companies should have become public. One of the reasons they did was this need to grow at an absurd rate. Ultimately, though I think it would have become possible to grow more like a traditional consulting firm, with a typical partnership structure.

Part of the problem is that your only asset in those companies is the consultants, and if their interest is primarily the stock price, then the whole company is at risk. It's in the interest of all the employees—whether it was Scient, Viant, Sapient, or Razorfish—to leave the company and go work for the competitor, because they get their options repriced. But that's also the worst possible thing for the relationships with clients. So you have this inherent contradiction at the root of the business. It's flawed and inappropriate.

———

It wasn't just Web shops: Even companies only tangentially related to the Internet hoped to capitalize on the dot-com boom. Artisan, an independent movie studio based in Los Angeles, tried to ride the Internet mania surrounding its hit film, *The Blair Witch Project*, to an IPO by rushing to produce a *Blair Witch* sequel without the original filmmakers' participation. Filing to go public on February 18, 2000, the company set the price at $16 to $18. On October 27, 2000, *Blair Witch* 2 opened. . . and bombed, big-time. Artisan withdrew its IPO on March 14, 2001.

DAN MYRICK

Artisan's original plan was five years to IPO the company, and *Blair Witch* accelerated that to two years. Without a doubt, *Blair* was Artisan's biggest success and put them on the map. Amidst all the hype, Artisan figured it would be a good time to IPO right after the sequel. We wanted to give it some time, and we tried to talk them out of it, but the mind behind an IPO is not the same as the mind behind your average filmmaker.

Despite the flops, the high-profile victories of recent college grads made those in the thick of the IPO madness—lawyers, journalists, and San Francisco real estate agents—wonder whether they should crash the party, too.

{LAWYERS}
PETER HEINECKE

One company I worked with asked me to come on as general counsel. They were about to go public in February of 2000, and they offered me an option package that they said would be worth four to six million. I looked at it and said, "Wait a second. These guys don't have any customers yet, and they're trying for a ten-*billion*-dollar valuation." I didn't take the offer and a couple of months later, the market crashed, they withdrew the registration, and they closed up shop. But it was tremendously tempting.

Rare Medium Stock Chart

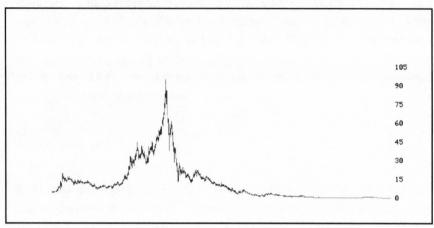

Razorfish Stock Chart

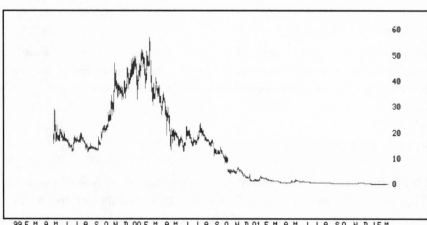

"It was insane for a public services company to have a two-billion-dollar market cap," says Rare Medium's Gon Szeto.

DAVID HORNIK

I think you couldn't help but say, "Well, maybe I should go work at a dot-com, rather than a law firm." You'd watch clients IPO and you'd think, Hmm. I had a number of different opportunities where I could have gone and joined Yahoo! Financially, obviously, it was a mistake not to. But I was learning, and I didn't want to leave my job.

At one point, I had a CEO at a board meeting ask, "So, David, when are you joining us?" I said, "It's about time!" And he said, "What are you talking about?" I said, "You're my last client to ask me to join. Every other client has asked me so far. I was wondering what I'd done to offend you!"

That's what it was like. In order to compete, law firms paid more and created a stock options pool. Eventually, they had to give in and let you invest your own money in these companies. There were some securities laws prohibiting what lawyers could and could not do, but a lot of people fudged them.

{JOURNALISTS}
PO BRONSON

I'd get offered jobs with stock options, but I was always like, "Oh my God! Are you crazy? I can't do this stuff!" I wrote op-eds for the *Wall Street Journal* and the *New York Times*, as well as pieces for *The New York Times Magazine*. I couldn't tarnish my reputation.

Then one day, in spring 1998, I went down to see Mike Malone, the long-time Valley writer. When Rich Kalgaard went to go run *Forbes*, Mike went to go run *Forbes ASAP*, so I had lunch with him. We went down to the parking lot, and Mike drove this nice, cherry-red, F150 supercab pickup truck.

I was like, "Nice truck, Mike, where'd you get this?" And he goes, "You don't know?" I said, "Don't know what?" He was like, "I was shareholder number six at eBay." I'm like, "You're the editor of *Forbes ASAP*, how can you be shareholder number six at eBay?" He said, "Come on, man, you gotta get in on the game."

He knew these guys at eBay, he was going to write about them, he decided not to write about them, and decided to help them instead. He introduced them to Knight Ridder. That was the only thing he ever did, other than just hang around and chit-chat, like I had done at a million other companies. But because of that, he was shareholder number six.

The company had done wonderfully since the early days when he was with them, and he was now cashing out as his stock vested. He was like, "You're a writer. You know these things better than anyone else." This is a guy that I had respected a great deal. Mike was the Valley's longest-standing business journalist, and he had written several books. That he had been able to do this with eBay, this famous company, and it hadn't tarnished his reputation one bit, just blew me away. He said, "I just never wrote about eBay. And that was okay at *Forbes.*" And I'm thinking, I am the stupidest person on Earth.

I agonized at great length, but I just couldn't get myself to do it.

REBECCA EISENBERG

I actually published a couple of pieces in the *San Francisco Examiner* stating I am really resentful of covering rich people, and I want to be rich myself. Goddammit, I went to Harvard Law School, so why am I not rich? You know, I was a poor columnist who had really given my heart and soul to this industry, but when I saw everyone getting rich off IPOs, I felt like I got nothing back.

I knew a lot of the players in these games. My whole freshman dorm ended up at Yahoo!: Jerry Yang; Tim Brady, who I think was employee number three; Steve Boom, who was maybe employee number thirteen; and Matt Rightmire. I think that if I had wanted to, I could have worked there. So I used to scratch my head a lot saying, "Why didn't I just do this?"

I did get to participate in one IPO, which is responsible for all the money I made. It wasn't a conflict of interest to get stock because it was in a publication for which I was writing—CBS MarketWatch.

CBS MarketWatch ended up being one of the best-performing IPOs at that time. I had a thirty-one-day lockup period, and I sold on day thirty-two. I was so broke for so long, and then I thought, "Oh my God, this is money!" So I sold it.

Pretty much any savings I have is because of the CBS MarketWatch IPO. But I'm not talking about a million dollars. I'm not even talking about $100,000.

{REAL ESTATE AGENT}
CHRIS DALLAS

Sure, you get tempted, but I didn't go overboard. I had a client who was worth a tremendous amount of money on paper. He bought a couple of buildings from me, which I thought was smart. Then he called me when his company went public. I bought some of the shares before they tripled and I sold them. He thought I'd made a mistake because it went up even further, but then it slammed down. Now that company is nonexistent and, ironically, his wealth is only in real estate.

———————

Unlike Dallas, however, many fell prey to what Alan Greenspan famously dubbed "irrational exuberance" in 1996—a term used to describe what the Federal Reserve Chairman viewed as an overvalued stock market poised to nose-dive. Perhaps Robert Shiller's 2000 book of the same name was published too late to make hopefuls think twice.

SHULI HALLACK

When I got to Rare Medium, our stock was trading at $50. Since I had 5,000 shares, for which I would have paid $6 apiece, I was going to make $220,000! We were hiring forty people a quarter, and everyone was making so much money. I thought, "Screw grad school, I'm making enough money here. It's the Internet revolution!" *Everyone* worked at an Internet company. *Everyone* had stock options, *everyone* had Aeron chairs, *everyone* had a Blackberry, *everyone* was getting rich. We were buying so many companies that I couldn't keep up with it. How could I lose?

TOM LAZAROFF

I took a substantial pay cut to go work at PayMyBills, and that was the excitement. Every other day, another company went public and had lots of paper millionaires, which was the carrot. Our incubator company, IdeaLab, had already created eToys and three or four others that had gone public. All those people had great stock options, and the sky was the limit. It was a badge of honor in '99 to take a pay cut and get stock options.

LEV CHAPELSKY

When we were talking about our option packages and negotiating at CarsDirect, the people inside the company actually said that each one of those stock options was going to be worth one hundred dollars. They said,

"That's going to happen. You're going to be cashing out at one hundred dollars." And people believed them. Today, they're debating whether the stock is worth a nickel.

JOANNE WEAVER

I got fifteen hundred shares when I started at Scient. Then the stock split, and I got options at $6.50 a piece. I believe that on paper I was worth $300,000! I was in a state of disbelief.

It was such a magical time, and when you're riding on this wave of optimism, it's really hard to imagine that ever coming to an end. I kept staving that off even though I thought I really needed to talk to a tax person to figure out these implications: If I sell this at 120 or 130, what does that mean? When the stock started to drop, it was all about, "Don't worry, this is just a blip in the economy." I didn't sell when I should have, and I came away with nothing.

The potential *ka-ching* rang louder in some people's ears than in other's. While many wanted nothing less than to become millionaire moguls, the former DEN video editor Matthew Klauschie hoped his company would IPO for much simpler reasons. Granted, admits Klauschie, the possible back-end "motivated people to work those kind of hours," but, he adds, "I wasn't counting on it making me rich. I was thinking, 'Hey, I could pay off all my student loans.'"

Still, says *The Industry Standard*'s Laura Rich, there existed an ambivalence between greed and restraint. Despite her colleagues' belief that "we weren't the people that we covered," she remembers that "when options were doled out, everyone was really concerned about how many they were getting."

Inevitably, concern turned into resentment.

ALAN CITRON

To me, there were two cycles. In the early cycle, when people got very rich, I didn't feel any animosity toward them, because it really was a surprise, and these were people who really loved what they were doing. With the second cycle, you started to get some snakes who were just in it as a way to get rich very quickly.

Then it got a little obnoxious, when you had standard business people putting on khakis because that's where the action was. It was very obvious. Some of them scored and some of them didn't, but it was very easy to feel animosity toward them because these people clearly didn't care about the Web.

LISA HENDRICKS

I'm known to my friends as one of the few people who got her money out. I remember very loudly in my brain—April fourteenth, when everything crashed and burned—how resentful people got, because they really thought it was easy. It was never easy. Building a company like I did was hard. You had to spend a lot of time thinking about what business we were in. How do we charge people and how do we make sense out of this? But so many people thought it was easy because they saw too many success stories of secretaries getting rich.

DEN's David Neuman and Inside.com's Kurt Andersen tried to temper these tales with a dose of reality. Good thing, given that DEN canceled its $75 million IPO in February 2000; while in 2001, the financially strapped Inside.com was acquired by Brill Media Holdings, only to be snatched up six months later by Primedia.

DAVID NEUMAN

I felt it was a moral responsibility of mine to say that DEN stock could be worth a lot or worth nothing. Both to investors and employees. Other companies did well, and there was a lot of optimism about it, but on a personal level, I never had any illusions. Yet people bought big houses and cars in anticipation of impending wealth. There wasn't any appreciable difference between the financial motives of a person who came in as an engineer and a director of photography for one of our videos. They both wanted to make a lot of money.

KURT ANDERSEN

There were people who had the get-rich-quick mentality, but in our case, because Inside.com was relatively late in the cycle, and the people that we were hiring were journalists and relatively older—thirty to thirty-five—the "Oh, we're all going to get rich" attitude was less part of our thing. The main round of our funding was on April 17, 2000, three days after Black Friday. From the very beginning, the temperament of skeptical, been-around-the-block journalists suppressed the we're-all-going-to-be-rich-overnight excitement. The initial pop of the bubble had happened before we even launched, so there was no extreme giddiness. We started our business and adventure without the crazy two years of profligacy, and the idea that capital is unending and free.

That was all to the good, because most of us at Inside were able to focus on creating something that hadn't been done before. The IPO idea was really never part of our calculation. Even in fall 1999, I think almost nobody came to work for us with IPO millions being anything like a major motivation. In fact, when we interviewed people, we were very careful to tell them not to do this if they thought they were going to get rich off it.

Not everyone wanted "to get rich off it," but a little dough might have been nice. An all-too-common lament was that of not having had the opportunity to get in at the right moment, which for many meant simply "pre-IPO."

CHRIS KINNEAR

The stock option package at eToys was decent, but I got fucked because I came in after the IPO. By the time I got my options, they were priced at $38. When I went there, my whole position was, "If this does take off, I just want enough to get a house." My goals were not dreaming of quitting work and getting a private jet. But I still got fucked.

TED KRUCKEL

Many times clients would want to negotiate their fees down and barter, getting me stock in their companies. I ended up executing two deals like that, but I didn't get in early enough. I got tens of thousands of shares which are worthless now. By the time I started to get the whiff that I should be doing this, everyone had IPO'd, and it was too late.

For Adeo Ressi, the problem wasn't just bad timing ("the market's too crowded") but too much *success*. While Ressi watched as a swarm of competing Web shops either went public or were in the planning stages, the IPO of Ressi's Methodfive got derailed because his company looked too good on paper.

ADEO RESSI

When we started to look to go public, we had nice profitability and fast-growing revenues. We had huge deals with major clients. We had great processes, everything. Here we are, the ideal candidate to go public, so I go out and start meeting with banks.

The most emblematic meeting was with Credit Suisse First Boston. That morning, CSFB had completed the merger between Whitman Hart and CS First West, which then became MarchFirst. So, here I am, walking into the room, and they're going, "We just announced the biggest merger in the Web's history. It's going to change the face of the industry."

And I said, "Well, I'm running a very profitable company, and if you look at our metrics, we hit them all"—revenue per employee was two hundred K; growth per quarter exceeded 20 percent; we had high client satisfaction from a usability standpoint. I'm walking through my presentation, and one of the bankers interrupts me with the following story:

"You know what you are?" he asks. I say, "No." He says, "You're a Cadillac driving on cruise control going fifty-five miles per hour." I say, "Okay." And he says, "That's a good thing. But I got jalopies with one tire loose, about to fall off, with a driver drinking beer passing you on the right." I know that he's representing Razorfish, so I'm like, "Yeah, you're right. They're not profitable, they have a lot of problems, they've rolled up a bunch of companies that they can't integrate."

So he goes, "You know what? They're going to beat you to the finish line."

I go, "If they don't fall off a cliff or blow up."

He comes back to me and says, "You don't know. In one quarter, these companies can turn a profit."

I was caught in this Catch–22, because I could continue this broken-down car analogy or counter with raw data. So finally I say, "The long and short of it is, you have a profitable company that's growing and wants to go public. And you have a whole bunch of public companies that are complete messes, that you're telling me can turn a corner and be profitable in one quarter. We'll see what happens with them, but I can tell you what's going to happen with us."

He ends the meeting with "I'm going to place my bets on these jalopies." He used some lame excuse about an overcrowded market. I was eventually proved right because MarchFirst goes bankrupt and Razorfish is facing horrendous problems.

Ressi's Methodfive eventually did go public, but not through an IPO. In fact, many private companies engaged in reverse mergers to reach the public market.

In a reverse merger, a private company becomes public through a merger with, or acquisition by, a public company. The end result is someone new in charge. Often, the existing public company is a shell corporation that had previously gone public, and lived now with little or no assets and liabilities. Rare Medium, says Gong Szeto, "reverse-merged with an air-conditioning company."

ADEO RESSI

To achieve scale at Methodfive, we wanted to reach the public sphere. We were ultimately approached by an "interesting" group of investors—and I don't mean that in the most flattering way—to do a reverse merger of a public company called Xceed. The concept was that Methodfive—a profitable company run very well—would take over a public roll-up to shape up Xceed to grow over the long term. They purchased us for over twenty times trailing twelve-month revenue—approximately $88 million in assets. It was an absurd amount of money, but they were really buying a management team that was going to help them succeed.

HELEN MAYNARD

A public biotech company called Procept became interested in Heavenly Door. Biotech stocks were going down and Internet stocks were climbing, so they decided to get into the Internet in January 2000. Procept bought Heavenly Door for $22 million, and we became the only public company in this part of the funeral industry.

I mean, this was a real dot-com story, and we rode it from the top right down to the bottom. Heavenly Door is no longer public. The weekend before Thanksgiving 2000, the Procept board of directors decided they no longer wanted to be in the Internet business—they wanted to go back to biotech. They still had $3.5 million in the bank, so they sold the Internet assets to a Minneapolis company called RememberedOnes.com and they turned the public shell on the Nasdaq OTC into Paligent, Inc.

Let's just say we had an interesting year.

It seems there were as many ways to get rich—or go broke—as there were strategies for playing Go. Taking one's company public wasn't the Holy Grail for every New Economy entrepreneur, including JustBalls.com's Jim Medalia. "Our goal was to execute our business plan, not just to take our company public." So what if his friend, Cyberian Outpost's Darryl Peck, "only wanted to have a public company"? All Medalia wanted was "to be the best-selling ball company out there. We wanted to be the Ball Kings."

Chuck D, however, just wanted bankers to get a clue.

CHUCK D

The bankers would say, "It's too small. Rap is just too small." I'd say, "It happens to be the music of choice," and they're all, "Oh, I don't know." And then they'd come back and say, "Okay, well, my daughter likes this hip-hop artist Ja Rule." I'd be like, "You *stupid*, I was just telling you."

The folks who really felt stupid might have been those who did go public to the tune of personal fortunes up to the hundreds of millions—only to watch much of it disappear. How did this happen? Chalk it up to "rational herding," the investor behavior pattern described by Yale University finance professor Ivo Welch in *Wired*: "People will continue to imitate each other until they come across some new bit of information, and finally it becomes pretty obvious to everyone, at the same time, that the herd went the wrong way."

Many herdsmen have since joined the "Hundred Million Club," a group of entrepreneurs who have lost nearly nine figures in the tech and dot-com crash. Adeo Ressi was a card-carrying member.

ADEO RESSI

For quite some time, I lost between one and two million every day. Just shwoot, shwoot, shwoot. I'd go to dinner with my friends, and it would be like, "I lost one million today. How you doing?" They'd say, "Great. I lost two million today. How you doing?" That was the beginning of the end.

I watched the market cap of the entire company of Xceed fall below the purchase price of Methodfive. Then I watched the market cap of Xceed fall below what I earned from the deal! The ultimate point of disgrace was when the market cap of Xceed fell below the cash that I still had left after paying taxes. That's a scary point.

All told, I lost close to thirty million dollars of value in Xceed. But the company thwarted efforts by employees and managers to sell their stock. They ignored clauses in agreements. They basically blocked transfer agents from transferring registered shares. So you were pretty much stuck with the stock.

DOUG SCOTT

At one point, I had $3.1 million on paper in Promotions.com, a company I cofounded. The day of the 2000 Oscar party, my wife said that we should sell tomorrow. I was like, No, No, No. And sure enough, six months later, all that paper money is up in smoke. The stock went from thirty-five dollars to getting bought by iVillage for eighty-seven cents a share.

GONG SZETO

People were given these stock options and they would have their special calculators to figure out what the stock was worth. But it's not like you have the stock. A lot of people, even at Rare Medium, lost their shirts. They exercised their options, went hog-wild and bought houses, cars, you name it, and then when it came tax time, they were like, "Whaddaya mean, I have to pay taxes on this?" They would end up owing hundreds of thousands of dollars, and we had some employees who just ended up completely ruined.

From cab drivers to college students to investment bankers, everyone seems to have an opinion about where the market will go next, but rarely is the verdict, "It can't go any lower." It can. It may not, but it can. Forces beyond John Q. Public's control—from terrorists to the Enron scandal—can dramatically affect people's financial lives.

We heard stories of soon-to-be-retirees who have had to extend their professional careers by five to ten years. Young investors rue their lost fortunes or justify them as "a very expensive education." Historians warn us that, like the Dutch tulip craze, the Mississippi bubble in France and the South Sea bubble in Britain, history is bound to repeat itself. But maybe this time, we've learned a thing or two.

ANDREW ANKER

If you could start a company, and have a billion-dollar IPO six or nine months later, then spending a few million here and there didn't matter. Normally, most of the dollars are spent toward generating revenue—dollars in and dollars out. The idea being that once you have revenue, you get to profitability, and those are things that the market will value.

But these Net startups skipped the revenue step, instead spending dollars *now* to get that money back in the public market. There were no underpinnings to the business. In fact, I remember quotes—"One in ten is going to a billion dollars, so one hundred million is the right amount to spend."

And, in a short-term way, it was a rational set of responses to the way things were going. It just wasn't a rational set of responses to the fact that things go up and down, not just up. We have to remember that.

Nowadays, it's easier to remember the downs than the ups. In recession-plagued 2001, only one Internet company, LoudCloud, cofounded by the former Netscape whiz kid Marc Andreessen, went public. But just as *Time* magazine was reporting in February 2002 that the startup's stock had since fallen approximately 40 percent, the online payment service PayPal.com raised $70 million for its much ballyhooed February 15 IPO; it gained 55 percent that day.

Will PayPal's success spur IPO fever again?

The industry's reaction remains cautious, but that won't stop the journalist Rebecca Eisenberg, who joined PayPal as an attorney just months before the company's IPO and subsequent steady rise, from feeling *slightly* less resentful of her Stanford buddies who cashed out big early on.

CHAPTER NINE THE LAYOFFS

I didn't really check the FuckedCompany site, but a lot of
people did on staff. I had to be told that there was an item on
me. Mine said, "Anyone know if that no-talent Laura Rich got
laid off?" I was touched! Somebody noticed me.
        —Former *Industry Standard* columnist Laura Rich

It is never an easy thing to close a company . . . [but] We
unanimously state that the Kibu team is one of the most creative, productive, and determined teams any of us has worked
with. You have built the foundation of a great product, and
your spirit and determination in this tough market has been
remarkable. The Kibu culture reflects your passion and commitment to the company and the team.
        —An excerpt from the closing letter sent by the Kibu Board of
        Directors to the entire Kibu staff, October 2000.

"If the queen had balls, she'd be the king," a good friend used to tell me when
I'd fall into a neurotic fit of "What ifs." But even if Kibu's investors hadn't asked
back for their remaining millions in October 2000 (leading worried dot-commers to exclaim, "Don't get Kibu'd!" lest they also be requested to return their
VC stash), I still wouldn't have been around for the potential IPO windfall.

Months earlier, I'd gotten canned.

———————

Upon Judy's return from her summer elopement in Bali, the management
team presented the results of our offsite meeting. To our surprise, both Judy

225

and Molly seemed pleased. In a bout of uncharacterisitic decisiveness, Molly even gave us the official go-ahead to implement the new plan. So off we went, pumped with purpose, charging into the Valley at the last second like the eCavalry.

While I probably should have been slightly suspicious of this sudden save-the-business brio, later that day, when Molly sent an e-mail asking if I'd meet with her and Judy at four-thirty, I naively assumed it was about the changes we'd outlined earlier. But as soon as I walked into the conference room, I was greeted not with the usual Kibu culture hoopla but with icy silence. I'd barely sat down when Judy announced somberly that instead of a strategy session, this was a "termination discussion."

"A what?" I replied with concern, never having heard the phrase, and thinking that someone—or perhaps Kibu itself—might have died.

"A termination discussion," Judy repeated matter-of-factly.

Lowering my armload of project folders, I stared back in disbelief. In the real world, I would have been fired, sacked, axed, shitcanned, laid off, downsized, cut—or, if the boss had an athletic bent, "released." But in e-speak, I was being "unhired."

Why?

Forget the laudatory e-mails that Judy had been sending me, like this one in late May: "Lori: In this and in many other communications I have seen from you, I have seen an incredible sense of how to motivate a team. Thanks so much for all you [sic] efforts to be a confident leader and a real cheerleader. That is SO important in a start-up environment, and it is a rare quality in management in my experience. Judy."

Or the press releases picked up by the national media in which Judy is quoted as saying that I was a "tremendous asset" and that "Lori's entertainment and publishing background" were "perfect for driving the editorial content and site experience for Kibu."

No, this termination discussion was all termination, no discussion. After being handed a boilerplate two-sentence letter, the closest I got to an explanation was that I had failed to "bond with the Faces."

"Bond with the Faces?" I felt like I'd been trapped in *Animal Farm* by way of *The Trial*.

"Yes," Judy said. "They needed coddling. They needed a mom."

I hated to admit it, but maybe she was right. If Kibu had hired a mom to watch over the Faces—say, Mother Teresa—she would have

July 10, 2000

Lori Gottlieb

████████████████

Dear Lori,

Effective today, July 10, 2000, your employment with Kibu is terminated. We wish you the best of luck in your future endeavors.

Sincerely,

[signature]

Judy MacDonald

Lori Gottlieb gets "unhired" at Kibu, after failing to "bond with the Faces."

written content for more than a dozen channels on her own each day, letting Kibu's Faces play outside the office, dithering about on their exorbitant salaries and company credit cards. In order to "bond," she would have asked the Faces to call her "Mommy Teresa," and she'd have looked the other way when members of her flock called her a "meanie" simply because she'd asked them to turn in their copy on deadline.

But I hadn't been so altruistic: I wanted to carry my own workload, see that others did too, and watch the company succeed. This clearly violated the sacred "Kibu culture."

Even so, perhaps the real reason for my unhiring had less to do with me and the Faces, or even me and Kibu, than it did with the dot-com world in general. I had, after all, violated the most important rule of the dot-com world: I'd said, loudly and insistently, that the emperor had no clothes.

So while part of me felt blindsided when I was handed that termination letter, deep down, I half expected it. Even though Judy was rarely around, she'd heard through her lackeys that I'd objected too many times to too many half-baked ideas, and attempted to establish too much of a "regular" work-place schedule. Most egregiously, I'd refused to cheer blindly at every empty interoffice email announcement, which I privately likened to Kibu's version of *Pravda*. Sustaining the illusion at all costs became the prevailing dot-com ethos, so that even on that fateful day, when I returned from the conference room to the cube farm, I mistakenly thought I'd been the only employee to get that innocent-sounding "Let's meet this afternoon" doomsday e-mail. All seemed like business as usual at Kibu Central.

So much so, in fact, that the next morning, according to some still-hireds, staffers who showed up at their nine-thirty departmental meetings—part of the newly implemented plan that management had presented just the day before—wondered where their bosses were. Had they gotten the time wrong? Had a carpool gotten into a fender-bender while pulling off the 101 freeway?

Rumors abounded until the All Hands meeting, when the unhirings were mentioned only in passing. On this day's whiteboards, where Judy posted each meeting's topics, next to the usual "most embarrassing story" item was something called "new agenda" to be handed out to the group. Reminiscent of the Susan Scarpa purging, we kiboshed Kibukis got nothing more than the brief valedictory "They've moved on" along with a cheery admonition that those remaining not "dwell" on the news. Meanwhile, the bullet-pointed new agenda included "Face's [sic] New Improved Role" (followed, predictably, by a happy face), and "Send new passwords. . . for security reasons."

Whatever the Faces' new role supposedly was, it couldn't save the entire Kibu staff from that final log-off in October. But while the site continued to operate, it wasn't a bad idea to take security precautions following this not-so-gracious goodbye. "Fired workers have always exacted revenge on their former employers," wrote *Business Week*'s Michelle Conlin in July 2001. But, she continued, "With more than 30,000 Web sites filled with hacking tools that any grade-schooler could use, today's brand of getting even is far easier for alienated workers to pull off."

According to Conlin, wreaking instant revenge had become so easy that Feds in San Francisco began routinely uncovering cyber sabotage, including the posting of a company's payroll on its Intranet; the sending of bawdy e-mails with pornographic attachments; publishing user IDs and passwords; sending data-destroying bugs; and forwarding intellectual property to competitors. And this was in addition to sneaking laptops, palming Palms, and bootlegging those nifty glow-in-the-dark pens past the beefy security guards at the door.

Obviously, reprisal was never an appropriate response, but laid-off digerati had reason to be disgruntled. Their main complaint wasn't so much that they'd been fired— after all, many were just-out-of-college liberal arts majors who, instead of slogging after a Ph.D., found themselves in groovy, high-paying—but high-risk—gigs. If their companies failed, well, some had to. Instead, what these former employees found so remarkable wasn't necessarily that the layoffs happened, or even that so many happened all at once, but that they were handled, in the words of *Salon's* technology and business staff, like "one massively botched-up amateur hour."

Salon cites a few of the acts. There was the executive assistant at Snowball.com who received the list of to-be-canneds from the human resources director, saw her own name in bits and bytes, and began e-mailing other people on the list to warn them of their fates. So much for Snowball executives' attempts at "controlling the flow of information."

Even those who hadn't been warned soon learned of their impending doom. Overhearing other employees' phone conversations ("Do they not realize how we all sit next to each other?" one worker asked), it became apparent that HR was going down the cubicles and toppling staffers like a row of dominos. Of course, once workers caught on, no one answered their phones: You can't fire me if you can't *find* me.

Salon also heard from a staffer at The New York Times on the Web, who read about his group's impending layoffs "in the very publication that was laying us off." All the news that's fit to print? At least reporters at *The Industry Standard* read about their publication's belt tightening on Inside.com rather than in their own pages. But who would be let go? As the just-axed flung their business cards on the street below, passersby were given a list in the form of red and white confetti.

A former Listen.com employee told *Salon* that despite management's adding staff as late as November 2000, on the Tuesday after New Year's Day,

2001, all employees received an e-mail asking them to report to one of two conference rooms for a mandatory meeting, where those in the inauspicious locale were asked to please disappear. Meantime, those who were getting back later from vacation arrived innocently at their cubicles, refreshed and ready to work, only to find their access denied. Other blunders included putting names on the wrong "to fire" list due to administrative fuckups; and telling folks there would be layoffs the following week but insisting that all employees meet their deadlines anyway.

We also learned about an online entertainment site that divided the staff into two groups, and sent those in the "made it" group off on a yellow school bus while HR fired the rest. A large e-commerce book site sent e-mails to senior management with a list of everyone who would be let go. . . and accidentally cc'd all the people who were to be, uh, let go.

Where it had been hip to talk about how many stock options you were granted, it soon became hip to talk about how badly you were mistreated when you were laid off. After all, even prisoners headed for the electric chair got a last meal.

"Just another bug smeared on the cyber windshield," is how one ex-dotcommer described the experience of receiving multiple e-mails from coworkers vying for her soon-to-be-vacant, closer-to-the-latté-machine cubicle the nanosecond word spread that she'd been "uninstalled."

As Internet and tech companies from Yahoo! to Cisco to Playboy.com, announced large-scale layoffs (euphemistically referred to as "restructurings"), the thousands who were "between opportunities" or "consulting" contributed to online layoff bitching boards like Philip "Pud" Kaplan's FuckedCompany.com, NetSlaves.com, and DotComScoop.com.

The accounts on these boards boast not merely alternately whiny and irreverent musings; they also constitute virtual case studies of the last days of many a dot-com. At first, the companies tend towards apologies, sending their victims consoling hugs, e-mails, and phone calls—the touchy-feely dirge of, "We tried, we were real *warriors*, we were such a great *team*, we'll help you in any way we can."

The laid off employees, meantime, respond to their loss by resorting—à la the psychiatrist Elizabeth Kubler-Ross's stages of grieving—to denial, but soon comes bargaining. "What, you've known about this for weeks, and you *still* told me to buy the car? How about severance? Health insurance?"

Few who post on these death-watch sites make it all the way to the final stage of grieving: acceptance. Most seem stuck between anger and depression. After all, death is for grandparents, not their too-cool companies—or *them*—right?

Wrong.

Even some of these layoff Web sites have been downsized. *The Industry Standard*'s online "Layoff Tracker," for instance, was a must-have bookmark on dot-commers' laptops until the magazine filed for bankruptcy in August 2001 and its site went dark.

Could we have seen the carnage coming? The attorney Peter Heinecke believes that better recruiting practices might have prevented the brutal bloodshed.

PETER HEINECKE

Companies had these headcount budgets early on, so their major accomplishment was recruiting a staff. But they kept on recruiting people despite the fact that they weren't meeting their revenue numbers. They assumed there would be more money, or the revenue would come in, but right then the most vital thing was getting the people—however many options you had to give, or however much money you had to spend on salaries. And then it turned out they couldn't pay the people, so they had to fire them.

These downsizings ranged from the good to the bad to the ugly. UBUBU's Josh Keller says of the firing squad experience that "the net effect was pretty good. No one got angry or anything, and friendships weren't severed." Not so sanguine is Sang Lee, who feels that Rare Medium handled the process "poorly." At the ugly end of the spectrum came cases of outright blackmail, as described by Adeo Ressi of Xceed (which had swallowed Ressi's Web shop, Methodfive).

ADEO RESSI

I had already left Xceed, but my brother was still an employee and he was down in Brazil working on a major client project for the company. It was earning seven figures of revenue for them. Meanwhile, back in New York, they were laying him off. They call all of his colleagues into a room and terminate them, and there was a packet on one of the chairs that says "Alex Ressi," but he has no idea.

So he goes into his hotel room in Brazil to log onto the Intranet, but his access privileges have been revoked. Then he calls someone in the office asking what's going on, and when he finds out, he's like, "Holy cow, I'm in Brazil!" He calls me up for advice, and I tell him that the chips are in his hand: He's with a client who's paying the company a lot of money.

So, he calls up the CEO to say, "I'm the front man on a huge account for you guys. If you want me not to sabotage it and get on the next plane home, I'm going to need an exceptional severance package, and all my access privileges turned back on. I want this in writing within twenty-four hours or I'm going to sabotage the whole account."

Sure enough, in twenty-four hours he got everything he asked for.

It wasn't easy being the executioner, and a difficult decision involved where to lead the dead man walk. The HR room? A conference room? Starbucks? In a clumsy attempt to spare feelings—or perhaps a selfish bid at preventing mutiny—many dot-coms herded employees "on the list" into one room, out of sight of the "saved" employees in another room. But according to J. Betty Ray, whether you got door number one or door number two, the situation just plain sucked.

"Most layoffs were standard-issue awful," she says. "It's just: You guys go into one room, you guys go into another room. And we have the All Hands meeting at the end. The rest of us left are sitting there going, 'Fuck.'"

Boo.com's Cameron Hickey, who watched his company go through several rounds of layoffs on two continents, agrees.

CAMERON HICKEY

The layoffs started in New York at Christmastime 1999. A good friend of mine was responsible for Miss Boo, and the last day before Christmas break, they fired him, gave me a raise, and gave me options. They told me about an hour before they fired him, because they wanted to know if he had any equipment. Laptops were always getting stolen.

Then in February 2000, I arrived in London to work out the plans for the second version of the site. After the day's meeting, I went to the area of the office where all the design and magazine people usually sit, and I found most of the area empty, except for a few of the designers who told me that they had all been taken out to breakfast that morning by Kajsa, the cofounder, while apparently the entire magazine staff back at the office was sacked! Kajsa didn't even tell them during the breakfast that this was happening, because she knew the two groups were close friends, and they wouldn't stand for it.

They also did this so that the magazine people wouldn't see the design people after they were let go, which would have been awkward. This was the rule: Once you were fired, you had fifteen minutes to pack up and get out. In the end, most of the magazine people came back for a whole day to gather all their files off the computers, because they wanted to use their creative work for their portfolios. And as a little bit of revenge, they completely wiped all the hard drives they had used, so that Boo no longer had any of their work.

I wasn't actually on the scene for the New York layoffs in February 2000, but I heard about what happened. In the customer service area, they told a bunch of people to leave and go to one room. They told another group of people to go to another room. They told those in room A that they were getting fired, and they told those in room B that the other room was getting fired. But they must have forgotten that there was a huge *glass wall* separating the two rooms! So, you're telling one room that they're getting fired due to financial reasons, but they're looking right at the group that's staying! There was yelling and screaming afterward, and those that were fired didn't leave.

At DEN that same year, layoff techniques applied in supposedly laid-back Los Angeles were similarly draconian and ham-fisted.

MATTHEW KLAUSCHIE

There were over three hundred employees at DEN in three different buildings, and an e-mail circulated in upper management about the list of layoffs.

One of the guys in the IT department got a hold of the list because he had access to all the e-mails, and he was giving people heads-ups. Of course, he got fired for that.

They laid off over one hundred people in one day. They invited you into a room, and while you were there, they closed down your e-mail account. Once you got laid off, they had lots of uniformed security there. They just gave you a box and you had to get your stuff out.

MATT WELCH

An eighteen-year-old girl started off as a glorified secretary and ended up working as the assistant to the legal department. She was one of the first dozen people to work there, and she really, really, really believed in the idea. And in the end, as it was all falling apart, not only was she fired but they accused her—falsely, she said—of having a sexual affair with one of the key founders. She wrote this to me in an e-mail, still believing in the idea and wanting to think it was a good experience.

DAVID NEUMAN

My most unpleasant memories at DEN are the layoffs. They happened in two major installments. One hundred twenty people were let go on the same day in March. Downsizing had to do in part with completing obligations we had to our investment bankers—restructuring our business model to adjust the burn rate of our company.

If you're going to lay off 120 people in a 300-person company, there's no great way to take care of it. We had a young female manager who weighed 100 pounds tell someone twice her size that your last day is today, and here is your severance. And she was genuinely fearful for her personal safety, so you have to have security present. But that creates an environment in which people are offended that you think they need to be escorted out by a guard.

The second wave was better: Everyone was fired, including ourselves. It was dramatic because we were negotiating bridge financing literally to the last minute. The clock struck five P.M. on a Tuesday in May of 2000, and according to our lawyers, if we didn't have a solid commitment to financing at five P.M., we had to let everyone go. But it was less agonizing because there was no survivor-guilt problem. There was no "Who's on the list, and who isn't?"

———————

Rare Medium's layoffs in 2000 and 2001 looked a lot like many startups' original hirings: based more on who you knew than on how well or how hard you had worked.

MARIA ISABEL GOUVERNEUR

The layoffs were done Mafia style: if you were a good friend of someone in the inner circle, you stayed. It wasn't based on any professional skill, your performance, merit, principle, nothing.

After about a year of layoffs, I went on vacation. They never contacted me to let me know I'd just been laid off, but I had a friend, who also got laid off, who had been the assistant to the president of the office. So she knew my name was on the list, and called me to let me know.

Well, I was on a tropical island looking at parrots and palms, and I felt a little weird and pissed off, especially because I'd worked hard. I knew it would happen eventually because I was the last person in the design department who wasn't part of the "Mafia," but still.

So I called several times, and nobody returned my call. Every day they somehow managed to have a "car accident" or "major tragedy" and couldn't make it in. After a few days, I got a call, not from Rare, but from this girl who was already laid off, who asked if I wanted to go back! For a public company that should be professionally managed, you get a call from your friend who is not even working for the company, asking if you want to go back to work?! At this time in New York, finding a job wasn't so easy. So I cut my vacation short and went back.

Later on, I asked my friend why they brought me back. She explained that the "Mafia" got into deep trouble because people were taking stuff home. Two or three monitors per person, twenty-five Aeron chairs. Laptops, video cameras, digital cameras, scanners, Palms, Blackberries. People who had a couple of G4s at their work-stations switched them with G3s and took the G4s home. Anyway, they all got fired, but Rare needed to finish a project, and that's why I got hired back.

I worked for another four weeks, then got laid off *again*. I saw the office manager very stressed out, so I thought something would happen on Friday, ten days after the World Trade Center. I called my friend and asked her to find out, and I heard they were closing the office the day after, "top secret." But when I found out, I looked around, it was two P.M., and everybody was already packing their stuff! They always did these things that were "top secret," but everybody knew.

My check from them bounced, I never got severance from the first time I got laid off, and the office closed down on September twenty-third. I got a lawyer and they finally sent me a new check. Of course, they counted vacation days that I never took, and comp days that had been promised became unofficial. They did whatever they wanted.

GONG SZETO

We first started doing the Rare layoffs by the book and people would get six weeks' severance. But it quickly turned into two weeks' severance, one week's severance, no severance. They were brought into a room, exit-interviewed, and had one hour to get out. We had to hire security guards to come in because there were a few exit interviews where people screamed, and yelled, and cried. But no violence or anything.

SHULI HALLACK

At the end, to boost morale, they paid for a motorized scooter for people in the office, but nobody showed up to work. There was nothing to do—how much can you surf the Net? The only people left at Rare were the highest paid, the management, the ones with the titles who did no work and just read the paper all day.

———————

If the digerati hoped to create new ways of doing business, they succeeded when it came to not doing business, i.e., firing people. Having labeled their

Old Economy counterparts "conventional," these New Economy successors found their own innovative ways to behave like assholes.

J. Betty Ray remembers a dot-com producer friend who was thinking of buying a house. "She had talked to her bosses beforehand," Ray says of her friend, who told them about her plans and asked if both the company and her job were stable. "They were like, 'Yes, we're okay,'" continues Ray, but two weeks after her friend signed the papers, the company was shuttered. "That was the most brutal one."

Was it?

"Deep in the bowels of the Florida home office," says a former employee of the entertainment news site Hollywood.com, "some moles built an all-new, alternative site to the Hollywood.com site that was currently live. They launched it themselves and then the next day fired most of the Santa Monica crew in California who had been working on the live site. Imagine if, say, the *Los Angeles Times* designed an all-new paper with a secret staff—unbeknownst to its current staff—and then fired everybody!"

The insensitivity didn't end there.

CHRIS KINNEAR

They weren't very cool about the whole thing at eToys. We came back from Christmas vacation on a Monday, and that Thursday, everyone got two different meeting times. If you were in one, you were gone. If you were in the other, you stayed. I was in the group that stayed.

There was some residual bitterness, particularly because it came out that Toby Lenk, the CEO, was getting $500,000 to stick around for three months, and the other senior managers were getting $250,000 a piece. Meanwhile, everyone else is getting laid off and getting nothing. And those were the people who *really* needed the money.

MICHAEL FELDMAN

A friend's company recently pulled the plug, and they required people to take a forced vacation to cut costs, and to take an additional week at minimum wage. It just didn't bode very well for morale. People were sending around e-mails saying that they could make more money working at Starbucks.

During the forced vacation time, the company had the audacity to send around an e-mail telling people that they could "volunteer" at work. Believe it or not, people actually *did*, which was a testament to the fact that people had worked so hard they really didn't have lives anymore. They would rather show up to a job where they weren't getting paid than stay at home!

Over at *Wired*, though, Steven Overman wanted nothing more than to be told to stay at home, as he tried to beat a seemingly Kafkaesque system before it beat him.

STEVEN OVERMAN

I thought they were trying to get me to quit, and I didn't even know who "they" were. It wasn't Louis—it was just some faceless management who didn't feel like we needed the TV property that I was working on. I was so mad, so I did this thing I call "designing my own severance package." I wasn't going to quit. Fuck it.

There was no HR department at the company, so they hired this woman from Menlo Park. I went to her and said, "Marilyn, how many days in a row do I have to not show up before it's considered a resignation?" She said that if you're not here three days in a row with no explanation and no contact, then we consider that a resignation. So I said, "Okay, I'll see you every third day." She said, "Great." I was just waiting for someone to say, "Bad attitude."

For two months, I showed up every third day. It felt awful, but I didn't want to quit because I felt like I deserved a severance package. I had never done anything wrong. I was so loyal to this place because I'd learned so much there. But eventually I had to let go.

I started moonlighting for another company in the same building, and I'd see people getting coffee. They'd say, "Why aren't you at your desk?" and I'd say, "Oh, I'm working at a different company." I did everything I could to get laid off. Finally I got axed when Louis and Jane did, and I got a package on top of what I'd already designed for myself. It was great! I started full-time at the other company the next day.

Not surprisingly, there were other facets to the layoff lunacy, like the inexperienced managers who had learned how easy it was to hire folks, now had to learn how hard it could be to let them go. While working at a dot-com may have been considered "business school by proxy," the syllabus involved not just managing people and projects for the first time, but also knowing to say, "We're eliminating the position" instead of "This is performance-based." For some, the excruciating experience was akin to gently breaking up with a lover, and trying to convince the jilted party that "it's about me, not you."

"This was my first experience letting people go," says FreeSamples.com's CEO Jeff Malkin. "I came out of it more tough-skinned, more leather-skinned. But looking back, it was just sad."

JOSH KELLER

I would like to think that we handled it well at UBUBU, because I was the one who mainly did it. I called different companies who had done it over time, and there are all kinds of theories about laying people off—down to what day of the week you should and shouldn't do it on. I think the answer is that there's no good day.

We really sat down and tried to think about it from the other side of the table. And obviously, respect was the most important thing. We gave the same message about why we did it to people who were getting laid off and people who were staying on: it doubled or tripled the life of the company. We also talked with our board about giving severance packages, and it kind of appalled us that people weren't doing that. Amazingly, most of the people who were laid off understood, and let us know that they'd be happy to help later on.

But not every company founder had the courage to break it off directly. Some dot-coms had their version of *Broadcast News*'s Paul Moore character, the news division president-cum–hatchet man. At *HotWired* it was *Wired* Digital's president, Beth Vanderslice.

STEVEN OVERMAN

There was a joke at HotWired: "The Beth-march." That was when you had to walk to Beth Vanderslice's office and get laid off. There was a gallows humor about the whole thing.

DOUG SCOTT

Unlike in other organizations, where they brought everyone into a conference room and said, "You're all laid off. Get your shit and leave," I had to lay off over forty people in my department one by one.

I met with everyone in my office, and by number twenty, they would say to me, "Look, everyone knows you're the hatchet man. I know what's going on, let's just shoot the shit for five minutes." It's not easy laying off a thirty-six-year-old guy with two kids and a wife who doesn't work. And I had to say, "I've got more good news for you—you only have two weeks' severance."

GONG SZETO

The first round, corporate headquarters at Rare Medium would just open up spreadsheets and start laying off people without consulting me.

But when it got to the point of 30 percent of the people being laid off, they turned it over to me and said, "Gong, you need to start doing them." My group was around 250 people and I was pretty much responsible for signing off on laying off 90 percent of them—after having been directly or indirectly involved in hiring most of them.

It was kind of a shitty position for me to be in, because while a lot of objective people understand that I had to do it, I have definitely made my fair share of enemies. It's a "shooting the messenger" type of syndrome. I'm not as beloved as I was three years ago.

Ill will aside, no one should have been surprised at the blizzard of pink slips. All the signs were there: nervous HR employees, extra brown boxes suitable for carting away one's life suddenly appearing in the storage closet, higher frequency of cigarette breaks.

Still, many reacted with disbelief when they got the tap on the shoulder, as if the Grim Reaper had showed up on their doorsteps several years too soon, or with the wrong address. So what if there's no revenue? So what if we can't pay our bills? Those shocked by the seeming abruptness of the final day truly believed, "This must be a mistake!"

TOM LAZAROFF

Nine months into my tenure at PayMyBills, we hired a CEO from a banking background, who brought in people from the banking world. About three months later, suddenly they realized that $30 million wasn't taking them very far. At that point, I could see things were changing. A month later, they announced the merger with Paytrust.

Some people were let go, but other people stuck around and were there until January 2000. I had left by then, but I heard about the layoffs secondhand. Apparently, employees walked in and the office wasn't there. There were literally people there saying, "Please gather your things, we're closing the office." And that was it. There were fifty or sixty customer-service people who were hourly-wage people, and they were just told, "Sorry, it's over." It was so sudden that no one could believe it, even though they all knew it was coming.

LAURA RICH

The Industry Standard was trying to cut costs, so they told us to go on paid vacation for a week. Of course, we all expected to come back.

I went sailing up in San Francisco for a long weekend, and when I got back to L.A. on Tuesday afternoon, there was this big story on my beat about the five movie studios doing video-on-demand. I thought that even though I was on vacation, I had to file this story. So I went into the office to work on it.

On my way into the office, I'm talking to the editor of "Web News" about vacation pay. He's saying how he didn't take it out, because he's working this week. I said, "That's good—if we shut down, you'll have more hours to get paid back." He said, "What, do you think we'll shut down?" I was like, "Are you blind and deaf? It's a *possibility!*"

So I get into work, turn on the computer, start the story, and get an e-mail from an old friend of mine from *Inside Media* who's now working at *Ad Age*. She said, "We're about to post a story that your company is for sale and suspending operations. I'm really sorry that you're hearing it from me first."

I'm now pissed off that I'm hearing it from this friend, but I also think she must be wrong. Why wouldn't I have heard it when I was pretty tapped in to the buzz network at work? About half an hour later, a story went up on the *Wall Street Journal* Online and everyone was on the phone just going, "Look at this site!" We were all reading about it, and I was sitting there with this half-written story that I didn't know if I should file. It wasn't until five P.M. that we got an e-mail from the COO confirming the reports.

The company was supergenerous—we were given cell phones, laptops—but I don't think it was because of the fact that we were sensitive to covering other people's layoffs. I think it was because we had deep-pocketed investors.

––––––––––––

"Sensitive to covering other people's layoffs"? David Neuman didn't find *The Industry Standard* particularly sensitive when DEN shut its doors. It was like Mel Brooks's definition of the difference between comedy and tragedy: comedy is when *you* slip on a banana peel and fall into a manhole; tragedy is when *I* slip on a banana peel and fall into a manhole.

DAVID NEUMAN

One of the ironies when DEN went out of business was that *The Industry Standard* and Inside.com were the two most vicious publications in terms of saying, "Look at these idiots and fools. Look at how they squandered their money." And now that they're gone, it's put a perfect end to it. They were very insensitive when we were telling 180 employees this was our last day. Inside.com was calling on my cell phone in the middle of it. Their conduct was uncivil. I wonder if anyone was calling *them* when they were telling all their employees that it was over. Was there any karma in the minds of these writers?

Unlike the gloating press corps, colleagues consoled each other with ample Kleenex wads and reassuring words. Yet despite the vain attempts of many to shrug it all away, getting laid off or watching your company fold tended to engender a combination of anger and self-doubt in even the most balanced personalities with the most pacific perspectives on life. After a while, logical explanations—"Everybody's getting laid off"; "It was a great learning experience"—seemed like the emptiest of bromides. It was still rejection, or—worse for these overachievers—failure.

In a column on the proliferation of therapy groups targeting downsized and demoralized dot-commers, the *New York Times* business reporter Abby Ellin half-jokingly described the emotional fallout as "Adult Survivors of Dysfunctional Dot-Coms." Yet Nicholas Hall, founder of the online support community StartupFailures.com, told Ellin that a recent survey on his site revealed rattled confidence and health problems—not to mention being "left without a personal vision"—as serious concerns for the unhireds.

In talking to displaced dot-commers, we discovered a wide range of emotions, from cynicism to sorrow to Schadenfreude—and everything in between.

LEV CHAPELSKY

You know what it is with these younger people, when they get laid off? The reason they cry in that meeting is because they have no options that vested, and they were told they would be worth two to five million. They lived for six or nine months believing not that they had paper money, but that they were multimillionaires! Then that one day, it all goes up in smoke.

CATHY BROOKS

Hell, yeah, I wanted to get rich, but I'm not bitter, angry, and throwing darts at people's pictures in my apartment. My company and I "mutually beneficially parted ways"—I think that's the way we spun it—which means they "fired my ass."

The day I got laid off, I went to Absinthe, where a friend of mine met me for champagne and oysters, because she told me that this was a celebration, not a sad moment. But when someone boots you out, even if you're just biding your time waiting for them to can you, it's still rejection. You still feel like shit.

CHRIS KINNEAR

It was a very emotional experience at eToys. A lot of us really believed in the company. We had sacrificed an enormous amount. I look at FuckedCompany and all the crapping on people that they do—"Your life was cushy and all"—but it wasn't like that. People worked incredibly hard. I didn't take a vacation for two years. There was a period where I worked thirty days without taking a single day off. By the end of it, people had a pretty deep respect for each other. There was a real sense of camaraderie through battle.

I broke down after they laid everyone off. I came home and realized that after the enormous investment we'd put in, it was all gone.

LAURA RICH

It really pisses me off, because I enjoyed what I was doing. It really is like someone died. The language that people used in their e-mails was one of sending condolences. The language that I used back was, "It's a big shock for us. . . it came suddenly." It was like a cancer.

DAVID NEUMAN

I was heartbroken and shattered that we failed, despite our best efforts. I was jealous that our sister companies were still operating. I thought, "Pop and WireBreak and Thirsty will succeed where we have failed. They'll get their next financing and we'll have been the shameful failure."

Someone looked at me and said, "David, the only difference between DEN and all these other companies is how much money they have in the bank." And I remember thinking, Can that be true? Is it that extreme? Every one of them? Now virtually every peer company to DEN is gone. In retro-

---

ETOYS "FLAMES" ON FUCKEDCOMPANY.COM

ARROGANT JERK #34   Mar 07 2001
These arrogant jerks deserve it. HA HA HA. LOSERS!

FUCK ETOYS.COM   Mar 09 2001
Fuck eToys. Actually, fuck the assholes and greed-heads who ran the place. The
company was doomed after its ill-fated battle with etoy.com
I mean, what the fuck...eToys thought they would be the next General Electric or
something, so they decided to try to kill a Swiss anarchistic electronic art consortium
which just happened to use a name similar to theirs – and which PRE-EXISTED
eToys, for Christ sake.
Ha. They got fucked up the ass, hard, without lube, for that bit of genius.
Fuck them. They're better off dead. I laughed when I saw their tombstone yesterday...I want to put my monitor on the ground and dance on it.

ETOYS.COM   Apr 27 2001
Kids: So KBToys bought the festering pile of crap that is eToys.com for like $3.4 mil-
lion or some ABSOLUTELY FUCKING RIDICULOUS number. Hint, you stupid
fuckheads at KB: ABORT MISSION and instead hire some high school kid to make
that site for you in 2 fucking months. As for the domain name... anything over
$35/year is too much.

"I look at Fucked Company and all the crapping. . . but it wasn't like
that," says the former eToys producer Chris Kinnear.

spect, they just had a longer and more prolonged agony, but I didn't see it
that way at the time.

Many dot-coms died the way they lived—as a family, huddled against the
world. Everyone would come together for one final All Hands meeting to
commiserate. Joanne Weaver, who fondly recalls the "Gooooooo Scient!"
cheers at the once high-flying Web shop, also remembers the moving
good-byes. "We were corralled into a big meeting room," Weaver says of
that day in December 2000 when about 25 percent of the company was laid
off. Scient chairman Bob Howe "got into the room on a speakerphone and
said, 'You're the best people I've ever worked with.' "

"When I got laid off from HomeGain, you could tell it was a very emotional thing for our CEO," says former Vice President Kal Deutsch. "He considered us his family."

Not every dot-com clan, however, behaved like TV's Bradys or Partridges.

ANDREW BRENNER

A company I worked with had a big meeting, and the CEO went on and on for an hour about all sorts of stuff, how they were family, etcetera. Everyone in the company was getting antsy because they knew there were going to be layoffs. So, finally they announce that the company is shutting down, and people race back to their desks to copy files and maybe snag their laptops and other goodies before bolting.

But here's the thing: The reason the CEO jabbered so long is that he had people go around during his speech and collect everyone's computer equipment so they couldn't abscond with it!

Fortunately, employees didn't have to live with these surrogate Addams families. But for many, the stress and long hours of the startup lifestyle had an adverse and irreparable effect on their actual families. In the end, some dot-commers didn't just lose their paper wealth, their dreams, their jobs and their businesses—they lost their loved ones, too.

ADEO RESSI

On April 19, 2000, I was in Europe on my first vacation in five years with a woman I was very serious with. I was meeting her family. I was about to walk into a restaurant to meet her mom, and someone phones me to tell me that Xceed's stock is at seven dollars. They said that I absolutely had to get on the next flight for a meeting to figure out what the hell to do. This is my first vacation in *years*. Basically, our stock had dipped from the forties two weeks earlier to fourteen, and from fourteen to seven in the last day.

So I had to fly back to New York to come up with an aggressive action plan. I actually met my girlfriend's mom for fifteen minutes, where I was extremely torn between making a good impression, and the fact that I had lost the majority of my illiquid wealth, and worrying about a company that I knew was in a lot of trouble and that I was managing. We've since broken up. Let's put it this way—it didn't help the relationship.

DOUG SCOTT

I'm in the midst of a divorce due to these last four years. I got married in April of 1997 and moved my wife out to L.A. in June 1997. We left L.A. in December 2000 and we separated in February of 2001. My marriage ran a parallel track to my business, and all that I have left from that is a two-year-old daughter, who is the love of my life. I regret a lot of the things that I didn't do, and how I put my business in front of my family.

I've attempted to have this conversation over and over with my wife. But when I look back at the so-called tulip craze here, I don't know if I would have been able to do it any differently. I'm looking around at my peers, I'm looking around at the opportunity, I'm looking around at the hype and the wealth, and I got caught up in the system.

Toward the closing stages of an Internet company's life, some noticed that this system was functioning differently, and that things were, in fact, changing. The Silicon Alley attorney Steven Masur says he heard the death knell of Kozmo.com, the once-popular home delivery service, "when this 10-year-old kid would show up on your doorstep with eighteen liters of Coke and a lobster dinner under his arm. That was grim."

Shuli Hallack knew the end was near at Rare Medium when the $1,500-a-day hot lunches from New York's finest restaurants were discontinued, along with the dollar-apiece mozzarella sticks for all employees. Then there was the photo wall that Hallack says the company had spent nine thousand dollars on.

"When we were growing quickly," explains Hallack, "each person took a picture of themselves that they could manipulate as they pleased in Photoshop. But after the first round of layoffs, you kept seeing people coming down off the wall."

Hallack's Rare Medium colleague, the engineer Kenny Lin, remembers his coworkers heeding these warning signs—and taking action while they still could.

KENNY LIN

Our full coverage for Lasik eye surgery was being reduced, so from November to December, many people were getting Lasik procedures. The running joke in the office was, anyone with glasses or contacts must be a new employee. People who were planning on leaving got their eyes done before giving notice—one guy even gave his two weeks' notice and got his eyes done the next day!

CATHY BROOKS

When I went out of town, I came back and had a new boss. I knew it was only a matter of time before I was out, so I started cleaning up my résumé and talking to friends, but I was going in and doing my basic job. Kind of like there were a lot of people in the industry just "skating" in the end.

Around that time I went to an industry event at the Filmore, and someone says to me, "So, Cathy, what do you do?" I don't even bat an eye and say, "Well, I'm a consultant." And they said, "Oh, what kind of consultant?" I said, "Well, public relations, but it delves a little bit into marketing." They said, "Oh, tell me more." So I took a deep breath, thought for a second, and said, "Well, it's a very niche practice. I focus completely on prelaunch companies, preannouncement companies for brand-new products, companies that are going into new markets or new directions."

They asked, "How long have you been in business?" I looked at my watch and said, "About five minutes." By noon the next day, I had five clients.

JOANNE WEAVER

Here's how I first knew that Scient was going down. We would always have these really posh, beautifully put on rallies with Veuve Clicquot champagne and a full spread of food—they were pretty much parties. When the industry was going downhill, someone said to me, "Do you notice that we're getting Bud Light and Glenn Allen instead of Heineken and Ankerstein?" That really hit me as pretty significant, because if they're scaling back on the little things, how bad are the *big* things?

JEFF GOODELL

Shortly before the crash, I went to go see my friend at Silicon Graphics. I used to ride my bike out to Silicon Graphics and remembered that it's just at the bottom of the Bay in Mountain View. I used to walk my dog out there in the fields. Well, the fields were gone, and in their place, one of the most fabulously designed corporate campuses was there. It's incredibly, exquisitely designed—it's the perfect workplace.

So I went there to visit my friend, but the place was *empty*. It was dead! A complete tomb. And it was so bizarre, because Silicon Graphics had been a once-glorious Silicon Valley company, and it was already a dead company walking.

FORMER PRODUCER AT DISNEY'S GO.COM

The last few months, we couldn't sell ads. Engineers and writers were quitting. The mood was definitely changing. We kept losing managers—they would just resign. We had like three or four GMs in the course of a year. We really started thinking, "Well, maybe this isn't going to work. What are we going to do?"

All of a sudden, we start hearing that Michael Eisner's been in meetings with senior managers, and he was given three options. One was to go to a site that just had a search engine, one was to end Go.com completely, and one was to sell the site. One way or the other, we thought the product was doomed. But all of the managers were telling us that wasn't true.

There was bullshit being thrown around everywhere. No one was working. There were all kinds of pools all over the office, and everyone was running around placing bets. It didn't matter what management said: We knew.

MATTHEW KLAUSCHIE

Gary Gersh, DEN's chairman, called a meeting and said, "You know what? The whole company is fucked up, the content is fucked up, and we have to change the way this is running." They seemed like they wanted to do the right things, but we knew that the company was too far gone. Gary is a knowledgeable guy, but at the point when Gary and his people took over, the morale and attitude of the general population was just, "Fuck it."

———

"Fuck it" was also the attitude of many embittered ex-employees. Revenge came in the form of theft, sabotage; and the equally injurious act of "flaming" and slandering on sites like Philip "Pud" Kaplan's FuckedCompany.com.

"I make over a million dollars now on FuckedCompany," says Kaplan, who laughs his way to the bank with revenue from ads, subscribers, and proprietary software. "It's beautifully ironic that I'm making money off a site that's premised on all these dumb companies and fucked-up managements."

DAVID NEUMAN

Once a down cycle starts and you're laying people off, you have all these angry people with axes to grind. If you looked at FuckedCompany, you'd see a thousand listings by all these people who have enormous grudges against their companies—"This person's an idiot and that person's an idiot."

We were among the beneficiaries, if you will, of this new phenomenon: employees get to vent on the Web. That never existed before. Let's say someone who got laid off from a GE plant had a visit from Jack Welch for forty minutes in 1993. All of a sudden, he becomes the new online authority on Jack Welch's ability level!

I'm not comparing myself to Jack Welch, because I have about one percent of his brainpower, but now there's an irresistible opportunity for people to even scores they feel they have with an employer. If you're out there raising money, and somebody who's got it in for you is up there on the message boards saying your company is fucked, you now have a situation to deal with that didn't used to exist in corporate history.

———

The industry's PR firms, party planners and outside agencies also got screwed—out of fees owed to them by their now-defunct Web clients.

TED KRUCKEL

We got stuck with over $100,000 in fees and expenses. In some cases, it wasn't their fault. The CEO of Ashford.com, Kenny Kurtzman, left and the new CEO didn't pay some of their bills. They had a great track record with us until then. BeautyJungle made all sorts of promises that they didn't fulfill. So we got stuck with a lot of bills.

Instead of feeling stuck, resourceful entrepreneurs took an if-you-can't-beat-'em-join-'em tack by turning their experience with failed dot-coms into thriving Web communities. Andrew Brenner and Michael Feldman found themselves out of work in early 2001 after Brenner was laid off from Mspect, a wireless Internet services company; and Feldman shut down Tools, Inc., his online marketing services company.

They might have sat around watching *Oprah* and pigging out on Häagen-Daz, but Brenner and Feldman decided to start Recession Camp (RecessionCamp.com), whose mission, according to their Web site, is "to help those downsized. . . to remain healthy, happy, and social while they look for their next job."

ANDREW BRENNER

Michael went away to South America, and I had gotten laid off a week or two before. When he got back, I called him and said, "Hey, let's go see a movie today." So we went to a matinee of *Lara Croft Tomb Raider*. While we were standing there contemplating Angelina Jolie's various outfits, we were talking about all the things that we wanted to do that summer. I wanted to go hiking and to museums, see some baseball games. I said, "There's got to be a lot of laid-off people in San Francisco, but there's no way to actually meet them."

The people that you knew in Silicon Valley were either through your company or dot-com parties. We needed to find these people who wanted to get out of the house. I said, "Let's call it 'Recession Camp,' " and for thirty-five dollars, I registered the name. I used my Web skills to create the site, and a week later, we were live.

We launched at one of Patty Beron's Pink Slip parties. We had business cards made up and told people to check out the site. People thought it was funny and sent it around to a bunch of their friends. The first event was the day after July Fourth, and we had only a handful of people, but people started to tell people, and then we started to get press.

It really was what the Net was magically good for. We get e-mails from people who want to start up Recession Camps around the world! We're riding the dot-com bomb all the way down! You live the excitement of the dot-coms all over again. Our mailing list is growing by a hundred people a week now.

People's conversations on the outings range from how they deal with their parents to what state has the best unemployment insurance—California does not. No subject is taboo. But we do ask that you not be negative. When you get people going on hikes and to museums, it's usually positive.

The most satisfying moment has been helping a lot of people. It sounds corny, but people thank us. We get e-mails from laid-off people who had been down in the dumps, but they think Recession Camp is cool. At the very least, they know they're not alone.

Still, Feldman and Brenner, like their Recession Camp bunkmates, remain jobless—and befuddled by the lack of action.

ANDREW BRENNER

You'd think that people would say, "Hey, these guys are clever, let's hire them." I would think that from all the press, and the fact that our résumés are on the site, we would get jobs. But *nothing!*

CHAPTER TEN

THE HEREAFTER

Dan Adler

Adler continues to run the New Media department at Hollywood's Creative Artists Agency, where since the early 1990s he has spearheaded ground-breaking deals by involving the agency's artists and corporate clients in Internet ventures.

> I remember going on the road early on and talking to John Hughes in Chicago about what was going on. I remember sitting down with Francis Ford Coppola in San Francisco and with Prince in Minneapolis, who at that stage was actually the "symbol." I had to put his little font into my Mac.
>
> We were doing stuff with Spielberg, Amblin, and Dreamworks. They were interested in seeing this new horizon and being an active part in its evolution. I think everybody knew—and knows—that something significant was—and is—going to happen. People who have a creative vision are passionate about letting that vision find its way to an audience.

Kurt Andersen

Anderson was editor-in-chief at *Spy* and *New York* magazines before starting his media news site, Inside.com, in May 2000. In 2001, Primedia acquired the site from Brill Media Holdings, which had bought Inside.com six months earlier. The author of the industry satire *Turn of the Century* (Random House, 1999), Andersen hosts *Studio 360*, a weekly radio show about "high and low art and culture" and serves, as a creative consultant to USA Entertainment.

The dot-com era was different because it was about being rich in addition to changing the world. But people will get over it. Still, as we all know, there are Baby Boomers who remain annoyingly and insanely nostalgic for their youths, when they were going to change the world. So probably for some young people now, the moment of 1998 and 1999 will be this thing that they remember bittersweetly and intensely forever.

Andrew Anker

Anker was CEO of *Wired* Digital from 1994 to 1998. He now doles out cash as a general partner at the Bay Area venture firm August Capital, where he focuses on Internet-related investments and serves on the boards of Emode, Guru.com, ImproveNet, Listen.com, and Topica.

I'm not going to tell my grandkids anything about this time. I mean, move on. The era comes and goes. The truth is, there are still far more interesting things going forward than there were in the past.

Steve Baldwin

Baldwin was a technology editor at Ziff-Davis from 1991 to 1994 and at Time Warner's online media site Pathfinder from 1994 to 1997. He has since built and managed both the Museum of E-Failures, an archive of dead dot-com homepages on Ghost Sites (disobey.com/ghostsites); and NetSlaves, a site that collects first-person accounts of Net workers. He is also at work on a follow-up to his first book, *NetSlaves: True Tales of Working on the Web* (McGraw-Hill, 1999).

Back in 1996, when I was working at Pathfinder, it was July Fourth and I was on a power sailboat crossing the Long Island Sound. Everyone was tired and went to bed, so my brother said, "Look, see this compass. Just keep the needle pointed east and you'll be okay. If you see a light ahead of you, it's a ship, so steer to the right." So, everyone's asleep, I see a light, and I steer to the right. But the light is a jetty! So I steer to the left. I violated the captain's orders and we all made it through.

I thought to myself, This is like the Net. We're all out here on our little ships, our sites. We're listening to the captain who doesn't know what the hell is going on, we're obeying orders, there's treacherous water ahead, and a lot of these sites are not going to make it, including the one that I'm working on. And, that's when I had the idea—Ghostsites! It's like the Flying Dutchman, which is like these abandoned ships, these ghostly presences, this undersea wreckage! I thought, this is a very risky thing we're all doing—we're betting our careers on the Web and there's no credibility. So I started to write about these derelict, defunct sites. I ran it on my little technology section and subtitled it, "Yesterday they ruled the Web, today they're Ghostsites."

Dave Bartis

A former senior programming executive at NBC, HBO, and 3Arts Entertainment, in 2000 Bartis cofounded Nibblebox.com, the college entertainment Web site, with his Brown University buddy Doug Liman, the director of *Go* and *Swingers*. Following the site's 2001 merger with Vivendi Universal's New Media production company, Hypnotic (Hypnotic.com), Bartis became CEO of the combined entity.

I feel like the Internet vortex stole a year of my life and I'm just catching up to reality. Someday I think people will look back at 1999 and 2000 and marvel at the insanity—no, wait, that's today. What's really surprising to me is that there were so many Internet "geniuses" identified and now everybody thinks the same people are idiots or frauds.

Jerry Blanton

Blanton was a branding strategist at Web shop MarchFirst during the mid-to-late 1990s. He now works at SBI, Inc., an e-business services firm that purchased a chunk of MarchFirst's assets at a fire sale.

I'll remember the stupidity that we were all a part of—a lot of people thinking that they were smarter than everyone else. And ultimately, nobody was. But that was the New Economy concept.

Andrew Brenner

An attorney at Wilson Sonsini Goodrich & Rosati in 1998 and 1999, Brenner later also did dot-com time at Contact Networks, eDaycare, and Mspect before joining the ranks of the downsized in 2001. With his buddy Michael Feldman, Brenner now runs Recession Camp, their networking organization and companion Web site for laid-off dot-commers. He welcomes any job offers.

I'm a geek. My niche is computers, so I'll be back.

Po Bronson

A Bay-area journalist, Bronson chronicled the outrageousness around him in the during the dot-com frenzy, most notably in *The Nudist on the Late Shift* (Random House 1999). He is currently working on a new book entitled *What Should I Do With My Life?*, a nonfiction journal exploring "how people face that question in all its various meanings." A feature film based on his novel *The First $20 Million Is Always the Hardest* (Random House, 1997), a comedy about Silicon Valley, is expected in theaters this year.

I've been recording stories of people trying to find themselves after having gone through tremendous crises in the past year, and the dot-commers are just not prepared for that degree of introspection. It's because of the very denial that's been drilled into them to ignore naysayers. I can't tell you the number of stories I've gotten from people who are traveling to, like, Vietnam right now—I'm waiting for one of them to actually have an epiphany or understand something about their lives.

A ton of people got married last year—that was another part of the fallout: "Okay, I've got no work, but I'm gonna fall in love." They put up a profile on Match.com, or they went after that guy they thought was cute, and it's like, boom!—they're married and they have kids. It's, "Oh, we've got these problems, but we'll work on these problems 24/7 and we'll fix them because we can fix things." It's the Internet mind-set.

Cathy Brooks

A veteran technology industry public relations executive, Brooks was laid off from TechTV in late 2001, where she had been the cable channel's Director of Booking since March 1999. She now runs Brooks & Associates, a media consulting firm in San Francisco.

People say, "I'm not in love with him, I'm in love with the *idea* of him." A lot of people weren't in love with the Internet, but got swept up by this idea: You got out of school, you had an $80,000 a year job, you cashed out of something, and then you're CEO of a company. There are people out there pounding the streets for jobs right now who have nothing but CEO on their résumé.

It's like, Get Over Your Bad Self! It's like the "little man, big car" concept. Let me show how much I've done by driving this big yellow Lamborghini twenty miles an hour through the city of San Francisco. You either need it because you're middle-aged and insecure or because you're twelve. I think if Freud had seen this era, he would have had a field day!

Deacon Carpenter

A project manager at the interactive consulting agencies Luminant Worldwide and Digitas in the late 1990s, Carpenter now works in Rhode Island for Silverlake Productions, an educational technology company. He dreams of moving to San Francisco, or somewhere in the Napa Valley, where he'd like to open a spa, or "do something a little more holistic."

Have you ever read *e* by Matt Beaumont, a novel about corporate backstabbing via a string of e-mails? That was my life. A lot of people working in New Media and the Internet don't move on from high school. They may have gone on to college, but they went right back to high school when they went to work for a Net company.

Lev Chapelsky

Armed with an MBA from UCLA's Andersen School of Business, Chapelsky
held senior marketing positions at CarsDirect.com and the online entertainment startup Icebox.com from 1998 to 2000. He is now a founding partner
of Blindlight, a Hollywood-based company that provides talent and production services to developers of video games.

> When I signed on with CarsDirect, I thought it had a really good proba-
> bility of succeeding, better than 50 percent. Not a sure thing. But it's a great
> story. I mean, Michael Dell made his first Internet investment in his life at
> CarsDirect. That was the peak.
>
> My new company is positioned to be an anti-dot-com. We picked an
> industry that's not going to collapse, an industry that has cash, from rev-
> enues and profits, not investment capital. So far, the total investment has
> been $3,000 out of our own pockets.

Alan Citron

After nearly two decades as a journalist, including thirteen years as a business
reporter for the *Los Angeles Times*, in 1995 Citron ventured into New Media as
president and chief operating officer of TicketMaster Multimedia. He left the
company in 1999 to work for Real Networks, and is now a senior executive
at Key3Media Group, Inc., a producer of worldwide technology conferences
and events such as COMDEX.

> I think the dot-com era is like the sixties: If you remember it, you weren't
> there. It was too much of a blur. It's been a feeling of being an observer and
> a participant at the same time. You've seen this whole industry spring up
> from nowhere, get chewed up, and begin the recovery process—all in a
> very narrow window of time.
>
> I still enjoy the industry, although it's not the rush it once was. It's cer-
> tainly not the conversation piece that it once was. It's sort of like saying
> that you sell insurance. People just shrug and walk away.

Alex Cohen

After founding Cinema Space (cinemaspace.berkeley.edu), the world's first World Wide Web film journal, in the early 1990s, Cohen went on to work as a technology executive at some of the leading Net companies, including Excite, Netscape, and CNET. He is currently vice president of engineering at OpenDesign.com, where he's working on a new distributed infrastructure technology for the Internet. He continues to edit Cinema Space and teach "Cinema and Beyond," an ultrapopular film course at UC Berkeley that explores the effects of computer technology on cinema, cultural expression, and society.

> In ten years, people aren't even going to think about Internet companies. It's not going to be a "thing," because it's a medium. That's going to be one of the biggest changes, because the Web is going to be embedded in everything.

Elizabeth Collet

After graduating from Harvard Business School in 1996, Collet moved from Beantown to the Bay Area to become Yahoo!'s senior director of Business Development & Strategic Planning—and one of the site's first forty employees. She left the Web giant in spring 2000, and is now "investing in non-U.S. and non-technology companies."

> I wanted to learn about markets overseas, so I started doing that from a technology perspective, then realized that the market had changed. I'm involved in some stuff in Belize, I'm on the board of a VC firm in London, I'm working on some real estate stuff in Canada, and odds and ends in Hong Kong. I'm not doing anything in the domestic technology market.

Chuck D

An early advocate of online music distribution, Public Enemy rapper Chuck D continues to preside over his online hip-hop empire, which includes PublicEnemy.com, RapStation.com, BringTheNoise.com and Slamjamz.com.

> People now are turning their heads and saying, "Well, there really is a viability instead of a liability in what the Net is all about." And there's a second onrush saying, "Hey, we can do this, but with a lot more people operating carefully and knowing they don't have to spend eighty million to have a super site."

Chris Dallas

A San Francisco real estate agent, Dallas still has an abundance of high-tech clients in the area, but few "dot-commers." And yes, he insists, there *is* a difference.

> Now people tend to take money out of the market and put it into real estate. People know that it's real. It's still a very good market even though the hey-day and the massive 30 to 40 percent appreciation a year are over. It's just a different market now. Buyers are in control, so they determine the value of the property.

Greg Deocampo

Deocampo cofounded COSA (the Company of Science and Art), which developed a popular digital video tool called AfterEffects that was acquired by Adobe in 1994. During the late 1990s he served as the chief technology officer at IFILM (ifilm.com). In 2000, Deocampo co-founded Tekadence, an L.A.-based software technology company, but he is probably best known as one of the original members of the multimedia performance art group Emergency Broadcast Network (EBN).

> One of the reasons I never thought the Web would take off is that I never imagined that people would actually type in "http://" and then some "www" URL address. I thought, "You expect someone to type *that* in? Good luck!" But they did.

Kal Deutsch

Deutsch was an executive at Price Waterhouse Coopers when he caught the Internet bug in 1999 and joined HomeGain.com, a real estate portal. He was laid off in 2001, but continues to ride the success of *Icevan.com*, a short film spoof he directed that satirizes the Internet industry and was featured at the 2002 Sundance Online Film Festival. Deutsch also consults in the Internet-TV convergence arena and helps companies "video-ize" their Web sites. He is codeveloping TVVillage.com as a community Web site for personal videos.

We modeled the whole *Icewan.com* film on VH1's *Behind the Music*. Except it's behind the startup. We said, "Let's find the stupidest thing you can sell on the Web," and I said it should be cinderblocks or bags of ice. We decided that selling ice, and offering one-hour delivery of ice, would be a good fictitious company to create.

We actually created a Web site for the film. It looks credible—pictures, login, information to buy stuff. Any guy could sit at a home computer and create this fictitious company and have it look like a real company. To me, that's what a lot of these startups were. I even got an e-mail from a biz-dev guy saying he could help me with Icevan.com. He thought it was legitimate! I ended up not writing him back, because what was I going to tell him?—"It's make-believe!" I didn't want him to feel like an ass.

Rebecca Eisenberg

After almost ten years of consulting, speaking, and writing about the Internet space for numerous media outlets, including the *San Francisco Examiner* and CBS MarketWatch, 1990 Stanford grad Eisenberg "went back to my roots and said, 'Oh yeah. I'm a lawyer!'" She is now in-house counsel at the online bill-paying service PayPal, Inc., which went public on February 15, 2002, and posted a 55 percent first-day gain.

There was a year and a half where a lot of kids dropped out of Stanford and other schools to become VPs of startups. Those are the people who quite possibly killed the industry. I don't think that they came until the money was there. Some of them did succeed, like at Google and Inktomi, but I found it distressing that so often these young people would think that the success of the company was due to something in *them*, rather than the fact that they had just won a lottery ticket. Then a lot of them went on to form second and third companies, and they had some really tough times facing the possibility that, whoa, maybe this really *had* been a lottery ticket!

David Epstein

When his Kansas-based Web shop, BlairLake, sold to Compuware in an all-cash deal worth over $18 million in 2000, Epstein stayed on to run the combined company until his contract expired. Making the move to New York City and still recuperating from a serious case of burnout, Epstein says he's exploring what will be his "next ride in life's carnival." But one thing's for sure: "The Internet roller coaster has been permanently closed for repairs!"

> I have bittersweet feelings, because the vast majority of my friends are unemployed. I would say to the grandkids that if you can get on the roller coaster, get on, but know when the hell to get off. By the luck of the Gods, we got off at the right time.

Chris Ewald

Former Balduccis.com CTO and fearless technology veteran Ewald is "getting ready to pitch a new company idea to the VC community."

> People right out of college were given five million based on a couple of pieces of paper. They weren't building businesses, they were trying to make money. It was a pyramid scheme. Like any pyramid scheme, people do see it, and they get out of it on top and make lots of money.

Michael Feldman

A former software developer at Oracle and Silicon Graphics, Feldman became director of partner marketing at the online sports retailer

Fogdog.com in 1998. After being downsized in 2001 along with the start-up he founded, Tools, Inc., a marketing services company, Feldman teamed up with Andrew Brenner to launch RecessionCamp.com.

> I've been thinking about what I really want to do next. I cowrote a screenplay, and I enjoy writing. I've been training for triathlons, sailing in the Caribbean. High-tech jobs do make me happy, but I'm kind of open to different things. Let's put it this way: I'm more open to different types of jobs now than I was six months ago!

Former Producer at Disney's Go.Com

After spending two years as a twenty-something producer at Disney's flame-out Go.com, he/she has taken a position with a small independent film and multimedia company.

> It wasn't even that everyone was *working* really hard at these Internet companies, but that everyone was *thinking* really hard. You always had to be thinking about the next big thing.

David Gilcreast

A former Food.com and DialPad.com public relations executive, Gilcreast is trying to sell *Free Lunch*, a screenplay he co-wrote about a flack who gets caught up in a scam. Featuring a company called MyPersonalServant.com, where employees will do any task requested by customers, the script, while eerily similar to parts of Gilcreast's life, is "purely a work of fiction."

> I'd gone to, like, my fiftieth launch party and it was just getting ridiculous—the whole "I work for a dot-com, I must be part of a new special breed of highly intelligent people." Two years ago, you'd say "dot-com" and people would think: success, making money, a real sharp-shooter. But I started to look at these people and realize that they were just full of shit.

Larry Glenn

The former CTO of the Web development company Liquid Digital in New York, Glenn is currently writing a novel.

> There are a lot of companies going into cockroach mode. I don't think it's unhealthy. There's a company that raised money and created a good product, but they had forty employees. They fired everyone except for two—a CEO and a tech guy. And that works just fine. They're going to survive. It's not an easy life for those guys, but it works. Their burn rate is only something like $3,600 a month.

Nicholas Goldsmith

A principal at the architectural firm FTL Happold, Goldsmith designed Boo.com's New York City office.

> As a designer, every project you do is a little part of you—just like a child. You're kind of sad to see it not used, but I was happy that Radical Media, the company that took over Boo's space, could use it the way it is.

Jeff Goodell

A Silicon Valley native, Goodell worked as a technical writer at Apple before running off to deal blackjack in Lake Tahoe. Although he missed the Apple IPO, he's since become a regular contributor to *Rolling Stone* and *The New York Times Magazine*, and recently published a best-selling memoir, *Sunnyvale: The Rise and Fall of a Silicon Valley Family* (Random House, 2000).

> Anyone with any kind of perspective knows that when you're figuring out a better way of selling bowling balls online, that's not changing the world. You're engaged in crass commerce. That was masked by that whole rhetoric, and, frankly, the money. You knew it had to change.
>
> There's something about the temporariness of the culture built into the geography of the whole area. It is, by definition, one of the most unstable places on Earth. The San Andreas Fault and the Hayward Fault run through it. It's only a matter of time before another big shake comes. You look at

the geological history of the Valley, and it's a place where change is just built into the very ground.

Maria Isabel Gouverneur

After her "interesting" stint as a designer at Rare Medium, Gouverneur, a native of Venezuela, is now working as a freelance graphic designer in New York City.

> It was an odd experience for me, as a foreigner, seeing these American kids who were very young, inexperienced, and full of themselves. This is a very curious culture. Some people were interesting and you couldn't understand how they ended up at an Internet company, but many of them were just very young people. It was like taking a bunch of kids into a huge Toys "R" Us store and saying to them, "You can do whatever you want."

Peter Guber

The films produced by former Sony Pictures CEO and chairman Guber have earned more than $3 billion in worldwide revenue and more than fifty Academy Awards nominations. Now chairman of Mandalay Pictures and cowriter of *Shootout* (Penguin Putnam, 2002), Guber is also a full professor at the UCLA school of Theater, Film, and Television, where he has been a member of the faculty for more years than the average age of a dot-com CEO in 1999.

> Like baseball teams, these companies were not profitable, but if you held them long enough, somebody would always buy them at a higher price. It reminded me of what happens when sharks feed on prey. One shark hunts the prey and takes it down and then another shark comes along and says, "Somebody's done my work for me. I'll start to eat." And then a bunch a sharks start swimming around and they get into such a frenzy, they start eating the other sharks, and some of them even start biting their own tails! I saw a lot of these companies who thought they were chasing somebody else who was winning. Well, they found out they were chasing their own tail and suddenly they disappeared up their own posterior.

My father could never get the Depression out of his mentality. It had such a profound effect on him. I'm not sure that this won't have a lasting effect on these people. They were the beneficiaries of a kind of galactic change, but they're also going to be the recipients of a new awareness. Can they take that painful lesson and use it as a tool? Many of them are talented and resilient and can look at what's happened. The question is, can they navigate in the current environment where there are mine fields instead of gold mines?

Nicholas Hall

Having bounced back from three startup failures in the financial services, beverage, and Internet industries, Hall parlayed his misfortune into StartupFailures.com, which offers "insight, resources, and support for entrepreneurs riding the startup roller coaster."

I've learned that you don't have to go-go-go in a big race to the finish. Life is a process, a journey. And some of your ideas will work and some won't, but enjoy the journey. The people trying to get rich quick, I wouldn't call them true entrepreneurs anyway. It's okay if they move out of that space.

Shuli Hallack

Hallack, now twenty-four, was an executive assistant at Rare Medium until 2000. She has since traveled to South America, participated in a four-hundred-mile AIDS ride from Montreal to Maine, and worked on a project with a journalist from Spain in which she interviewed families of victims of a real disaster, the WTC tragedy. She plans to pursue a masters degree in photography.

I had just graduated college and was trying to figure stuff out. Internet companies sounded kind of cool. A lot of us felt like we could be whatever we wanted to be.

Lew Harris

The former editor-in-chief of *Los Angeles Magazine* (1974–1995), E! Online (1996–2000), and IFILM (2000–2001), Harris is using the downturn as an opportunity to start a new site, one that he calls "a soapbox for alternative viewpoints on the Web, a revival of the political broadsides of the forties and fifties." He is currently consulting for *Us Weekly* magazine.

> The same thing on the Web has to be as true as it is for a magazine or for the corner minimart. You have to have a business plan. That's why E! Online's commerce shop failed. It had no plan. The idea was to sell all things entertainment. I tried to put the breaks on it, but they kept going. I said, if this were a brick-and-mortar store, people wouldn't shop in it, so why do you think people are going to shop there on the Web?

Lynn Harris

More than a year after selling BreakupGirl.com to Oxygen and joining their ranks herself, Harris left Geraldine Layborne's New Media empire when the online community for women changed its business plan . . . again. Harris has since returned to print, and is now the advice columnist for *Glamour* magazine. She continues to perform stand-up comedy in New York City, for which, we're betting, she has quite a bit of new material.

> We want the rights to BreakupGirl back, at the very least to give her a proper burial, if not to launch a scaled-down version of the site. We can't run the site the way it was. We don't have the money, the staff, the building, the technology. People had no idea how much work it was. It was one of the only properties of its time to have Flash-based animation that aired on TV and the Web. It was very newsworthy. It's painful to have her be nowhere. We just have to get her back!

Peter Heinecke

Heinecke lived through the IPO craze as an attorney at the Silicon Valley law firm Wilson, Sonsini, Goodrich & Rosati, where, unlike many of the clients he represented, he remains gainfully employed.

> Everybody was happy to be working at Wilson at the center of it, but nobody had the illusion that we were doing anything that much different from what we'd been doing before—which was taking companies public

and doing VC finance. It was just that we were doing it during some truly amazing times.

I think there will be a "revenge of the nerds." The Internet culture grew out of—and then sort of overwhelmed—the tech culture, but we'll come back to the tech culture. There's still a tremendous amount of true creativity here. People are trying to solve difficult problems and are spending the time to solve them—which is a lot different from announcing that you're going to sell kibble online.

Lisa Hendricks

A former music manager and early online entertainment pioneer, Hendricks leads the team that creates, develops, and produces talent-driven content for TV and the Web at Tidal14, her convergence entertainment company. Clients include Alanis Morissette and MuchMusicUSA. She's not quite sure how she'll explain all this to her new baby.

My dentist has an eight-year-old son, and they were cleaning up their closet, and they came upon an electric typewriter. The kid said, "What's that?" The dad said, "It's a typewriter." So the kid said, "Oh, you mean, it's a computer without a screen." I'm going to feel like my mom who told me what life was like without radio and TV.

I don't know how I'll ever explain what life was like before computers and the Net. I'm only grateful that I understand it. So many people I know don't want to come near it, don't want to know anything about it. But this whole experience taught me that you're actually able to reinvent yourself three, four, five times in your life. Coming from a management perspective, I was frightened because I thought that my skill set was so limited. But I realized that as a manager, you do a little bit of everything, and that's what the Internet is about. You're IM-ing, chatting on the phone, checking your stocks. That's what our kids will be used to.

Cameron Hickey

Following his "Web innovator" gig at the fashion flameout Boo.com, the twenty-two-year-old Hickey is doing computer animation for the film *Naqoyqatsi*, to be released by Miramax in October 2002. Once the film wraps, he plans to move to Greece with his girlfriend to work on a documentary about the 2004 Athens Olympics, and relax in the warmth of the Mediterranean.

People were always focusing on the extraneous stuff, like how cool it would be for a shoe to rotate, rather than how to build a database that serves our business needs. I started to lose faith in all the glitzy, flashy stuff early on.

We had really big zoom images on the site so you could see the laces of the shoe, but when you zoomed in that close, you couldn't see the shoe anymore. And no one ever holds a shoe an inch from one's face! So without anyone's permission, I took four or five hours and created a set of code that pulled different images. Then I got in a whole lot of trouble for it, because I was circumventing the paths of authority. But I felt it was necessary to do. I spent many nights working on the technology, because I didn't want my name attached to something that was worthless. I mean, I couldn't have made it any *worse* than it already was.

Auren Hoffman

After founding Kyber Systems in 1995 as a U.C. Berkeley undergraduate, Hoffman, now twenty-seven, runs the online staffing exchange service, BridgePath.com; and hosts Silicon Forum, a monthly Silicon Valley round-table luncheon event that'll cost you forty-five bucks for Chinese food at Ming's in Palo Alto—if you're lucky enough to be invited.

I believe that San Francisco is still the most exciting place to be when you have an idea. It's more of a meritocracy than any place that I've ever been to. Certainly, discrimination exists in the Bay Area, but I think less so on age, gender, sexual orientation, race, who your father is, whether you've got sixteen earrings, or if you have purple hair.

People here have much more discrimination on your brain. And I like *brain discrimination*. I believe that the Net started here for a reason. The taxicab drivers here are incredibly intelligent. If you go into a bar, you'll invariably have a conversation about Bosnia, or ancient Rome, or some sort of Shakespearean plot. It's a very transient city where people are coming and going very quickly. Because of that, you've got this insane networking where people meet each other and constantly exchange ideas.

David Hornik

A former intellectual property and corporate attorney at Cravath, Swaine & Moore; Venture Law Group; and Perkins Coie LLP, Hornik is now "happily a VC at August Capital, investing in enterprise software, as well as Internet infrastructure and services."

> When I left New York to go the Valley, my wife was skeptical. She didn't say, "You're the man with vision, I will follow you." It was, "You can always go back to representing tobacco companies when it fails."
>
> I can tell you, having worked in Washington, D.C., where the drug of choice was politics, and having worked in New York City, where the drug of choice was money, that technology is just better. Politics and money can be completely devoid of either substance or intellect. To my mind, technology cannot. People are proud of what they're building. I love that.

Bernardo Joselevich

Since stumbling upon the industry in 1996 when he learned to sell Internet advertising on a small Portuguese island off the coast of Africa, Joselevich went on to start both DutyFreeGuide.com and Bernardo's List, an online networking and party guide for "the schmoozing classes." Joselevich acknowledges, however, that his party list is used more as an information tool for conferences and panels these days, and less as a source for sizzling soirées.

> Even though I was exposed to some of the early adopters, I'm not prone to fads, so I didn't think this thing was going to be very big. Especially because of the lean-forward, lean-back thing with the TV. Most people grew up with their families telling them never to get too close to the screen because of UV radiation. So I was skeptical of something that demands that a source of UV radiation should be a way of the world.

I had this image that when I grew up, we'd all be flying on rocket ships. That's a great disappointment. The planes are the same now as they were when I was six years old. We were supposed to be going to Tokyo in thirty minutes. We were supposed to wear rocket shoes. Except for a cell phone and a couple other things that are really magical, nothing else really materialized. What ever happened to flying cars?

Elizabeth Kalodner

After leaving her senior executive position at Walt Disney to seek out fame, fortune, and a soul mate as chairman and CEO of the San Francisco startup SocialNet.com, Kalodner says that she "did pretty well on the fame, but not so well on the fortune." The popular online dating service MatchNet.com acquired SocialNet in January 2001, and although Kalodner is still available, romantically speaking, she's since gotten hitched to Sesame (as in Street) Workshop as senior VP of global consumer products and international television production. Before landing at that company, however, Kalodner told us:

For my next job, I'd like to go somewhere where all the furniture matches.

Philip "Pud" Kaplan

A former project manager at the Web consultancy Think New Ideas, Kaplan founded his own shop, PK Interactive, and most notably, FuckedCompany.com, the popular death-watch site for dot-gone startups. As somewhat of a geek celebrity, he has been featured in national magazines and on network talk shows, while his FuckedCompany.com, which generates over $1 million a year, has been expanded to the page in his *F'd Companies: Spectacular Dot-Com Flameouts* (Simon & Schuster, 2002).

I had a front-row seat to all the bullshit that went on.

Heather Keenan

An event planner since 1982, Keenan and her company, Key Events, coordinated some of the most memorable launch parties in the Valley and San Francisco during the boom.

With few dot-com clients still dancing, Keenan has gladly returned to relying on more established corporations for event gigs.

I now work with pharmaceuticals and financials. Period.

Josh Keller

Harvard Business School grad and UBUBU cofounder Keller became the poster boy for twenty-something dot-commers when he landed on the cover of *Fortune* magazine in August 1999. Although the article had little measurable influence on UBUBU's business, it did make Keller's parents extremely proud. Keller left UBUBU in January 2001 and joined the San Francisco consulting firm foreAction.

My personal value is on learning. I felt like the learning that could be had in another situation could be higher.

Chris Kinnear

A producer at the former e-commerce giant eToys, Kinnear relished the excitement of the boom enough to join another dot-com, becoming manager of product development at the domain name registry DotTV. "Between opportunities" again, he has just returned from a month-long trip to Thailand.

The most valuable lesson from leaving eToys was that you can't just disappear from the rest of your life. The things that are enduring in life are friendships. So you can either kill yourself for a job, or you can get some perspective and realize that it's just a job and your entire identity is not tied up with that. At the end of day, what's really going to matter is to be well-loved, not how many twelve-hour days you worked in a row, not how long you went without a vacation.

Matthew Klauschie

Since graduating from the University of Southern California in 1999, Klauschie has worked at three online entertainment companies. The first two, DEN and Pop.com, went under in 2000. The third is IFILM.com, where Klauschie manages the site's digital video encoding. In the event of strike three, he can always fall back on Los Angelitos, his Afro-Cuban band.

> After I lost my job at Pop.com, I was like, "I'm going to Cuba, and take two months off." I didn't go. My loans keep me in check. People looked for work for a long time and couldn't find stuff that made it worth it for them to stop freelancing, or collecting unemployment. If IFILM goes down, I have doubts about coming up with something that pays what I make right now, and gives me the control and independence that I have. I'll just do my thing.

Michael Krantz

Time magazine's former San Francisco bureau chief, Krantz is the editorial director for Keen.com, the Benchmark-backed "eBay of 900 numbers."

> I remember thinking, "Gee, being part of New Media means going to parties where everyone gets wasted, does drugs, and looks for someone to fuck. You don't even need to know HTML to do that!"

Ted Kruckel

A veteran PR and marketing executive, Kruckel is the president of Ted, Inc., a boutique firm specializing in the magazine publishing, entertainment, fashion, and beauty industries, which he founded in 1993. Deluged in the late 90's with dot-com clients including Ashford.com, Homestead.com, SmarterKids.com, CondeNet, Style.com, BeautyJungle.com, and Yahoo! Internet Life, he now devises strategic campaigns for Old Economy clients like *The New Yorker*, L'Ermitage Hotel, Shiseido, and *InStyle* magazine. Although Kruckel spins stories for the press, he didn't mince words when asked about his New Economy clients.

My experiences were varied, but I definitely resented the young dot-commers telling me what to do when they had no sense of what my experience was. They would talk about their advertising and PR strategies, and they would be so top-line and basic and lacking of the teeth to make the thing chew. I found that annoying. Many young people showed a lot of ingenuity and great promise, but they were so arrogant that now they can't get the time of day with someone like me on the phone. No ex-dot-commer wants to go work for fifty thousand and be a brand manager, but that's what they all should do.

Tom Lazaroff

A former Disney and Hard Rock Café marketing executive, Lazaroff has been in the trenches at two dot-coms, PayMyBills.com and ClickTex, a B2B start-up in the textile industry. His consulting firm, Lazaroff, Dundore & Associates, provides marketing support to companies who are launching or relaunching products and services.

At the end of the day, I wouldn't trade the experience for anything. You could ask anybody in the company on any given day their opinion on any aspect of the business and people would actually listen—wow! Just because that person does HTML doesn't mean they can't tell you whether they think it's a good idea to offer our service for free. When I was at Disney, I loved it, but the spirit, fire, and excitement that you felt every day at PayMyBills was something I'd never seen before and would be surprised if I ever see again.

Sang Lee

After repeatedly putting off his MBA "to pursue the dot-com craze," Lee, a former senior producer at the New York Web shop Rare Medium, is now working for RiskClick.com, a Web-based application provider in the B2B—and more mellow—insurance space.

I basically saw through the fluff, but the money and potential were too huge to resist.

Doug Levin

A twenty-one-year veteran of the high-tech industry, Levin held senior management positions at Microsoft from 1987 to 1995 in Seattle and Germany. Since leaving Microsoft, he has served in executive management positions at, or as a consultant to, six technology startups in the Boston area. He is now the CEO of Message Machines, a company that develops cross-device messaging solutions.

> Bell-bottoms came back! I never thought I'd be wearing bell-bottoms again, but I did! In the software business, there are also all these cycles. IBM went through big waves of success and retrenchment. The same thing will happen again. It's just now in its right place.
>
> We've gone through a telecom infrastructure expansion, and the next phase will be people actually starting to use it more. And I think that may happen in the aftermath of September eleventh: telecommunications will help defeat the terrorists. It's clear that wireless played a huge role in September eleventh. I think one of the big things is that a next-generation wireless service, called 3G, will really take off. People will be able to stand around in coffee shops and not need to dial up. The Internet will come back in a different form—in a grounded form, not hype.

Kenny Lin

After working as an engineer at Rare Medium, Lin tells us he's "collecting unemployment insurance, catching up on movies and DVDs, taking a long-overdue drive across the country, and looking for work along the way."

> What I've learned is, trust your own BS filters.

Bob Makela

Former DEN producer Makela is producing a basketball-themed reality TV pilot with David Duchovny, doing the occasional freelance magazine article, working on a screenplay, and trying to finish his book about the hundred-day bar-hopping journey he took around America.

> Everyone at DEN said, "This is so early in the game. Wait until the technology comes around and more people get broadband." The one-liner was supposed to be that this was like being at NBC in the 1950s or MTV in 1985. It was the early stages of something that would become a staple in people's lives. But I was never sold on online entertainment because I could never watch the damn shows. It was always jumpy, and I *had* broadband!

Jeff Malkin

A former guitarist in a New York City rock band, in 1999 Malkin founded FreeSamples.com, an online marketing services site that closed shop in March 2002. He is now reviewing business plans for his next Internet startup.

> I got twenty years of business experience in three years. That's what I'll describe to my kids: in a matter of six months, going from being on top of the world to scraping by, just surviving.

Harold Mann

After graduating from U.C. Berkeley, Mann cofounded the San Francisco Internet consultancy Mann Consulting in 1990.

> I've got people interviewing with me now who've got a couple years of experience with ridiculous salaries and titles. My brother and I use the term "ruined" when we interview them. They're ruined! They're having to take a $30,000 pay cut, and they don't understand why. But as an employer, I can't help but feel that it's a certain amount of karmic justice.

Steven Masur

Silicon Alley attorney Masur is a partner at Masur & Associates, LLC, a boutique firm founded in 1995 which provides legal services to entrepreneurs and businesses in the entertainment, media, and technology industries. The firm's clients include Digital Club Network and Mouse, Inc., but Masur offers us the following tip for free:

> There are a lot of really good deals now. You don't have to be smart to realize that in a down market, things are cheap. For example, there's a company called Onsite Access that had raised $185 million during the boom and built infrastructure in large buildings in major cities, including New York. These are buildings with solid businesses in them, some that have been here for twenty years and will be here for twenty more. And they're going to need Internet access. It's a good business, not exciting, but solid. The company recently went into bankruptcy and sold to one of their competitors, eLink, for six million dollars. So someone paid only six million dollars for a completely built network with paying customers in Chicago, New York, and L.A.!

Helen Maynard

A former executive in the home appliance and uniform businesses in New Zealand, Maynard continues to work at HeavenlyDoor, Inc., a once-public company, but not one in need of its own cyber casket. The startup is one of the last remaining funeral services dot-coms.

> At first there was no business plan that made sense, and I found that difficult because I come from a product base. But I said, they must have something going—I just don't know what it is!

Dennis McMahon

San Francisco Peace Corps spokesman McMahon's creative campaigns to recruit out-of-work dot-commers have gained national attention and resulted in a deluge of volunteers who've been stripped of their cell phones.

> We felt that many of the people drawn to the dot-com industry were the sort of people that would be very good Peace Corps volunteers because they were drawn to a nonconventional work environment, and one that

values creativity and innovation. Some people are coming to us saying, "I heard you have an IT sector," then other people say, "Get me as far away from a computer as possible, and if I have to dig ditches, I'll do that." A lot of dot-com people aren't geeks punching code—they're people with English and journalism backgrounds who have good communication skills and could serve as English teachers.

Jim Medalia

Prior to founding JustBalls.com, Medalia founded and was president of Digital Exchange, Inc., a computer graphics and Internet communications company in New York. He is currently CEO of nWatt, a home energy management startup.

Sure, there were some foolish things. Like guys who raised money on the back of a napkin and spent it on furniture. But it was also a very meaningful time. In the human sense, I think that I was part of one of the great revolutions of mankind. Who knew you could change the world by selling balls online?

Jennifer Musillo

A former sales representative at *Us* magazine and Disney Publishing Worldwide, Musillo is weathering the advertising lull as an account manager at Ziff-Davis's Yahoo! Internet Life.

I can't remember if it was eToys or ToySmart.com that had great broadcast creative. It was the one where the little kid would draw a crayon fish, and then his mom would buy him a fishing pole from the site. Well, I guess the creative wasn't *that* good if I can't remember the brand!

Dan Myrick

After cowriting, directing, and producing the hit film *The Blair Witch Project*, Myrick now runs Gear Head Pictures, a production company formed "to help facilitate various solo projects, ranging from feature films to Internet content or whatever else flips our switch."

Everyone was on the cusp of a new wave of technology and a new wave of making movies. I'd like to think that we had this grand plan for *Blair Witch*, and that we had instituted this grand marketing strategy, but, honestly, we got lucky. Getting feedback from our audience was so key with *Blair Witch*. People were constantly updating us online with what they liked, disliked, and what improvements we could make.

I had no resentment toward anyone. I was like, more power to you if you have fifty million dollars, and some rich guy's going to give you a chance. Because, what's ultimately going to happen is that the good ones will be left standing. That's free enterprise, man. That's what America is about! Some people, there were stars in their eyes. But some people really know their shit.

David Neuman

After stints as president of Walt Disney Network Television, programming president at Channel One, vice president of comedy development at NBC, and a producer of Peabody Award–winning shows, Neuman reigned over DEN during its frenzied rise and demise. He is currently consulting for Turner Networks in Atlanta.

A major investment banker once looked at me and said, "You realize you're going to have sixty million dollars." I didn't believe it. I thought, it's possible, but a lot can happen between now and then. I remembered the cycles that I went through with network TV. You're up, then you're down. Successes and failures.

Two weeks after DEN failed, I had a commitment to go to one of those conferences in New York, streaming media or something. I was a keynote speaker and I was thinking about canceling: My company failed, what right do I have to speak? But the conference was pleading with me: Please come speak. So I had to do inventory and I decided I'll keep the commitment, but I'm not going to blame anybody except myself.

Brad Nye

In 1995, Nye cofounded VIC, a popular New Media networking event in the Los Angeles area, and turned it into a nonprofit in 1998 before it shut down in December 2001. Now living in the Bay Area, Nye has launched a non-profit organization called aMuse, whose mission is to promote creativity for children.

> VIC used to be a place for ideas, but then it became a feeding frenzy. A lot of people stopped coming to VIC after they realized that everyone was there for the deal. We had people in insurance, car salesmen, real estate people, massage therapists. Anyone who had a product that they felt they could sell to people. It became this obnoxious marketplace.
>
> We were creating a community where people could exchange information and ideas. Little did we know that people with the *real* ideas would get forced out the door when people looking for a business opportunity showed up.

Steven Overman

Overman plunged headfirst into the industry as a twenty-something executive assistant at *Wired* in 1994. In 2001 he founded Brandism, a San Francisco consulting firm, where he serves as "chief brandist." Having supervised innovative strategy and branding projects in a range of industries, from high-tech financial services to Hollywood filmmaking, Overman tries to prevent his startup clients from making the same mistakes he's witnessed over the years.

> There was a feeling at *Wired* that anything was possible, and I felt it when I walked into the office the very first time after just arriving from New York City. The mix of people, the energy, the windows were broken, the place was crap, and they had just won the National Magazine Award for General Editorial Excellence! I'm seeing this clubhouse, this patched-together space where everything was crooked, and everybody was young. My phone didn't work and there was no computer at my desk. I said, "Where's my computer?" They said, "Oh, you have to get all that stuff set up." That's when I realized everything was possible, because everyone was doing it for themselves. No bureaucracy, no hierarchy. A shared mission and everyone doing their part.

Ashley Power

The founder, president, CEO and cochair (with her stepdad) of the teen entertainment site Goosehead.com, Power couldn't become a twenty-some-thing dot-com millionaire because she's only sixteen. The eleventh-grader has a development deal with NBC for Goosehead TV, and in her spare time, she's finishing high school.

> I'm definitely going to college. I'm a junior, so I'm looking at colleges now. I'm at the point where I've been through so much and I'm trying to take control of who I am and what I want to be. There's so much I can't control. I can't control the studios, I can't control the networks, I can't control the Internet, and I can't control who's coming to my site. It's a weird situation to be in, y'know?

Courtney Pulitzer

A Silicon Alley veteran, Pulitzer still writes her online party column, "The Cyber Scene," and hosts "Cocktails with Courtney," New York's leading net-working event, which she founded in 1995.

> I've felt like an oddball the last couple of years, because people would say "What's your exit strategy?" And I'd say that I didn't have one, because I'd like to own my company for a few years and see it be profitable and keep it existing. I never fit into the get-rich-quick crowd because I just wanted to keep doing what I was doing. I wanted to grow my business, Courtney Pulitzer Creations, more organically. They didn't quite have a response to that.

Andrew Rasiej

After launching one of New York's top concert halls, Irving Plaza, in 1997 Rasiej cofounded the live music site Digital Club Network and the non-profit MOUSE (Making Opportunities for Upgrading Schools and Education), which provides technology equipment centers to public schools.

I think that of the people involved in the last couple of years, only 25 percent were truly committed. If you're twenty-two years old and the Net doesn't pan out, you're probably thinking, "Okay, how am I going to start a new career?" But if you're older and committed to technology and the Net, you're thinking that you're going to starve for several years, but you're going to see this thing out. I'm going to see this thing pan out.

J. Betty Ray

Before heading up the content and community departments at San Francisc's Internet radio site Live365.com, Ray founded Soul Pants, an interactive television startup, and freelanced for numerous publications.

There were some successes. Phil Kaplan. *The Onion* is a huge success story. I think humor on the Web is huge. Streaming media could be interesting. It circumvents the FCC and that's a particular interest of mine: information getting out there unmitigated by traditional players.

Adeo Ressi

Shortly after graduating from the University of Pennsylvania, Ressi cofounded one of the first Web companies, Total New York, which AOL and Tribune acquired in 1997. He then founded a Web shop, Methodfive, that sold for a cool $88 million three years later to the Nasdaq-listed Xceed, where he served as chief strategy officer and executive vice president. Now a partner at Sophos Partners, a management consulting firm for Internet and technology companies, Ressi hosts a weekly poker game for current and former CEOs whose bank statements have lost up to nine digits in the economic downturn. But despite having once been worth over $100 million, Ressi says, "The stakes at these games have always been low, because we're all cheap bastards." Besides, he may need that money for his next big project: The Life to Mars Foundation.

We decided that we wanted to do something that gives back to civilization and humanity, and has historical importance. We think that space is one of the most meaningful areas that a group of smart, technology-savvy individuals who have wealth and means can contribute to. If we can do a meaningful private mission to Mars, we can capture the public's imagination with space again, like in the sixties.

We've done an initial feasibility study that says it will cost between ten and twenty million to fly a lander to Mars. We'll probably put a seed on that lander and attempt to grow plants on the Martian soil. We'd like to launch in 2003, but we may have to launch in 2005. There's a twenty-four-month window. The analogy between space and the Net certainly holds true.

Laura Rich

A former columnist for *The Industry Standard*, Rich's book about Microsoft cofounder Paul Allen will be published this year by John Wiley & Sons.

People had been looking for some new religion. I read somewhere that the dot-com movement was essentially a religious movement. There was all this coverage of New Age stuff, but the Net gave people this replacement belief system. It was an order, a New World Order. It seemed chaotic, but it was an order. The Internet became a system of beliefs for a lot of people.

Dan Roach

A former director of high-technology services at Price Waterhouse Coopers and former managing director at the venture-capital firm Garage Technology Ventures, Roach is now working with the VC firm MassVentures two days a week, and as "chief financial officer at a couple of startups the other days."

A lot of the dot-coms bet the farm on a fast move of consumers to an online world, but the lack of a truly fast home connection turned many people off. A big factor, IMHO [in my humble opinion], is that the company valuations were silly. That made what should have been a soap bubble bursting turn into the *Hindenberg*—expectations were way too high.

Doug Scott

In 1993, Scott cofounded the Internet industry magazine, *Red Herring*, and subsequently served as senior vice president of sales and marketing for the

Hollywood Stock Exchange (HSX.com). In 2001, he became vice president of marketing at Hypnotic, a Vivendi Universal-backed interactive production company.

> There's no sure thing in this world anymore. I worry that Hypnotic isn't going to make it, just like I'd worry if I were at Intel that I'd be one of seven thousand to be laid off. I don't think that there's anyone out there at Lucent, Hewlett-Packard, or AT&T who's not worried that they'll come in tomorrow and there will be padlocks on the doors.
>
> But knowing that I love what I'm doing and I'm passionate about it, and it's a platform for me to showcase my talents, I'm willing to take that risk. I came to Hypnotic and took a 40 percent pay cut.

Peter Seidler

After serving as chief creative officer of the Web shop Razorfish in New York, Seidler founded Seidler Ventures LLP, a holding company for his new ventures. Oh yeah, he's also learning how to sequence genes at MIT and Harvard.

> I think digital genomics is the most important thing right now. The Internet isn't anything on its own anymore. In ten years, it will probably be said that the most valuable aspect of computers is that they enable us to work with genomics. Every area of our lives will be radically changed based on this. Whether it's material science, military, insurance, legal, health and medicine, reproduction, or new designer plants. Everything.

Jesse Sheidlower

A former senior editor for Random House Reference, Sheidlower is the first American lexicographer to be appointed a top editor at the *Oxford English Dictionary*. Now the principal editor of the North American unit, he was kind enough not to correct our grammar during his interview.

> Internet language has spread extremely quickly and is extremely pervasive, but I think that if you look at other periods—for example, the growth of steam locomotives or of automobiles—you'll see a not-too-dissimilar pat-

tern. It was probably faster in the case of computers because the ability to spread vocabulary more quickly had changed.

Amanda Sherman

After a stint at Hugo Boss, Sherman became a buyer at Barney's New York, where she has tried to wean the dot-commers off their Banana Republic khakis and baseball hats. Sherman applauds the return of the suit and tie.

> Ties are the only accessory for men—the one way to express themselves. If a guy isn't wearing a tie, it's difficult to tell what he's about. And when men weren't wearing ties anymore, they were lost.

Gong Szeto

The former chief creative officer at Rare Medium, Szeto is a board member of two nonprofit organizations: the Van Alen Institute for Public Architecture, which is working on the New York New Visions initiative to rebuild Lower Manhattan post–9/11; and the American Institute of Graphic Arts. He is also the editor of *Gain*, an online journal, and has a private consultancy, formandcontent.

> This whole FuckedCompany.com and TheVault.com thing has been a really brilliant expression of free speech in our country. But the degree of slander, threats, and defamation that happens there is frightening. I'm actually starting to work with some attorneys on a defamation suit against some individuals who are posting things on these boards, because it's starting to screw me up. Someone really slams you, and then you get a call from a VC who says he doesn't want to give you money because, according to those boards, you're an asshole.

Richard Titus

In 1996, Titus founded [tag] media, a Web consultancy whose client roster included Intel, Microsoft, Jim Henson Entertainment, 20th Century Fox, and NASA. Two years later, the company was acquired by Razorfish, where Titus served as managing director of the L.A. office and vice president of strategic investments. After a three-month sabbatical in Chile in 2001, he cofounded Plinyminor, a technology consulting firm, and executive produced *On-Line,* an independent feature film.

> If you look at Razorfish as a business, the reasons that it began to fail are completely different from the reasons that most others failed. They were profitable. They were making money. They were financed. And yet, the core business mistakes were largely due to their inexperience. This was a $2.5-billion-dollar company, and only *one person* had worked for a Net company before! Think about that.

Joanne Weaver

Since her days as Scient's receptionist and the owner of $300,000 of Scient stock, Weaver has lost it all—the money, the job, the San Fran zip code. No worries, Weaver's young—she's now in New York discovering her inner rock goddess and tells us she's "in discussions with a band who's auditioning singer-songwriters."

> I thought I'd be a natural at the rock-star thing, but it's actually pretty tough! I guess that's what I get for lip-synching to Barry Manilow and Melissa Manchester growing up instead of Led Zeppelin or Frank Zappa or somebody a lot cooler who would better prepare me for this. But I'll keep on keepin' on.

Matt Welch

At twenty-two, Welch started *Prognosis,* an English-language daily in Prague. He returned to the United States in 1998 to get involved in Internet journalism, and has since gained a reputation as one of the Web's best columnists. Now thirty-three, Welch writes about New Media for the *Online Journalism Review,* where he chronicled his short but memorable experience at DEN, and pens "the odd column about whatever" for the *Los Angeles Daily News.* His popular e-zine, MattWelch.com, is chock full of cool stuff.

> I'm a big New Economy cheerleader. Largely, it's because of the experience

of working at a startup company. I had that experience in central Europe—
I started a newspaper when I was twenty-two years old. And once you do
that, it never stops, it's never out of your blood. You always have that
instinct when you're dissatisfied with your job. You feel like, "Shit, I'd better start a thing up."

Kevin Wendle

The first senior Hollywood executive to make the move to the Web, Wendle
cofounded the Fox Broadcasting Network in 1986. He then went on to
cofound CNET in 1993, E! Online in 1996, and IFILM in 1999, where he
serves as CEO.

So many of those people who went from college to CEO really got
extraordinary experience, in spite of the flameout. There's no better way to
learn about business than by going through that experience. When a baby
first learns to walk, he falls down. He then realizes that if he doesn't want
to fall down, he stands like this. Similarly, there's plenty of people who
might one day make great CEOs, but stumbled, and next time around may
be brilliant. There's some disenchantment, and maybe they're in a one- or
two- or five-year reality check. But if they had the ambition and drive once,
they'll have it again.

Ted Werth

Werth cofounded the online city guide Total New York with his University
of Pennsylvania buddy Adeo Ressi in 1994. Since 1998 he has been the chief
strategic officer at the live-music site Digital Club Network. He is also a partner in Original Sin Hard Cider and a Board member of Harvestworks, a non-
profit group bridging the art and technology worlds.

I think back to the early Internet conferences like Jupiter, which was a startup itself. They had never thrown a conference before and the presenters
had never presented before. And you would end up with people on panels
who would say "shit," "fuck," and other profanities. There wasn't that much
decorum because people who were on the panels weren't politicians.

Nowadays, when you go to a conference, you have senior executives at big companies who are as much politicians as anything else, and they know how to deflect questions. But the first couple of times that some of these senior people were getting onto panels with these young upstarts, the young guys would be like, "What are you talking about, man?" The older guy would use some lingo, and the younger guys would just snicker and look at the old guy. The older guys were trying to fit in, but it was hopeless.

I think that struggle is still going on today and is in some ways a metaphor for the whole industry.

ACKNOWLEDGMENTS

It should take a number of people to get a book reported and written in a mere five months. Strangely, in a moment of irrational optimism not dissimilar to the flash of idealism that led me to join Kibu, I signed on to produce this book with a single cowriter, Jesse Jacobs. Of course, several friends, colleagues, and random goodhearted souls pitched in with moral support and caffeinated beverage deliveries. I owe them something extremely valuable, which I hope to make good on when I actually have more than my childhood marble collection to offer. Meantime, despite my enormous gratitude, a wimpy but heartfelt thanks with a capital "T" is the best I've got.

Thanks especially go to my editors at the late *The Industry Standard*, Bob Cohn and Mark Robinson, for letting me write about my Internet escapades in the first place; Stanford Medical School, for granting me a leave of absence that may well make the *Guinness Book of World Records*; my parents, for handing me a "Get Out of Family Occasions Guilt-Free" card, at least until this book was delivered; Carl Kugel, who knows why; Neal Karlen, who likewise knows why, but also for reading every word in the span of a week and being the best partner-in-crime on the planet; the talented folks I worked with at Kibu, who used to say, "We'll laugh about this someday" — and with whom I've been doing exactly that since the "unhirings"; Judy MacDonald, for being gracious enough to invite me to the Kibu reunion parties; and our generous, insightful, and highly entertaining contributors, who not only poured their professional guts out on tape, but promptly replied to a barrage of follow-up e-mails that screamed, "FINAL DEADLINE!" enough times for the Boy Who Cried Wolf to get a bad case of laryngitis.

The admirable Julianne Lamarche, a.k.a. the most organized chick on the planet, looks like a supermodel, is a real-life supermom, and has a superbrain that stores more information — more accurately — than my hard drive. I hope to become half as together as her one day. Julianne single-handedly coordinated every interview, produced the funkiest file folders and spreadsheets I'd ever seen, kept Jesse and me in our respective play-pens, and somehow made everything happen when it needed to. Julianne's efficiency and implacability, however, belie her apparent masochism. After assisting Barry Diller for four long years, she told Jesse, "I think it would be interesting to be part of the process of getting a book published." If there were "take backs" in life, I'm guessing this would be at the top of her list. (Fortunately for us, there aren't.)

Jill Grinberg is supposed to be my agent, but she managed to keep me saner than my shrink could at what seemed like crucial moments in the process. Which is to say, virtually every moment. The highest compliment I can pay her is that she's the most un-agent-like agent I know, except when it comes to the business side of being an agent. If it weren't for Jill, I'd have spent the last several months churning out more "How Much You Should Tell Your Mother About Your Sex Life" articles, reviewing other people's books, or taking a job at the New Economy's most popular temp gig, another startup.

The Perseus team first duped Jesse and me into believing that we could meet our deadline and have fun doing so ("It'll be a wild ride!" said our persuasive editor, Nick Philipson), then miraculously made their claim come true. I'm especially grateful to our publisher, David Goehring, for shepherding this project through the pipeline with a level of personal attention that seems as rare nowadays as a doctor who still makes house calls; Nick Philipson for his wisdom, constant stream of e-mail encouragement, mastery of all things intellectual despite his admitted *Survivor* obsession, care with our contributors' words, and ability to make us laugh at the eleventh hour by emailing a photo of him editing the manuscript with his two-year-old daughter, Rachel; Elizabeth Carduff, for sparing us humiliation by nuking our dopiest title suggestions; Chris Coffin and David Wienir, for watching our backs; Arlinda Shtuni, for her smarts, and more behind-the-scenes magic touches than I can list or probably even know about; über-copy editor Kate Scott, for helping us to say what we meant; Zen-like production guru Marco Pavia, for making the whole process run smoothly; publicist Leigh Weiner, for "getting it" afer living through her own dot-com drama; and the entire sales team, for a level of enthusiasm usually reserved only for proud parents who've lost all objectivity.

Jesse Jacobs, a stranger who contacted me via e-mail and whom I came to know through the shotgun partnership that resulted in this book, turned out to be an incredibly impressive twenty-something with the networking skills of a seasoned politician, a self-deprecating sense of humor, and a heart of gold underneath it all. He taught me far more than how painfully unhip I am, or what the "computer stuff" means in a way that makes sense to a thirty-something Luddite like me. Which just goes to show that the old adage "Never talk to strangers" doesn't apply in the Internet Age.

Lori Gottlieb
Los Angeles
March 2002

Special gratitude goes to the nearly one hundred interviewees who shared their stories, anecdotes, quotes, quips, lives, and, most graciously, their time with us. A testament to their civility and dedication, they never complained when I reached them on their cell phones while they were away on vacation or when I e-mailed them at 3 A.M. with another "time-sensitive" request. This book is as much theirs as anyone's.

My family: My uncle Stephen and aunt Ruth Hendel for their life-long support; Nancy Utley Jacobs and Bernie Shaikin, whose care and loyalty belie all myths about evil stepparents; Emma, Hannah, and Mia—my "little" sisters—for teaching me firsthand about the Instant-Messaging Generation; my brother Stacy, for reminding me that it's okay to get off the computer and have fun every once in a while; and my sister Abra, who worked a lot harder than I during the past six months. Writing a book is a small feat compared to caring for our mother during her fight against breast cancer.

My friends: Alma Bune, Anna David, Noam Dromi, Matthew Fogelman, Brandon Friedman, Allon Hellmann, Billy Parks, and Alex Umansky—whose words of wisdom and shoulders of support kept me from going crazy. Whether it was an interview referral, an inspiration for a word, a bourbon on the rocks or just not hating me for being a hermit for the last several months, I owe you all.

My professional inspirations and mentors: Lew Harris and Paul Turcotte, whose belief in me gave me the confidence necessary to tackle this project; Kevin Wendle, Skip Paul, Frank Voci, Roger Jackson, Melissa Zukerman, and everyone else at IFILM, for supporting me in my desire to moonlight as an author.

My agent Jill Grinberg, whose unyielding belief in our vision and world-class negotiation skills are the primary reasons this book got published. Perseus Publishing, which, despite my disbelief, did not misspeak when they asked us to deliver the manuscript by December 2001, not 2002. I have the utmost regard and esteem for our publisher, David Goehring; Arlinda Shtuni; David Wienir; Marco Pavia; and our editor, Nick Philipson, whose irrefutable certainty that we could meet the task at hand kept me from falling asleep at the keyboard many a wee morning hour. His ability to push Lori and me forward when we were on the brink of exhaustion is most admirable.

True friendship is selfless. Josh Swartz and Brett Varsov are two of my closest friends and two of the most brilliant people I know. Josh spent valuable time providing me with countless hours of legal support and advice. Brett provided constructive feedback and put me in touch with numerous interviewees. I hope I can repay them both one day.

Read this book, and you'll see Julianne Lamarche's impression in between the lines, on the flypaper, within the seams, and in the ink. She was the blood, sweat, and tears of the endeavor. She conducted her research with unparalleled attention to detail, communicated with each interviewee with great aplomb, and never failed to tell me to snap out of one of my mood spells. And she did this with the best attitude I have ever seen, all while raising two adorable kids, kicking ass at IFILM, and going out eight nights at week.

To Joanna Murstein, whose energy, creativity, love, patience, and tolerance for my many imperfections allowed me to write: Not to mention the research she conducted, the ideas she proposed, the feedback she provided and the bedside support she gave me.

To my father, who opened up his home and his heart to help me acclimate to Los Angeles. His advice, professional and personal, guide me through life.

To my mother for raising me, loving me, and supporting me. We should all be so lucky to have her joie de vivre. I dedicate this to you, Mom.

And, finally, to Lori Gottlieb, to whom I will be eternally grateful for devoting her valuable time, her creative mind, and her inexhaustible energy to this project. Before I met her, I knew that she was a talented writer. But after several months of editing–cum–rap sessions, I now know her also as a trusted friend.

Jesse Jacobs
Los Angeles
January 2002

The authors gratefully acknowledge permission to reproduce materials from the following sources:

Page 1. Excerpt from *Death of a Salesman*. From *Death of a Salesman* by Arthur Miller, copyright 1949, renewed © 1977 by Arthur Miller. Used by permission of Viking Penguin, a division of Penguin Putnam Inc. Territory: U.S., Canada, P.I., Open, E.E.C.

Page 61. Melisssa Daimler job solicitation email. Used by permission of Melissa Daimler.

Page 99. Bernardo's List emails. Used by permission of Bernardo Joselevich.

Page 105. The Fresh Air Fund's "Silicon Alley's First Black Tie Benefit" invitation. Used by permission of Courtney Pulitzer Creations.

Pages 118-120. *The Industry Standard* article excerpt. Used by permission of Alan Citron

Pages 140 and 141. *Salon* magazine article excerpt. Used by permission of Ruth Shalit.

Page 154. Nibblebox.com logo. Used by permission of Dave Bartis.

Page 167 and other Matt Welch excerpts in text. Online Journalism Review article excerpts. Used by permission of Matt Welch.

Page 208. Excerpts from "The History of Shallow Esophagus." Used by permission of Joanne Weaver and Chas Watkins.

Page 245. FuckedCompany.com postings on the eTtoys.com board. Used by permission of Philip "Pud" Kaplan.

INDEX